Counseling Youth

Counseling Youth

Systemic Issues and Interventions

RICHARD S. BALKIN, AMANDA WINBURN,
ERIKA L. SCHMIT, AND
SAMANTHA M. MENDOZA

OXFORD
UNIVERSITY PRESS

Oxford University Press is a department of the University of Oxford. It furthers
the University's objective of excellence in research, scholarship, and education
by publishing worldwide. Oxford is a registered trade mark of Oxford University
Press in the UK and certain other countries.

Published in the United States of America by Oxford University Press
198 Madison Avenue, New York, NY 10016, United States of America.

© Oxford University Press 2023

All rights reserved. No part of this publication may be reproduced, stored in
a retrieval system, or transmitted, in any form or by any means, without the
prior permission in writing of Oxford University Press, or as expressly permitted
by law, by license, or under terms agreed with the appropriate reproduction
rights organization. Inquiries concerning reproduction outside the scope of the
above should be sent to the Rights Department, Oxford University Press, at the
address above.

You must not circulate this work in any other form
and you must impose this same condition on any acquirer.

CIP data is on file at the Library of Congress

ISBN 978-0-19-758676-1

DOI: 10.1093/oso/9780197586761.001.0001

Printed by Marquis, Canada

Contents

Preface   vii

PART I AN OVERVIEW OF THE SYSTEM

1. Defining a Systemic Approach to Working with Youth   3
2. What Is Normal?   21
3. Our System of Care   38
4. Addressing Youth Interventions in Schools   56
5. Immigrant and Refugee Youth   80

PART II ISSUES AFFECTING YOUTH

6. Stress, Depression, and Suicide   101
7. Sex and Sexuality   121
8. Bullying and Violence   141
9. Antisocial Behavior and Addiction   163
10. Abuse and Trauma   196

PART III AFFECTING CHANGE

11. Engaging Communities in Need   215
12. Putting It All Together: Systemic Change for Positive Mental Health in Youth   237

Index   251

Preface

Our goal in this text is to address the needs and factors influencing youth development and mental health from a systemic perspective for clinicians and clinicians-in training across disciplines (e.g., counseling, marriage and family therapy, psychology, social work). Throughout this text we address the various systems that influence and impact development and mental health for children and adolescents. We focus on a biopsychosocial model to address how various systems such as schools, community, juvenile justice, medical, and social services interplay when addressing concerns from early childhood to emerging adulthood. Throughout the text we address models, systems, concepts, and interventions that are interwoven into youth development and mental health.

Organization of This Book

The text is derived from four authors with varied experiences delivering youth services, from the roles of schools to counseling services, the juvenile justice system, and issues and interventions for undocumented immigrant minors.

Dr. Richard S. Balkin is Professor at the University of Mississippi in the Department of Leadership. His counseling experience working with at-risk youth in psychiatric hospitals and outpatient settings was formative to his research agenda, which includes understanding the role of counseling and relevant goals for adolescents in crisis and counseling outcomes.

Dr. Amanda Winburn is Associate Professor at the University of Mississippi in the Department of Leadership and Counselor Education. Dr. Winburn has more than a decade of experience working with children in various settings, including schools and clinical settings; she has licensure as an educator, counselor, and administrator, as well as a clinical specialization in play therapy.

Dr. Erika L. Schmit is Associate Professor at the University of Mississippi in the Department of Leadership and Counselor Education. Her experiences include working with children and adolescents in numerous settings including schools, agencies, and inpatient hospitals.

Dr. Samantha M. Mendoza serves as a Federal Field Specialist, employed through the Office of Refugee Resettlement, and is Adjunct Professor in the Counselor Education Department at the University of St. Thomas and the University of the Southwest. Since 2008, Dr. Mendoza has worked with vulnerable populations, particularly children and individuals with intellectual disabilities or mental health needs.

The book is organized into three sections.

Part I includes Chapters 1 through 5, focusing on the systemic perspective, biopsychosocial model, and the various systems that play a role in youth development, intervention, and treatment.

Chapter 1 introduces the systemic perspective and the collaborative role that agencies, organizations, and services must play to address youth mental health.

Chapter 2 focuses on youth development models, including both common and unique aspects of developmental models with respect to physiological, psychological, and social development. We provide an overview of how the common developmental models address healthy development.

Chapter 3 provides an overview of various systems of care, including levels of mental health care and juvenile justice system. The multifaceted nature of youth interventions is addressed.

Chapter 4 focuses on how schools address youth mental health. The interwoven nature of public health and schools is addressed, along with the policies and limitations of addressing issues affecting youth and the need to revise policies and processes to ensure the health and well-being of youth.

Chapter 5 provides a framework to guide mental health providers who work with refugees and immigrants. We examine the complex ways in which culture impacts the refugee experience, barriers to engagement in mental health practice and strategies for overcoming them, collaborative and integrated mental health interventions, and efforts to increase resilience in children, families, and communities.

Part II, Chapters 6 through 10, highlights issues affecting youth mental health. Issues of depression, stress, suicide, antisocial behavior and substance use, sex and sexuality, and trauma are highlighted. We selected topics that represent current issues with youth requiring awareness and consideration, particularly in the present sociopolitical climate and during emergence from a pandemic in which we saw increases in youth depression, stress, suicide, and substance use, as well as exposure to trauma. We focus on the variety of settings influencing resources and care for youth.

Chapter 6 focuses on youth stressors, depression, suicide, and how these three interact and impact each other. Protective factors, risk factors, and effective counseling services are addressed.

Chapter 7 provides an introduction to the diverse and complex issues involved in counseling LGBT youth. Additionally, this chapter covers many issues in sexuality that affect today's youth, including sexual activity, sex trafficking, and teen pregnancy and parenthood.

Chapter 8 focuses on bullying and violent behaviors and their implications for adolescents. Exposure to these behaviors can certainly hinder academic and social development in youth. Mental health, prevention, and interventions are discussed.

Chapter 9 provides information on aggression, antisocial behavior, and addiction in youth. Major types of aggressive and antisocial behaviors are addressed along with their interplay among neurobiological processes, protective factors, and gender variables. In addition, we cover both process addiction and substance abuse in this chapter, highlighting the genetic predisposition for and behavioral components to addiction from a biopsychosocial model.

Chapter 10 highlights the short- and long-term impact of abuse and trauma on children and adolescents within a cultural context. We provide guidelines for trauma-informed care with youth.

Part III concludes this text with two chapters on affecting change. We highlight community engagement and challenges and essential components to providing youth services from a systemic perspective.

Chapter 11 provides an overview of issues, challenges, and services to communities in need and lack access to care. We highlight differences in urban and rural poverty and methods to increase resources and services to affected areas.

Chapter 12 concludes the text with a focus on mental health promotion, prevention, and intervention when working with youth in schools and community settings. We emphasize the importance of developing positive mental health through a focus on risk and protective factors promoting prevention activities, developing collaborations, and advocating for change.

PART I
AN OVERVIEW OF THE SYSTEM

1
Defining a Systemic Approach to Working with Youth

Talk with any clinician about what they do, and you will likely hear a story—not about an amazing turn-around or a typical case—but probably about a difficult case, perhaps one in which the clinician questioned the outcome or did not feel very successful. Client failure is a real phenomenon. Unlike medical care, where a physician assumes responsibility for treating, and often, curing an illness, addressing mental health concerns is not so cut and dried.

Clients enter counseling with histories. Some of the problems are more recent, such as sudden grief or a disaster. Other problems are more long-standing—issues such as addiction, chronic pain, depression, anxiety, or abuse. The road to success with a client is often difficult—and even against the odds. It is not just the failure of the clinician or the failure of the client. Sometimes, the systems that are already in place make success truly difficult to achieve.

Consider the multitude of systemic issues affecting youth and adults:

- Abuse and neglect
- Addiction
- Poverty
- Immigration
- Access to mental health services
- Public health
- Absentee parents
- Underresourced schools
- Youth violence
- School violence
- Technology/social media
- Discrimination/oppression
- Childcare

Counseling Youth. Richard S. Balkin, Amanda Winburn, Erika L. Schmit, and Samantha M. Mendoza,
Oxford University Press. © Oxford University Press 2023. DOI: 10.1093/oso/9780197586761.003.0001

Adults often have the luxury of autonomy—more freedom (though not necessarily complete freedom) to alter their cycle. But youth lack that power. A dysfunctional family system, such as an abusive relative, can set events in motion that, once encountered, are difficult to heal. An ineffective placement in a school, a negative peer group, an unsupportive community can negatively impact youth, setting the stage for further problems down the road. And when resources are sought, they may be difficult to obtain or ineffective as isolated interventions. Consider what happens when a student skips school. The student might be referred to a truancy officer. The truancy officer might discuss the situation with the parent(s) or caretaker(s), who could be overwhelmed with work, bills, and stress. The ability to seek outpatient counseling services might be limited, thereby falling to the responsibility of the school counselor, who often carries unrealistic caseloads, with hundreds of students or perhaps even more.

Agencies and organizations essential to youth development are often underresourced or perhaps even hindered from providing effective services. For example, a community mental health center may be understaffed and unable to see a family in need on a weekly basis. In addition, schools are not only responsible for educating children but also are tasked with the responsibility of overseeing a variety of public health issues. A nonexhaustive list of these issues includes vaccinations, vision and hearing screening, sex/abstinence-based education, free/reduced breakfast and lunch, early or after-school childcare, transportation, and medical services for children with special needs. While the efforts and resources put forward are pertinent and noteworthy, the effectiveness and accountability of services are often called in to question. If time, money, and resources are going to be utilized to provide services, the public wants to see that such services are effective.

Our Systemic Failure

Despite years of training and experience working with youth in a variety of mental health settings, whether counseling in an office, detention centers, psychiatric hospitals, or residential treatment settings, and after conducting numerous studies on counseling outcomes specifically related to youth, if a judge asked us to, "prove to the effectiveness of mental health treatment in addressing problems with youth," it might be a difficult case to win. The evidence of positive mental health outcomes is clear, as numerous studies have been conducted to show that counseling services are effective in helping youth address a variety of social, emotional, and developmental problems. For example, Fedewa et al. (2016) evaluated 468 effects across 140 studies for school-aged youth across eight outcomes:

- School attendance
- School achievement
- Internalizing problems, such as anxiety, depression, and trauma
- Externalizing problems, such as conduct, aggression, impulsivity, and disruptive behaviors
- Psychosomatization, including any kind of body pain
- Self-concept
- Stress
- Overall behaviors, such as any global assessments of emotional well-being

Students who received counseling services experienced noted gains in self-concept, school attendance, and overall positive behavior and noted decreases in internalizing problems, externalizing problems, psychosomatization, and stress.

On the other hand, there may be a feeling of inundation when faced with unresolvable mental health issues affecting youth. Since the Columbine High School shooting in 1999, where two high school seniors murdered 12 students and 1 teacher, there have been 7 school shootings in which a student or young adult murdered youth in a school setting. Livingston et al. (2019) cited 179 school shootings occurring between April 1999 and May 2018, while the US Naval Postgraduate School study cited 657 violent incidents during that same time period. Furthermore, youth suicide represents the second leading cause of death for individuals 15–24 years of age, and prevalence increased by 56% between 2007 and 2017 (Curtin & Heron, 2019). Even more alarming is the rise of suicide attempts in Black youth, which increased by 73% in 26 years, from 1991 to 2017 (Lindsey et al., 2019). Thus, the ability to identify problems in youth and prevent tragedies is both imperfect and limited.

In addition, no specific interventions demonstrated notable gains over other interventions. Simply the presence of counseling services appeared to make the difference in positive outcomes (Fedewa et al., 2016). So, although we might understand that counseling is effective, we do not have a strong idea of why counseling is effective (Kottler & Balkin, 2020). Much of the research (e.g., Duncan, 2014; Lambert, 2013; Wampold & Imel, 2015) conducted in the area of counseling outcomes indicates that predictors of success lie not in techniques, interventions, or client hope, but more in the relationship that clients and clinicians share. Moreover, the largest contributing factors to client outcomes are external—things we have no control over. External factors refer to those aspects of an individual's life that can impact change, such as an individual's support system, environment, even random events in a person's life (Thomas, 2006). So, issues such as support systems, personal crises, and interpersonal relationships can impact the course of therapy more than anything happening in the therapeutic process.

And that brings us to the systemic issues affecting youth and their mental health. By *systemic*, we are referring to the various services, agencies, and organizations that youth may come into contact with when receiving mental health services. The medical model endorses a practitioner-treatment approach to healthcare. A person feels ill, seeks a medical professional, receives a diagnosis, and obtains treatment. And although this approach is widely applied to mental healthcare, the application is a poor fit, especially for youth who are involved in multiple systems affecting health and well-being. Consider examples of how a variety of systems integrate with youth well-being and affect youth when their needs are unmet.

Schools and Connected Systems

The average school day is approximately 7 hours (National Center on Education and the Economy, 2018). Aside from weekends, youth may spend at least 50% of their waking hours on school/education-related activities (US Department of Health and Human Services, 2019). Schools have an integral role in public health for youth, providing morning and evening care and supervision, meals, health screenings (e.g., hearing, vision, scoliosis, vaccinations), and extracurricular/leisure activities. When youth experience school failure or difficulty within the school environment, a major portion of their life and development may be impacted.

Success in school often depends on a stable family system, whether the family system is nuclear, extended, blended, joint, or family by choice. Unfortunately, many kids in school do not have access to any type of family system, and their situation is further complicated through the Division of

Human Services (DHS) and foster care. These systems are often limited in personnel and resources, which further deteriorates the disposition of youth involved in these systems.

> ### Case Study: Jackson
>
> Jackson was a 16-year-old boy who at the time of our introduction was a sophomore in high school and living at home with his biological mother and her live-in boyfriend. Jackson had a history of academic difficulties; he was retained in the second grade due to low classroom grades and underperformance on state exams. Since then, he has struggled to earn passing grades but has managed to stay out of trouble for the most part, with only a few minor behavioral issues along the way. However, during his freshman year things seemed to change; he was often tardy for school and his appearance seemed disheveled at times. A teacher who had developed a relationship with him would check on him often, and Jackson would report that he was fine. Jackson seemed "off" to his teacher and was falling asleep in her class so she attempted to call, email, and text the mother but got no response.
>
> After several failed attempts the teacher reported to the school counselor her concern and need to communicate with Jackson's mom to ensure that everything was OK at home and report his behavior in class. The school counselor then attempted to call, email, and text. After the school counselor was unsuccessful, the school administrator was contacted. The principal also attempted contact, with no success. The administrator, counselor, and school resource officer decided to conduct a home visit. It was at this point that they determined that Jackson had been abandoned by his mother. Once the discovery had been made a DHS report was filed and Jackson admitted that he came home from school 4 weeks prior and found that his mother and her boyfriend had packed up and left during the school day. During this 4-week period all the utilities were shut off to the mobile home and the fridge was empty. Jackson insisted that he was fine and he was "better off on his own."
>
> That evening, Jackson was taken into protective custody by DHS. Unfortunately, a foster family could not be located within his current school district so Jackson was transferred to the high school in the next town. Over the next year, Jackson struggled socially and academically, so

much so, that he was rehomed three times in 12 months. Each time came a new school and new issues. By his seventeenth birthday he was physically aggressive, skipped school, and his grades plummeted. He ran away from two foster families, and, on the day his mother signed away parental rights, he was arrested for burglary.

Upon entering his fourth foster home and working with the court system regarding his arrest, Jackson moved in with a foster family living in his original school district and returned to his old high school once again. When he met his school counselor, she asked him what she could do to help. Jackson stated "I don't need anything, from anyone. I told you I am better off alone." Jackson resisted attempts at assistance and continued to skip school. On his eighteenth birthday he came school to officially drop out.

This is a case where limited resources in the DHS, foster care system, and public school system failed to provide adequate support and stability for Jackson. These entities are overwhelmed with caseloads, underfunded, and understaffed. At their current status, they are destined for failure unless significant changes are made. Jackson was a by-product of the system, passed from family to family and school to school with minimal support, communication, or tracking of services. Just one example of this is that, during Jackson's time in the foster care system, his case was handled by four different case managers due to high turnover rates.

Community Mental Health and Youth Services

The focus on child mental health can be traced back to the work of Alfred Adler establishing the first child guidance clinic in Vienna, Austria, in 1921. Rudolf Dreikurs, a student of Adler, established the first child guidance center in the United States in 1938, in Chicago. Despite these advances, federal initiatives were more focused on adult mental health and deinstitutionalization, with the signing of the National Mental Health Act in 1946. Almost 20 years later, the Community Mental Health Centers Act was passed in 1963. Beyond training and providing care, case management became a major emphasis in 1986, with the passing of the Mental Health Planning Act in that year, which also established a mandate to provide services to the homeless and add rehabilitation services.

Modern trends include funding challenges, given the exhaustive services provided by community mental health centers. In addition to counseling and case management, community mental health centers provide medical mental health services and medication management, in-home care, assessment, testing, and evaluation. Resources tend to be focused on populations who cannot access private services due to financial constraints or simply the lack of services in their communities. In addition, client-centered outcome research is lacking. Most data appear focused on points of service provided (e.g., number of sessions, types of diagnoses, or client satisfaction), as opposed to actual outcomes demonstrating the efficacy of care.

Case Study: Anthony

Anthony is a 10-year-old boy in fourth grade. His mother cleans houses, and his father works as a handyman doing work when he can find it. Anthony has been experiencing difficulty at school. His teachers report that he requires numerous cues throughout the day to stay on task. His work is disorganized, and he is missing a lot of assignments. Anthony has difficulty socializing with other kids, and he often eats by himself during lunch. He was recently in a fight with another child and received in-school suspension. The school counselor suggested Anthony might benefit from counseling. Because the family does not have insurance, the school counselor made a referral to the community mental health center. The earliest appointment available was in 3 weeks.

When Anthony was finally able to get to his appointment, his situation had worsened, with more behavior problems in school and noncompliance at home. The counselor recommended that Anthony be evaluated for medication management. The psychiatrist was at the community mental health center once a week, and the earliest possible appointment was in 4 weeks. In the meantime, Anthony could be seen by the counselor once every other week. Anthony's father mentioned that they had only one car and, when both parents are working, getting to appointments and taking time off work can be difficult, especially if the psychiatrist appointment and the counseling appointment were at different times. However, given the limitations in scheduling, getting both appointments at the same time was not possible.

> The length of time between appointments, the difficulty in scheduling, and Anthony's escalating behavior frustrated both Anthony and his parents. Anthony missed several appointments, was never able to see the psychiatrist, and eventually his case was dropped from the community mental health center.

Psychiatric Hospitalization

Psychiatric hospitalization for children and adolescents occurs when outpatient counseling is deemed insufficient and the child or adolescent is a danger to self or others, requiring crisis residence. *Acute care* is a brief inpatient psychiatric hospitalization for children and adolescents requiring crisis care, generally 14 days or less. *Partial hospitalization* represents day-long treatment, but the patient does not reside in the hospital but returns to the parent(s)/guardian(s). For this reason, partial hospitalization is considered subacute—intensive but less restrictive. *Residential treatment* is often reserved for chronic problems, in which the average length of stay is much longer, from 4 weeks to several months, and the patient resides on the unit. Generally, residential treatment may be used when neither outpatient nor inpatient counseling is effective.

Outcomes in psychiatric hospitalization are difficult to track due to Health Insurance Portability and Accountability Act (HIPAA) regulations and the inability to track long-term outcomes from patients previously hospitalized. Family participation is considered an integral part of treatment success because some intervention is often necessary at a systemic level. In addition, youth requiring crisis residence often experience dysfunctional family systems, so collaboration with children and family services is essential. Because patients will receive educational services within the hospitalization, coordination with schools and school districts is needed.

> **Case Study: Terry**
>
> Terry was a 17-year-old girl who lived with her mother and was on probation due to selling drugs. After testing positive for crystal methamphetamine and THC on her most recent drug screen, the probation officer told her she could go to treatment or have her probation revoked and go before

the judge in juvenile court with a potential to be placed in detention. Terry indicated she would prefer treatment. She was evaluated at a psychiatric hospital and admitted to the adolescent unit.

Terry's mother signed the admission paper. During the pre-admission assessment, Terry's mother admitted to being an alcoholic, actively using alcohol, but also being supportive of her daughter's treatment. "It hasn't worked for me, but maybe it will work for her."

With a history of methamphetamine use and the presence of withdrawal symptoms, justifying Terry's admission was easy. She appeared motivated in her treatment. An important moment during her treatment came when she was talking about her drug use and drug dealing during group therapy.

"I can get drugs any time I want," Terry boasted.

"Why do you say that?" asked Camille.

Camille was a 16-year-old who was also admitted for drug use and threatening suicide. This was her second treatment in the hospital inside of 6 months. After her first treatment, she had a period of 2 months where she did well, but she resumed her old friendships and relapsed back to her previous high-risk behavior.

"It's because it's true," Terry said emphatically, as if responding to a challenge.

"So people just give you drugs for free?" Camille asked.

"Yes. I just go to my dealer. He will offer me drugs any time I want them."

Camille paused and leaned forward in her chair, making certain to close the space with Terry and look her in the eye. She said gently, but with confidence, "It's never free, Terry. You're paying for it. You know he is getting something from you." Camille's eyes began to tear.

Terry froze for a moment. Then she brought her hands up to cover her face and leaned down toward her legs sobbing. "I never wanted to think about that," Terry cried. "It's been horrible."

The session was a turning point for Terry. She quit glorifying her drug use and began to talk about the toll it has taken on her. She identified goals and felt she had the capacity to succeed academically if she could get clean. Terry also knew that going home was going to be difficult. "I wish treatment could be longer than just a week. I need more time," she said. "With my mother's drinking and the neighborhood I live in, I am just not ready. Are there longer treatments?"

> Terry and her counselor talked about different options, but the reality is that a residential treatment program was not possible. Her hospitalization was paid for by Medicaid through a court order. But Medicaid would not pay for long-term substance abuse treatment without documented outpatient failure in counseling.
>
> "But I know that won't be enough," Terry stated. "I need more than that." Terry's counselor agreed, but options were limited.
>
> It was a case where the available resources in a rural state simply were not present for individuals who lacked insurance benefits, and the state would not pay for treatment with the absence of any documented outpatient counseling. In other words, Terry would have to return home and fail in outpatient counseling before further treatment would be considered.

Refugee Services

The State Department identifies refugee children overseas who are eligible for resettlement in the United States but do not have a parent or a relative available and committed to providing for their long-term care. Upon arrival in the United States, these refugee children are placed into the Unaccompanied Refugee Minors (URM) program and receive refugee foster care services and benefits. The program establishes legal responsibility, under state law, to ensure that unaccompanied minor refugees and entrants receive the full range of assistance, care, and services that are available to all foster children in the state. A legal authority is designated to act in place of the child's unavailable parent(s) (ACF Office of Refugee Resettlement, 2022). Reunification of children with their parents or other appropriate adult relatives is encouraged, through family tracing and coordination with local refugee resettlement agencies. Additional services provided include indirect financial support for housing, food, clothing, medical care, and other necessities; intensive case management by social workers; independent living skills training; educational supports; English-language training; career/college counseling and training; mental health services; assistance in adjusting immigration status; cultural activities; recreational opportunities; support for social integration; and cultural and religious preservation. Children eligible for the URM Program are younger than 18, are unaccompanied, and are confirmed as refugees, entrants, asylees, or victims of trafficking. Similar to many social service programs such as child protective services and community mental health agencies, refugee programs and services face challenges, including funding, infrastructure, and human resources, all of which contributed to the disposition illustrated in the next case study.

> **Case Study: Yasmin**
>
> Yasmin was a 17-year-old girl who immigrated to the United States from her country of origin, El Salvador. Yasmin yearned for a life outside of the community in which she grew up, which was rampant with cartel violence and gang threats. At the shelter where she is being held, Yasmin disclosed no history of drug use and denies current suicidal ideation. However, she did disclose prior self-harm, as recent as within the past 3 months.
>
> Yasmin disclosed to an on-site counselor that she was sexually assaulted by a family member at the age of 8, physically abused by her caregiver from age 7 to 14, and was sexually assaulted by an unknown gang member at the age of 16. Yasmin became pregnant as a result of the sexual assault and lost the pregnancy in her seventh month. When asked how she handled her grief, or if she sought therapy or counseling in her home country, Yasmin replied, "No one really asked me how I was doing. My teacher said it was probably better this way, because I wouldn't have to become a mom."
>
> Yasmin arrived in the United States with intentions of residing with a family friend. Upon her arrival, the family friend declined to sponsor Yasmin. She said her home was too small and she couldn't worry about another person to feed and care for. Yasmin was certain she did not want to return to her country of origin—the threat of gang and cartel violence was too much to bear.
>
> "I can go to a foster home, can't I? Some of my cousins have done that," Yasmin suggested.
>
> "Unfortunately, no. You are 17½ years old, so it is too late for us to refer you to a foster home before you age out and turn 18. It's a rule," her caseworker explained. Yasmin has lived a very traumatic life and has no reliable caregiver in the United States or in El Salvador. She could greatly benefit from a stable foster home and ongoing services (group therapy, counseling) if only she weren't so close to "aging out."
>
> Yasmin's caseworker and counselor talked about different options, but the unfortunate truth is that her options were limited. She could remain at the shelter until her eighteenth birthday, but she is not eligible for foster

care due to her age. With no viable caregiver in the United States, she would be forced into repatriation to her country of origin.

"I can't go back. They will hurt me again," Yasmin cried. "I don't want to get hurt and I don't want to feel hopeless and cut myself again." Yasmin's counselor agreed, but options were almost nonexistent.

This is a case where the available resources were not available for individuals of Yasmin's age. Yasmin could have received treatment and a foster care referral if she had arrived in the United States just a few months earlier. Unfortunately for Yasmin, her options are limited, and she will be forced to return to her country of origin on her eighteenth birthday.

What Is a Systemic Approach?

A variety of systems are identified in the case scenarios. Neither the scenarios nor the services below represent an exhaustive list, but you can see that caring for youth requires a complex number of agencies, organizations, and services. Moreover, in each of the case studies, two major challenges were evident: (a) the efficacy of resources and (b) the sufficiency of resources. Consider the multitude of systems that provide services to youth:

- Schools
- Community mental health centers
- Psychiatric hospitals
- DHS/Child Protective Services
- Refugee services
- Juvenile court
- Abuse shelters
- Residential facilities (e.g., youth homes, group living)
- Foster homes
- Homeless shelters
- Child care facilities/after-school programs
- Youth programs (e.g., YMCA, Boys' and Girls' Clubs, community centers)
- Religious centers (e.g., churches, synagogues, mosques)
- Healthcare providers

Efficacy of Resources

Some of the systemic failure noted in the case scenarios occur due to the perceived lack of effective treatment. Such an assumption can be dangerous because mental health providers are well-trained. In fact, the 60-hour master's degree in counseling is among the highest number of hours required for any master's degree. Training does not appear to be a problem. Rather, difficulty facilitating change with a challenging population is a primary obstacle (Kottler & Balkin, 2020). How do we know that the services a youth is receiving are effective? Of course, there are myriad of measures that look at client progress, such as symptom and problem checklists, client satisfaction questionnaires, and the tracking of therapeutic goals (Balkin, 2014). Duncan (2014) promoted the concept of feedback effects, along with the common factors of therapeutic alliance, client hopefulness, counselor's theories/techniques, and external factors. *Feedback effects* refer to the client's communication of therapeutic progress and the quality of the therapeutic relationship. Sometimes youth can be inundated with resources—a school counselor, mental health counselor, case manager, primary care physician, psychiatrist, child protective services case worker, probation officer. It can be hard to know what is effective, helpful, or even detrimental. The antithesis is that resources are limited, contact points are few, and the youth is not connected with the resources that are available. So, a good place to start to determine what is effective is to simply ask. This can be done in the form of client interviews, discussions within the course of counseling, or use of standardized measures. Some examples of measures that help evaluate feedback effects include the following:

- Session Rating Scale (Duncan et al., 2003)
- Working Alliance Inventory (Hatcher & Gillaspy, 2006)
- Ohio Scales (Ogles et al., 2004)
- YOQ-TA (OQ Measures, n.d.)

Effective care with youth must go beyond referral and even treatment or offering of services. Rather, careful monitoring is essential, and incorporating feedback effects into the standard of care is essential.

Sufficiency of Resources

The case studies in this chapter point to the insufficiency of resources. Sometimes insufficiency is due to systemic factors, such as human resources, fiscal resources, or environment (e.g., rural areas lacking services). At other times external factors interfere with the ability to initiate assistance for youth, such as dysfunctional family systems, aging-out, or inability to qualify for services. How do mental health practitioners address these limitations? A focus on advocacy, a collaborative mindset, and a knowledge of resources are essential.

Could any of our case scenarios been turned around? Some cases are inherently difficult when external factors, such as legal proceedings or age of the youth, control the narrative. But at other times there is a breakdown in communication or a lack of understanding regarding needs. For example, Anthony may have qualified for in-home visits if his case manager and counselor communicated about transportation and employment difficulties for the parents. Keeping Jackson in the same high school may have been a higher priority. Certainly, limitations of resources are a problem in providing services. Sometimes, the answers appear obvious but the ability to obtain the necessary resources for the optimal disposition may seem out of reach. Engaging in advocacy and collaboration is not a foolproof method to ensure positive outcomes, but becoming aware of additional resources to assist in dispositions for youth is necessary to increase success with difficult populations.

Operating from a Systemic Paradigm: Systemic Collaboration

Given the various systems that may influence youth, how would an effective systemic paradigm operate? We refer to such a paradigm as *systemic collaboration*: a group of systems (e.g., agencies, organizations) that operate and openly communicate as advocates and stakeholders for the common clients they serve. For example, an effective systemic collaboration might include a school counselor and administrator actively communicating and working with child protective services, a youth shelter, and a professional counselor to streamline care and monitor progress and goals for a youth working within all of these systems.

Of course, the same policies that are meant to protect youth often hamper systemic collaboration. Two pertinent policies to understand are the Family Educational Rights and Privacy Act (FERPA) and HIPAA.

FERPA is federal legislation initially passed in 1974, which covers consent for testing and release of education records to parent(s)/guardian(s) or students over the age of 18. Schools must have permission to release educational records. Schools may release records without consent under the following conditions (US Department of Education, 2018):

- School officials with legitimate educational interest
- Other schools to which a student is transferring
- Specified officials for audit or evaluation purposes
- Appropriate parties in connection with financial aid to a student
- Organizations conducting certain studies for or on behalf of the school
- Accrediting organizations
- To comply with a judicial order or lawfully issued subpoena
- Appropriate officials in cases of health and safety emergencies
- State and local authorities, within a juvenile justice system, pursuant to specific state law

Important to the issue of systemic collaboration is that records from schools may be shared in the case of "health and safety emergencies."

HIPAA is a federal act created in 1996 and last modified in 2002; it addresses the protection of individuals' health information. HIPAA established standards for health plans, healthcare clearinghouses, and healthcare providers. Protection of health information and limitations to conditions in which healthcare information may be disclosed are highlighted in HIPAA. There are two conditions in which identifiable health information may be disclosed (US Department of Health and Human Services, 2013):

1. A specific request from an individual or legal representative of the individual to disclose protected health information, or
2. Under a compliance investigation from the US Department of Health and Human Services.

HIPAA guidelines serve as an important privacy protection, but when an adverse event affects the health and well-being of youth, HIPAA guidelines may prevent the sharing of identifiable healthcare information that may be pertinent to providing interventions, treatment, and services to youth in need. With these issues in mind, clinicians who provide services to youth have the primary responsibility of initiating systemic collaboration. The chapters that follow will provide information about the issues and challenges that lead to systemic failure, as well as processes to enhance systemic collaboration. However, the overarching concepts to systemic collaboration include the following:

- A comprehensive assessment of services being offered to the youth
- A detailed history of systems that have engaged with the youth and family
- Consent to obtain information from previous agencies and organizations related to the youth's disposition
- Consent to release information to present and future agencies and organizations related to the youth's disposition
- Initiating communication to present and future agencies related to the youth's disposition and agreement to unified goals for a positive disposition and outcome
- Maintaining unified collaboration and services to monitor outcomes

Summary

In this chapter, we identified the importance of a systemic approach to working with youth. Examples of systemic failure were presented as was an introduction to the variety of agencies, organizations, and resources that serve a variety of youth in challenging circumstances. An orientation toward advocacy, a collaborative approach from a multidisciplinary perspective, and a knowledge of resources are essential to address the challenges of today's youth. Mental health professionals must be aware of the variety of services and environments that serve youth, including outpatient services, inpatient services, schools, and agencies and organizations that specialize in targeted and marginalized populations such as refugees, LGBT youth, homeless youth, and youth in foster care. In addition, clinicians must be aware of federal laws and structures that protect privacy and actively advocate and initiate consents and communication to establish systemic collaboration among the variety of youth services.

References

Administration for Children and Families [ACF]. (2022). Unaccompanied children. Author. Retreived December 2, 2022 from https://www.acf.hhs.gov/orr/programs/uc

Balkin, R. S. (2014). *The Crisis Stabilization Scale manual and sampler set*. Mind Garden, Inc.

Curtin, S. C., & Heron, M. (2019, October). Death rates due to suicide and homicide among persons aged 10–24: United States, 2000–2017. NCHS Data Brief (No. 352). U.S. Department of Health and Human Services, Centers for Disease Control and Prevention, National Center for Health Statistics. Retrieved December 2, 2022 from https://www.cdc.gov/nchs/data/databriefs/db352-h.pdf

Duncan, B. (2014). *On becoming a better therapist: Evidence-based practice one client at a time*. American Psychological Association.

Duncan, B. L., Miller, S. D., Sparks, J. A., Claud, D. A., Reynolds, L. R., Brown, J., & Johnson, L. D. (2003). The Session Rating Scale: Preliminary psychometric properties of a "working" alliance measure. *Journal of Brief Therapy, 3*(1), 3–12.

Fedewa, A. L., Ahn, S., Reese, R. J., Suarez, M. M., Macquoid, A., Davis, M. C., & Prout, H. T. (2016). Does psychotherapy work with school-aged youth? A meta-analytic examination of moderator variables that influence therapeutic outcomes. *Journal of School Psychology, 56*, 59–87. https://doi-org.umiss.idm.oclc.org/10.1016/j.jsp.2016.03.001

Hatcher, R. L., & Gillaspy, J. A. (2006). Development and validation of a revised short version of the Working Alliance Inventory. *Psychotherapy Research, 16*, 12–25. http://dx.doi.org/10.1080/10503300500352500

Kottler, J. A., & Balkin, R. S. (2020). *Myths, misconceptions, and invalid assumptions in counseling and psychotherapy*. Oxford University Press.

Lambert, M. J. (Ed.). (2013). *Bergin and Garfield's handbook of psychotherapy and behavior change* (6th ed.). Wiley.

Lindsey, M.A., Sheftall, A.H., Xiao, Y., & Joe, S. (2019). Trends of suicidal behaviors among high school students in the United States: 1991–2017. *Pediatrics, 155*(5), 1–10. doi:10.1542/peds.2019-1187

Livingston, M. D., Rossheim, M. E., & Hall, K. S. (2019). A descriptive analysis of school and school shooter characteristics and the severity of school shootings in the United States, 1999–2018. *Journal of Adolescent Health, 64*(6), 797–799.

National Center on Education and the Economy. (2018). Statistics of the month. Retrieved January 19, 2020, from http://ncee.org/2018/02/statistic-of-the-month-how-much-time-do-students-spend-in-school/

Ogles, B. M., Dowell, K., Hatfield, D., Melendez, G., & Carlston, D. L. (2004). The Ohio Scales. In M. E. Maruish (Ed.), *The use of psychological testing for treatment planning and outcomes assessment: Instruments for children and adolescents* (pp. 275–304). Lawrence Erlbaum.

OQ Measures (n.d.). Retrieved December 2, 2022 from https://www.oqmeasures.com

Thomas, M. L. (2006). The contributing factors of change in a therapeutic process. *Contemporary Family Therapy: An International Journal, 28*(2), 201–210. https://doi-org.umiss.idm.oclc.org/10.1007/s10591-006-9000-4

US Department of Education. (2018). Family Educational Rights and Privacy Act (FERPA). Retrieved February 21, 2020, from https://www2.ed.gov/policy/gen/guid/fpco/ferpa/index.html

US Department of Health and Human Services (2013). Summary of the HIPAA Privacy Rule. Retrieved February 21, 2020, from https://www.hhs.gov/hipaa/for-professionals/privacy/laws-regulations/index.html

US Department of Health and Human Services. (2019). A day in the life of a high school teen. Retrieved January 19, 2020, from https://www.hhs.gov/ash/oah/facts-and-stats/day-in-the-life/index.html

Wampold, B. E., & Imel, Z. E. (2015). *The great psychotherapy debate: The evidence of what makes psychotherapy work*. Routledge.

2
What Is Normal?

Overview

Common models of youth development often focus on maturation, development, and learning, culminating in the "storm and stress" of adolescence—a term first coined by G. Stanley Hall in 1904. Theorists such as Freud and Erikson propagated this approach with their focus on psychosexual development and the struggle to achieve identity. However, later theorists, spearheaded by Havighurst (1972), highlighted developmental tasks and the normalization of this period of development and identity formation. In this chapter we highlight the normal attributes of adolescent development and emphasize a movement away from conceptualizing adolescence as a time of storm and stress.

Defining Normal

Let's begin this chapter by simply cutting to the chase. Do we really have any idea of what *normal* is? Defining normality can be an elusive concept. We have numerous models and theories that define various aspects of normal development. We might see stages or explanations of behaviors. But rarely does one go through their day-to-day life identifying what is normal. Rather, we do the opposite, preferring to identify what is not normal. What stands out? What is the exception? What draws our attention away from the mundane?

Think about a time when you were in a grocery store or restaurant and you saw a child throwing a temper tantrum. The child is on the floor screaming; tears are flowing and there is no response to a reasonable or calm tone. The parent of the child stands looking at their kid trying to maintain some type of dignity, talking in a reasonable tone and looking exasperated. Other people are walking by this scene. Some of those individuals walk away with a scowl, nodding disapprovingly and perhaps thinking, "My kid would never behave this way!" Or perhaps their response is more toward criticism of the parent: "If my kid did this I would make sure they never did it again!" Yet other people might witness this scene and have a more empathic perspective, "I've been there!" The entire situation draws our attention because the ongoing behavior seems extreme; yet many people have not only witnessed this situation but have also experienced it themselves. But would anyone look at the situation and think to themselves, "Hmmm... that's normal"?

"I Know It When I See It"

Hence, rather than identify what is normal, pointing out what is *not normal* might be far more common. Perhaps one of the better-known colloquialisms occurred under a 1964 Supreme Court case, *Jacobellis v. Ohio*, in which the court was attempting to rule whether the state of Ohio could ban a film that the state identified as obscene. In this case, Supreme Court Justice Potter Stewart declared that the Constitution protected obscenity as free speech, with the exception of hard-core pornography, which could not be readily defined.

> I have reached the conclusion ... that under the First and Fourteenth Amendments criminal laws in this area are constitutionally limited to hard-core pornography. I shall not today attempt further to define the kinds of material I understand to be embraced within that shorthand description; and perhaps I could never succeed in intelligibly doing so. But I know it when I see it, and the motion picture involved in this case is not that. (*Jacobellis v. Ohio*, 378 U.S. 184 [1964])

Yet defining *normal* through the identification of *what is not normal* does not really work. Perhaps one way to think about normal is by considering what we might expect. An outcome that is expected is normal. When something happens that we don't expect, that's not normal. This idea was first postulated by Abraham de Moivre, in 1733. De Moivre was a statistician who was trying to solve a gambling problem, as he often consulted with gamblers to create lengthy computations of probability. De Moivre noted, for example, that if a coin were flipped many times, noting heads versus tails, the shape of the distribution created a curve; this would eventually be referred to as the *normal curve* (Lane, n.d.).

So what does any of this have to do with youth development and, more importantly, counseling youth? We can look to the *Diagnostic and Statistical Manual of Mental Disorders* (5th ed., tex rev., American Psychiatric Association [APA], 2022) for an answer. When does a problem become a problem? A key criteria is *impairment*, defined as an obstruction in or interference with daily living, such as school, work, relationships, and social and emotional functioning. So, when is a behavior not normal? The APA stipulated that psychiatric diagnoses are not merely identified with impairment, but that the impairment must be "clinically significant." Hence, there is not simply the notion of a problem being present but also the allusion to that problem being severe in nature.

Absent from this discussion, however, is context. Let's go back to our previous example of the crying child in the grocery store. Maybe you have either experienced a crying kid in the grocery store or you have witnessed it. And maybe you even thought, "no big deal." Or you stopped, paused, and looked empathically at the parent. Regardless, this was not a disruption to your life. But what if the child is crying in a place of worship? Again, no problem. Some places of worship even have cry rooms. It's as if to say, "Kids cry during services. We did, too. We expect it. So, here is a place you can go!" Now, what about a child crying in a movie theater? That's a bigger problem. If the parent or guardian does not walk out of the theater with the crying child, someone is probably going to get a manager and a removal will occur. What is the difference? It is the significance of the disruption and who is affected by it. A temper tantrum in a place of worship might seem normal; a temper tantrum at the grocery store might be a little less expected. But a temper tantrum in a movie theater? No, that is not going to sit well. We continue to see these issues as children get older. What about opposition? Is that normal? Or what about rolling the eyes at a parent or teacher?

As we consider what is normal in youth, it might be helpful to consider these points:

1. Identifying what is normal is a statement of probability, an indication about what is expected.
2. What might be considered *not normal* or *abnormal* should demonstrate chronicity and evidence of impairment.

The frequency of a problematic behavior and the evidence of impairment are important considerations because not every behavior that is outside the mainstream leads to impairment. Creativity may not be normal, but the effect of creativity would certainly not qualify as impairment and can even lead to healthy social and emotional behaviors. In essence, not all behavior that is outside the norm is bad. However, as clinicians, we are primarily concerned with behaviors and developmental issues that are more indicative of impairment in social, emotional, and cognitive functioning. A review of prominent models in child and adolescent development may be helpful to add context to understanding normal development, as well as to highlight developmental tasks in context with age and stage (Havighurst, 1972).

A Primer on Theories of Development

To provide a comprehensive overview of developmental models would be exhaustive. Here we highlight prominent developmental models specific to youth development, but also provide the following cautions:

1. Theories of development are not necessarily empirically validated. Freud's psychosexual theory of development was a forerunner to subsequent theories but was monocultural, with a focus on the development of White males and a lack of empirical support. The models presented in this text survived the test of time but may not necessarily be developed through rigorous empirical research (Carducci, 2009).
2. The age and stage categorizations are not static; rather, some stages occur much later than initially theorized. For example, Piaget noted formal operational reasoning begins around age 11, but the understanding of abstract thought and the complexity of emotions might actually happen years later (Ray, 2016).
3. Stages in developmental models are generally presented as a hierarchy. Later stages build off earlier stages, and being at a higher stage at an earlier age is not necessarily important or favorable (Ray, 2016). For example, a fifth grader reading at the college level may have the cognitive capacity to comprehend a novel but lack the emotional maturity to internalize the experiences.
4. Many theories of development were conceptualized in the early to mid-20th century. Hence, developmental theories were conceptualized

outside the scope of diversity, equity, and inclusion. Many of the values espoused in developmental theories, such as autonomy, may be White, Westernized values that lack inclusivity or consideration of cultures outside of the culture of power (Evans et al., 2015).

Psychosocial Identity Development: Erik Erikson

Erikson's 1950 theory on psychosocial identity development included eight stages across the lifespan. From these eight stages, five stages focus on birth through adolescence.

- Trust versus mistrust, birth to 1½
- Autonomy versus shame and doubt, 1½ to 3
- Initiative versus guilt, 3 to 5
- Industry versus inferiority, 5 to 12
- Identity versus role confusion, 12 to 18
- Intimacy versus isolation, 18 to 40
- Generativity versus stagnation, 40 to 65
- Integrity versus despair, 65+

Guided by Freud's theory of psychosexual development, Erikson believed individuals to be motivated to develop socially (Ray, 2016). Beginning at birth, infants learn to trust in the care they receive through affection, comfort, and sustenance. In other words, basic needs are provided by the parent, which results in a trusting relationship. When such basic needs are withheld, physical maturation, social development, and attachment may be stalled. At around 2 years of age, children transition from total dependence to the development of some independence. This includes learning and eventually controlling bodily functions and the opportunity to make choices, perhaps with food, toys, or clothes. Mastering these skills can lead to more positive social and academic functioning (Erikson, 1950/1963). With newfound autonomy, children may begin to engage in new activities and behaviors. When such initiative is encouraged by parents or caregivers, children gain confidence and are willing to take more risks or try new things; conversely, children who were discouraged from such independence may be reluctant to try new behaviors and may express less confidence. In the next stage, around age 5, children may start school and begin activities that revolve less around immediate family. As a result, children expand their social environment. The increase in socialization and activities beyond the home and immediate family have the potential to increase self-concept and further expand their physical and emotional abilities. In the final stage of youth development, which includes adolescence, youth attempt to establish identity or sense of self through an exploration of beliefs, values, and relationships. During this period, adolescents may negotiate between differentiation from parents, family, or caregivers and undertake an adoption of values. Youth who are not encouraged to explore their identity may experience frustration in forming and sustaining relationships or suffer from lower self-esteem (Arnold, 2017).

Adolescent Identity Development: James Marcia

Marcia (1966) expanded on Erikson's stage of identify versus role confusion, choosing to address adolescent development. Marcia did not propose a hierarchical model of development; rather, Marcia proposed four identity statuses based on a semi-structured interview developed for research purposes. Within adolescence, Marcia noted the following identity statuses: diffusion, foreclosure, moratorium, and achievement.

Marcia believed that adolescent identity was established through decisions and commitment to social roles, values, beliefs, and vocational interests and goals (Kroger & Marcia, 2011). Adolescents in identity diffusion may not view themselves as having choices. *Diffusion* may occur as a response to authoritarianism or through stagnation in previous stages of development. *Foreclosure* describes adolescents who may have explored some values, beliefs, or goals but essentially conform to external expectations. Such expectations may be from parents or caregivers, community, or cultural expectations. Sometimes, adolescents are ready to make choices but lack commitment to such choices; this is known as *identity moratorium*. This identity status might be characterized as exploration of a variety of choices. When choices and commitment converge for adolescents, Marcia describes this status as *identity achievement*. Not only was Marcia's theory of identity statuses developed through research, but further validation is also apparent, confirming the identity statuses that Marcia developed (Potterton et al., 2022).

Cognitive Development: Jean Claude Piaget

Unlike Freud and Erickson, who were concerned with personality development, Piaget focused on cognitive development. Piaget initially studied intelligence with Alfred Binet, who invented the first intelligence test, and developed a theory of cognitive development based on observations of his own children, a small, limited, and privileged sample of three! In 1936, Piaget theorized that children learn through either acquiring information and placing it into categories, referred to as *schemas*, or by revising and changing existing schemas, known as *accommodation*. This process included four hierarchical, developmental stages.

- Sensorimotor, birth to 2
- Preoperational, 2 to 7
- Concrete operational, 7 to 12
- Formal operational, 12 to adulthood

In the *sensorimotor* stage, children acquire knowledge through the senses and the development of bodily functions. The *preoperational* stage is characterized by language development, communication, and socialization. The *concrete operational* stage describes children's ability to think logically, follow rules, and understand order, whereas *formal operational* development includes the ability to formulate abstractions and reasoning.

Though Piaget provided a framework for intellectual development, a limitation of Piaget's theory is its lack of emphasis on social interactions (Ray, 2016). Whereas Piaget felt children construct their knowledge through their own acquisition of experiences and stimuli, Vygotsky (1978) believed that children develop knowledge primarily through social interactions and interactions with their environment. Both theorists make a strong point, and, because clinicians view child development from a systemic perspective, both the quality of the environment and the opportunity to engage in experiences and social interaction may help or hinder development.

Moral Development: Lawrence Kohlberg

In 1958, Kohlberg expanded Piaget's theory by focusing on moral development as a component of cognitive development. Kohlberg proposed three hierarchical stages of moral development, with two phases in each level, that were linked to Piaget's theory of cognitive development.

- Preconventional, young children to 9
- Conventional, 9 to adulthood
- Postconventional, few adolescents and adults

In the *preconventional* stage, behaviors are shaped by the expectations of parents, caregivers, and other essential adults (e.g., teachers, authority figures). The early phase is characterized by adherence to rules and punishment for disobedience, whereas the latter phase is characterized by how engagement in a behavior may satisfy one's needs. In the *conventional* stage, the individual accepts rules based on social norms. In the earlier phase, typically adolescents and adults engage in moral behaviors based on the approval of others; in the latter phase, there is an awareness of the broader rules of society and the law. The final stage, *postconventional*, may be achieved by a few adolescents and adults; Kohlberg estimated that about 15% of adults reach this stage (Kohlberg, 1984). In this final stage, moral reasoning is depicted internally, rather than externally. In the earlier stage, individuals recognize that some social rules may disenfranchise others. For example, a public school holds a Christmas assembly, and a Jewish student does not wish to attend. In the latter stage, individuals develop their own sense of morality. This could apply to diversity, equity, and inclusion.

Some of the criticisms of Kohlberg's theory focused on his research design, in which different individuals were interviewed at the various stages, but later longitudinal research with the same participants across years of development confirmed Kohlberg's stages (Colby et al., 1983). In addition, the focus on justice as opposed to care of others was noted to be sex-biased by Gilligan (1977). Gilligan asserted that, for females, care for others was more highly developed and socialized and therefore represented an aspect of morality equivalent to justice.

Developmental Tasks: Robert J. Havighurst

A less discussed theory of development attributed to Havighurst (1972) focuses on developmental tasks. In developmental task theory, Havighurst integrated the roles of biology and maturation; beliefs, values, and goals;

and culture and environment to formulate a biopsychosocial developmental model. According to Havighurst, individuals develop across six stages of the lifespan, and, within each stage, the achievement of developmental tasks leads to enhanced self-concept, successful progression in the next developmental stage, and contribution to society. Because of the focus on a biopsychosocial model, successful achievement with developmental tasks may be influenced by biological, psychological, and social factors. Below are Havighurst's six developmental stages across the lifespan, three of which focus on childhood through adolescence.

- Infancy and early childhood, 0 to 5
- Middle childhood, 6 to 12
- Adolescence, 13 to 17
- Early adulthood, 18 to 35
- Middle adulthood, 36 to 60
- Later maturity, over 60

Box 2.1 provides an overview of examples of developmental tasks at each stage with youth developmental tasks in bold (Havighurst, 1972).

A Systemic Perspective on Development

Although each developmental model provides a theory of development that may be generalized, conceptualizing the intersection of developmental theories can be challenging. Figure 2.1 provides a framework on how these various developmental theories intersect with one another.

Figure 2.1 essentially demonstrates that, throughout the lifespan, at each phase, development is multifaceted with a lot going on throughout each of the age categories depicted, and this is particularly true for infancy through adolescence.

Developmental processes cannot be sped up, but barriers can appear through the family, educational, and community systems that can hinder development. In other words, positive environments have the capacity to foster and support development; negative environments put barriers in place that obstruct normal, healthy development. Consider the implications of growing up in areas inundated by poverty and/or violence and the extent to which such circumstances impact education, behavior, and wellness.

Box 2.1 Examples of Havighurst's (1972) Developmental Tasks

Infancy and Early Childhood:
  Learning to walk.
  Learning to take solid foods
  Learning to talk
  Learning to control the elimination of body wastes
  Learning sex differences and sexual modesty
  Forming concepts and learning language to describe social and physical reality
  Getting ready to read

Middle Childhood:
  Learning physical skills necessary for ordinary games
  Building wholesome attitudes toward oneself as a growing organism
  Learning to get along with age-mates
  Learning an appropriate social role
  Developing fundamental skills in reading, writing, and calculating
  Developing concepts necessary for everyday living.
  Developing conscience, morality, and a scale of values
  Achieving personal independence
  Developing attitudes toward social groups and institutions

Developmental Tasks of Adolescence:
  Achieving new and more mature relations with age-mates of both sexes
  Achieving a masculine or feminine social role
  Accepting one's physique and using the body effectively
  Achieving emotional independence of parents and other adults
  Acquiring a set of values and an ethical system as a guide to behavior; developing an ideology
  Desiring and achieving socially responsible behavior

Developmental Tasks of Early Adulthood:
  Selecting a mate
  Achieving a social role

> Learning to live with a marriage partner
> Starting a family
> Rearing children
> Managing a home
> Getting started in an occupation
> Taking on civic responsibility
> Finding a congenial social group
>
> Developmental Tasks of Middle Age:
> Achieving adult civic and social responsibility
> Establishing and maintaining an economic standard of living
> Assisting teenage children to become responsible and happy adults
> Developing adult leisure-time activities
> Relating oneself to one's spouse as a person
> Accepting and adjusting to the physiologic changes or middle age
> Adjusting to aging parents.
>
> Developmental Tasks of Later Maturity:
> Adjusting to decreasing physical strength and health
> Adjusting to retirement and reduced income
> Adjusting to death of a spouse
> Establishing an explicit affiliation with one's age group
> Meeting social and civil obligations
> Establishing satisfactory physical living arrangement

Within the various paradigms of youth development is the role of executive functioning (EF), which describes children's abilities related to memory, self-control, and adaptability (Chen et al., 2020), and it is these very same functions that become adversely effected due to trauma, including neglect, abuse, and violence. Childhood trauma might induce a state of hyperarousal, which can impact EF in such tasks as paying attention or time-on-task behaviors (Kavanaugh et al., 2017). Chen and colleagues noted an association between trauma experiences of children and an increase in behavior problems. However, the effects of trauma on cognitive development and EF were not evidenced, as other variables such as maternal education appear to have more impact. This is not to say that trauma does not impact EF; rather, other variables also play a role.

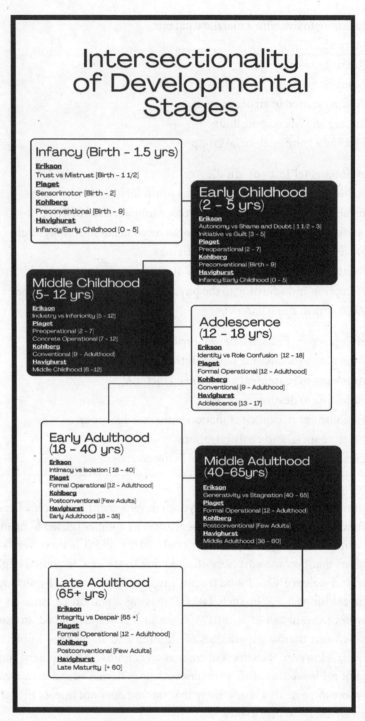

Figure 2.1 A sequential framework of the intersectionality of developmental stages.

For example, simply in terms of the effect of low socioeconomic status, access to books may be obstructed and thus the habit of reading may not exist or be a priority in the home. But reading is highly correlated with the acquisition of vocabulary. Vocabulary is one of the strongest predictors of standardized test scores related to ability, including scores on tests measuring intelligence, aptitude, and achievement (Balkin & Juhnke, 2018; Ibrahim et al., 2016; Masrai & Milton, 2017; Ramsook et al., 2020). But what does this have to do with the stages of development? Let's take a look.

One of the best ways to acquire vocabulary is to read. Access to books and the habits of reading, whether reading to a child or the child engaging in independent reading, are associated with stronger vocabulary (Duff et al., 2015; Ibrahim et al., 2016). Why does that matter? Besides the potential for enhanced self-efficacy and achievement in academic tasks (Masrai & Milton, 2017; Ramsook et al., 2020), children's growth in vocabulary is associated with communication skills and self-regulation. As early as preschool, children with greater vocabulary skills show greater skills in self-discipline, maintaining attention, compliance with rules/expectations, memory, and communication with others as exhibited by initiating, maintaining, and terminating conversations (Ramsook et al., 2020). Hence, within this evidence, we see the incorporation of Havighurst's developmental tasks in early childhood, including preparation for reading and learning socialization, language, and concepts. Both Piaget and Erikson emphasized increases in language development, autonomy, socialization, and an expansion of one's social environment, whereas Kohlberg emphasized learning and adherence to rules.

Two points are worth mentioning here. First, notice the commonalities and crossover references among the various theories of development. Socialization, learning, communication, and adherence to rules are mentioned in each of the theories. Second, we started this illustration with citations related to how access to books and increased reading habits could enhance vocabulary skills and the associations that vocabulary has to educational and developmental outcomes. Could an early intervention to improve access to books and reading really enhance development?

Complex problems rarely have simple solutions; complex problems have complex solutions. So, simply suggesting that providing opportunities for children to (a) be read to more frequently and (b) have more access to books oversimplifies a complex problem. Such an intervention might be helpful but would not likely be sufficient to obtaining better educational and developmental outcomes if undertaken as a sole intervention. Remember, we are looking at problems from a systemic perspective.

For example, a lack of access to books might be due to income inequities, which often exacerbate environments where there may be larger social issues such as increased violence, food insecurity, and less stability in the home. These issues go beyond what an early childhood reading program might address. An organization can provide more access to books, but that pales in comparison to the effects of poor nutrition or trauma that may be occurring.

Hence, educational interventions that ignore the systemic issues might be limited in their accomplishments. Consider the following study by Ray et al. (2015) in which a meta-analysis was conducted using 23 studies evaluating the effects of child-centered play therapy (CCPT) in schools. Small effects were noted for children who received CCPT in schools, with improvements in behavior and academic outcomes and decreases in emotional distress when compared to children who did not receive an intervention. However, no differences were noted between children who received CCPT in school and children who received a different therapeutic intervention in school. Notice that the effects of CCPT in schools were beneficial when the child was not receiving any intervention at all, but the effects were not large. Certainly, some effect—even a small effect—is better than none, but would the provision of a therapeutic service have been even more effective? Perhaps not. All studies utilized in the meta-analysis met the following requirements:

> (a) studies appeared in print between 1970 and 2011; (b) at least one experimental group utilized a clearly defined CCPT intervention; (c) the intervention was conducted in the school; (d) the CCPT intervention was conducted by a mental health professional (school counselor or other mental health professional); (e) participants were between pre-kindergarten and seventh grade; (f) participants had to be selected into treatment, control, or comparison groups by either random assignment or other quasi-experimental method; and (g) the study included data sufficient to calculate an effect size. (Ray et al., 2015, p. 110)

From these inclusion criteria, we do not have information on the frequency of the intervention or the extent of problems outside of the school environment. In other words, with the best efforts made from the school, addressing issues outside the school setting remains challenging and results in limited gains from interventions. Change does not come easily, and lasting change over a long period of time, referred to as *quantum change*, is not an easily attainable outcome (Kottler & Balkin, 2020).

Summary

In this chapter we provided an overview of keys principles underlying developmental stages across the lifespan with an emphasis on child development. We illustrated the key components of each stage related to child development and provided an understanding of the commonalities and intersections of various theories of development. We examined examples of how educational and therapeutic interventions may fall short, particularly when they only include one facet of a complex system to address barriers that may impair development for youth. We conclude by providing context for youth workers to consider when addressing the holistic health of youth. Particularly when we are talking about child development, the removal of barriers that may impede development is challenging, and one intervention within one system may not be sufficient to create quantum change. Again, our emphasis is on the point that child development cannot be accelerated but barriers can be removed so that development is not impeded.

Particularly with youth, developing an understanding of barriers in home and educational settings and beyond is essential. For example, consider the following:

- Does the child have access to medical, dental, and vision care?
- Is the home in a safe environment?
- Has the child encountered or is encountering traumatic experiences, and how are those experiences being dealt with? What resources can the school provide?
- What resources need to be provided outside of the home and school settings?
- Are such services accessible to the family?

There are perhaps even more questions to add to this list, but this is a start when looking at the various facets that contribute to child development from a systemic perspective.

References

American Psychiatric Association. (2022). *Diagnostic and statistical manual of mental disorders* (5th ed., text rev.). https://doi.org/10.1176/appi.books.9780890425787

Arnold, M. E. (2017). Supporting adolescent exploration and commitment: Identity formation, thriving, and positive youth development. *Journal of Youth Development,12*(4),1–15. https://doi.org/10.5195/jyd.2017.522

Balkin, R. S., & Juhnke, G. A. (2018). *Assessment in counseling: Practice and applications.* Oxford University Press.

Carducci, B. J. (2009). *The psychology of personality: Viewpoints, research, and applications*. Wiley.

Chen, S. H., Cohodes, E., Bush, N. R., & Lieberman, A. F. (2020). Child and caregiver executive function in trauma-exposed families: Relations with children's behavioral and cognitive functioning. *Journal of Experimental Child Psychology, 200*. https://doi.org/10.1016/j.jecp.2020.104946

Colby, A., Kohlberg, L., Gibbs, J., & Lieberman, M. (1983). *A longitudinal study of moral judgment. Monographs of the Society for Research in Child Development, 48 (1–2, Serial No. 200)*. University of Chicago Press.

Duff, D., Tomblin, J. B., & Catts, H. (2015). The influence of reading on vocabulary growth: A case for a Matthew effect. *Journal of Speech, Language, and Hearing Research, 58*(3), 853–864. https://doi.org/10.1044/2015_JSLHR-L-13-0310

Erikson, E. H. (1950/1963). *Childhood and society*. W. W. Norton.

Evans, M., Duffey, T., Erford, B. T., & Gladding, S. T. (2015). Counseling in the United States. In T. H. Hohenshil, N. E. Amundson, & S. G. Niles (Eds.), *Counseling Around the World* (pp. 323–331). https://doi.org/10.1002/9781119222736.ch34

Gilligan, C. (1977). In a different voice: Women's conceptions of self and of morality. *Harvard Educational Review, 47*(4), 481–517.

Havighurst, R. J. (1972). *Developmental tasks and education*. David McKay.

Ibrahim, E. H. E., Sarudin, I., & Muhamad, A. J. (2016). The relationship between vocabulary size and reading comprehension of ESL learners. *English Language Teaching, 9*(2), 116–123. http://dx.doi.org/10.5539/elt.v9n2p116

Jacobellis v. Ohio. (n.d.). Oyez. Retrieved April 17, 2022, from https://www.oyez.org/cases/1963/11

Kavanaugh, B. C., Dupont-Frechette, J. A., Jerskey, B. A., & Holler, K. A. (2017). Neurocognitive deficits in children and adolescents following maltreatment: Neurodevelopmental consequences and neuropsychological implications of traumatic stress, *Applied Neuropsychology: Child, 6*(1), 64–78. http://doi.org/10.1080/21622965.2015.1079712

Kohlberg, L. (1958). *The development of modes of thinking and choices in years 10 to 16*. PhD Dissertation, University of Chicago.

Kohlberg, L. (1984). *The psychology of moral development: The nature and validity of moral stages (Essays on moral development, volume 2).* Harper & Row

Kottler, J. A., & Balkin, R. S. (2020). *Myths, misconceptions, and invalid assumptions about counseling and psychotherapy*. Oxford University Press.

Kroger, J., & Marcia, J. E. (2011). The identity statuses: Origins, meanings, and interpretations. In S. J. Schwartz, K. Luyckx, & V. L. Vignoles (Eds.), *Handbook of identity theory and research* (pp. 31–53). Springer Science + Business Media. https://doi.org/10.1007/978-1-4419-7988-9_2

Lane, D. (n.d.). Online statistics education: A multimedia course of study. Rice University. Retrieved December 2, 2022 from http://onlinestatbook.com/

Marcia, J. E. (1966). Development and validation of ego-identity status. *Journal of Personality and Social Psychology, 3*(5), 551–558. https://doi.org/10.1037/h0023281

Masrai, A., & Milton, J. (2017). Recognition vocabulary knowledge and intelligence as predictors of academic achievement in EFL context. *TESOL International Journal, 12*, 128–142.

Piaget, J. (1936). *Origins of intelligence in the child*. Routledge & Kegan Paul.

Potterton, R., Austin, A., Robinson, L., Webb, H., Allen, K. L., & Schmidt, U. (2022). Identity development and social-emotional disorders during adolescence and emerging adulthood: A systematic review and meta-analysis. *Journal of Youth and Adolescence, 51*(1), 16–29. https://doi.org/10.1007/s10964-021-01536-7

Ramsook, K. A., Welsh, J. A., & Bierman, K. L. (2020). What you say, and how you say it: Preschoolers' growth in vocabulary and communication skills differentially predict kindergarten academic achievement and self-regulation. *Social Development (Oxford, England), 29*(3), 783–800. https://doi.org/10.1111/sode.12425

Ray, D. C. (2016). *A therapist's guide to child development: The extraordinarily normal years*. Routledge.

Ray, D. C., Armstrong, S. A., Balkin, R. S., & Jayne, K. M. (2015). Child centered play therapy in the schools: Review and meta-analysis. *Psychology in the Schools, 52*, 107–123. https://doi.org/10.1002/pits.21798

Vygotsky, L. S. (1978). *Mind in society: The development of higher psychological processes*. Harvard University Press.

3
Our System of Care

Overview

Our system of care for youth is distinct in that the health of a minor is very different from the health of an adult. For instance, factors that may affect youth include reliance on family factors (e.g., a minor cannot drive to healthcare appointments) and physical and emotional changes (i.e., puberty). In addition to this, systems such as provider networks, communication, insurance, and knowledge of different health fields can all affect the strength of continuity of care. Given that approximately 8 million youth aged 3–17 are diagnosed with a mental health condition (NSCH; Health Resources and Services Administration, 2020), those working with youth should have an increased awareness of these barriers and begin advocating for change in the system.

In this chapter, we examine the continuum of care across multiple spectrums—from outpatient counseling to long-term residential treatment. Furthermore, we provide an overview of how youth enter into the justice system, the likely outcomes of the system, and the need for reform and implementation of mental health services. Last, we highlight where the system of care fails and what might constitute effective services for youth.

Defining Care for Youth

Before we move on to how our system may be currently failing children and adolescents, it is crucial to know what the system of health currently looks like. Generally speaking, systemic care for youth involves all individual people (e.g., parent/guardian, teacher, counselor) and systems (e.g., community, social, healthcare) working together in a coordinated and integrative system of care for the child. Few programs and communities achieve this level of unification, usually for reasons including a lack of a cohesive definition, funding, resources, and stigma. There are several variations of what we consider *integrated treatment* (e.g., coordinated care; integrated behavioral and primary healthcare treatment; Watson & Schmit, 2019). In fact, each healthcare field may have its own specific term for this type of care. In addition, this level of collaboration would likely take governmental funding and resources. All of these issues together could potentially impact disintegration within healthcare for youth.

Instead, if you were to walk into any system that may involve care of youth you would likely see (a) professionals knowledgeable about that area, (b) physical space for that field, and (c) separate treatment planning efforts. A common example is related to medical care. Imagine a parent taking their child to the medical doctor for a wellness check. In that medical office, you would see medical doctors (MDs), registered nurses (RNs), and administrative teams all in the same building. These individuals all have knowledge about the medical treatment of children. At the end of the visit, the doctor and/or nurse types up a treatment plan and/or note for the child patient. In that note, the doctor writes what was discussed and what the child may further need. Now imagine this added consideration: the child is physically in great health, no issues, growing well, meeting developmental milestones; however, she has started to show signs of difficulty concentrating at school, becoming really irritable with peers, and, for the past 2 weeks, has told her parents that she is scared to go to school. What then? In that scenario, the family would likely be referred to (or have to find themselves) a different provider specializing in a different field and the aforementioned list (a, b, c) would start again.

You may even see this separate nature of things in other areas. Examples include (a) keeping extracurricular activities independent of elementary schools, (b) sending at-risk children to alternative schools, (c) prosecuting juveniles based on developmentally appropriate yet risky behaviors, and (d) prescribing psychiatric medication for children with no follow-up to counseling services. This is not to say that every provider should know everything about every field. That would be impossible and improbable. We need medical doctors who specialize in specific areas of the body and age ranges. We need licensed counselors who specialize in childhood anxiety. We need teachers to educate our youth. These are all important jobs that aid in the healthy development of youth. However, communication and collaboration between these fields would yield a more positive result than the current system provides.

Mental Health in Childhood

A national survey on the mental health of children found that approximately 13.2% have been diagnosed with a mental health disorder (8.5% anxiety; 6.8% behavior disorder; 3.8% depression; Health Resources and Services Administration [HRSA], 2020). These numbers are likely higher given that the entire population has been affected by the COVID-19 pandemic that began in early 2020. About half of those diagnosed with a mental health disorder receive counseling services. According to Ali et al. (2019), youth aged 3–17 commonly utilized only medication for mental health treatment. This in and of itself is an issue, given that research has shown that counseling can be just as effective as medication and is very effective when used along with medication for mental health disorders. This also highlights the need for professional advocacy to remove barriers that many face to receiving treatment.

Some common mental health issues that youth may face in their lives include but are not limited to the following:

- Anxiety
- Behavior issues
- Depression
- Substance use
- Suicidality

Because these are discussed further in other chapters, we only introduce overall mental health topics here. Contrary to what mainstream society may believe, mental health issues can and do start in childhood, although symptomatology may look different than that seen in adults. Just as in adults, however, there is no known singular cause for mental health disorders, and they are likely a mixture of genetics, brain chemistry, and environmental factors such as trauma or stress. Unlike adults, children and adolescents are in a constant state of change. They go through major physical, emotional, and psychological changes throughout childhood. These changes may thwart mental health diagnoses and treatment. What complicates things even more is that some of the symptoms seen, especially in adolescents, can also be considered typical behaviors (e.g., isolation and irritability in teenagers). Now that we have discussed the system of care and childhood mental health, it is important to look at where and how the system fails and what may be missing.

Where the System of Care May Fail

As stated in Chapter 1, research is clear on the fact that counseling is effective in helping youth with a variety of issues. At this point you may be asking why, if mental health clinicians are facilitating successful outcomes, particularly when it comes to mental and emotional health, are there so many unanswered questions related to decreasing mental health issues as a whole in our society? It is true that there have been numerous increases in events effecting the mental health of youth. For example, school shootings, suicide attempts, family violence, and mass incarceration have all increased. Unfortunately, as much as we would like to say the answer to this mystery is here in this text, there is no simple answer. Instead, a multitude of factors are at work, some that we are hoping to shed light on here.

First, the lack of integration between the many systems affecting youth is a main failure of the system of care itself. For the most part and although all healthcare providers care about the progress of their clients, we all work in silos. Even with the best intentions, many providers will provide referrals to clients for issues outside of their expertise. This is certainly needed—but is it enough? This is not to place blame on the providers themselves. Again, a long line of systemic flaws persist.

Second, one huge issue is the shortage of mental health clinicians. Wainberg et al. (2017) found that approximately 75% of people around the world have no access to mental health treatment. There are just not enough of us to keep up with mental health needs (American Psychiatric Association [APA], 2021; National Council for Mental Wellbeing [NCMW], 2020), especially since these needs have increased during the past few years. Furthermore, those who live in rural areas have an even harder time obtaining services due to lack of resources and scarcity of providers. This further highlights the challenge caused by the fact that approximately 57 million people live in rural communities (HRSA, Federal Office of Rural Health Programs [FORHP], 2022).

Last, withdrawal from services could also be related to a lack of proper continuation of care. Reasons why minor clients may stop attending mental health services include moving, parents changing jobs and/or insurance change, and family illness/death (Bornheimer et al., 2018). Try to remember a time in your life when one of these events may have happened. These transitions are hard. Now add on top of that the specific barriers related to mental health. At that point, counseling services understandably may no longer be a priority for families. Imagine a child having issues transitioning after a move. They begin a new school, have to make new friends, everything seems new and difficult. However, their new school is in a district that is well-funded, with several clinicians in the school setting (i.e., school counselors, school psychologists) and every new student is mandated to seek counseling from one of the many counselors housed in the school. How do you think this may impact the child's well-being? In addition to this, research has consistently reported that children in poverty have a higher degree of mental health diagnoses and are less likely to obtain healthcare (Cree et al., 2018; Ghandour et al., 2019). This might suggest that healthcare is a systemic rather than just an individual issue. Below we discuss the importance of continuity of care and how this may help with some of the systemic issues.

Continuity of Care

One of the proposed answers to the lack of a holistic system of care for clients is what we call *continuity of care*. According to the American Academy of Family Physicians Foundation (AAFP), continuity of care has to do with the quality of a person's healthcare over time. The purpose of continuity of care is to have a shared knowledge of and goal for the health of clients in order to provide a high quality of care. This aids in communication between professionals (e.g., medical doctors, counselors, social workers, etc.). Imagine a family receiving health services without the major barriers of navigating referrals, lack of communication between providers, and lack of knowledge about health information.

In a more integrated system of health (i.e., physical and behavioral health), health information is shared between health providers such as medical doctors, licensed professional counselors, and psychiatrists (Schmit et al., 2018) and may even be provided in the same building (see Heath et al., 2013). Although rare, this is seen as the gold standard of continuity of care. Taking the example above, imagine that none of those barriers exists and healthcare is provided in the same building, allowing clients to receive both physical care from a medical doctor, psychiatric care from a psychiatrist, and counseling services from a licensed clinician, all of whom are communicating with each other to develop a treatment plan.

Next, we explore the more common settings in which youth may receive treatment services.

Treatment Settings

Clinicians may see clients in a multitude of settings. Here we discuss outpatient counseling, inpatient counseling, and long-term residential treatment. Of course, these are not all-encompassing as children and adolescents may also receive services from schools and medical practices. However, it is crucial for those working with minors to be knowledgeable of all types of treatment settings so they can have a more holistic picture of possible care options.

Outpatient Counseling

Outpatient counseling settings are likely the most common way for youth to receive services outside of schools. Outpatient services include counseling usually at an agency, private practice, or group practice. Clients utilize outpatient counseling for mental healthcare when safety does not pose a risk (i.e., suicidality).

There is no specific modality used in outpatient settings as this will depend on the type of practice and client needs and issues, as well as on clinician theoretical orientation. Common services in outpatient settings are individual counseling, group therapy, family therapy, and play therapy.

Strengths of outpatient counseling include clients being in the least restrictive environment (i.e., live at home; go to school) and giving the family the ability to choose sessions/clinicians based on availability. Outpatient counseling is a good modality for children and their families who are struggling with mental health issues or life stressors. Common issues may include anxiety and depression or changing schools and bullying.

Inpatient Counseling

Inpatient counseling settings are necessary when youth are a danger to self or others and need 24/7 surveillance and care. There are different types of inpatient settings including acute care, crisis residence, and residential treatment. Residential treatment will be discussed in more detail below; however, acute care and crisis residence are briefly defined here and further discussed in Chapter 7. *Acute care* generally means that clients need treatment on a short-term basis. Acute care in a behavioral hospital has four overall goals: safety, reducing harm to self or others, discharge planning, and providing resources for outpatient services (Balkin & Roland, 2005). The need for inpatient counseling for children specifically may look a little different from that for adults or adolescents who may have better communication skills. Of course, the main reason your client may need inpatient care is if they are in an immediate crisis (e.g., showing suicidal behaviors). In some cases, children become a threat to others (e.g., consistently throwing chairs in a school classroom where other children are present). Children may also experience hallucinations or feelings of being out of control. In such situations, outpatient counseling may be inappropriate, thus necessitating the need for hospitalization.

Residential Treatment

Residential treatment, while rare for children, may be utilized for those who are not in an immediate crisis (i.e., suicidal) but who need a longer period of treatment. These settings are normally used when a child has a severe mental health disorder. For example, a developmental and/or neurocognitive disorder along with suicidal ideation, having active hallucinations (auditory or visual), or conduct-related disorders along with suicidality. At times, psychiatrists may refer children to residential treatment programs when they have been seen in inpatient hospitals (i.e., acute care) several times without making progress, thus necessitating longer treatment. During their time at a residential treatment center, clients may learn more about their disorder and coping skills to manage symptomatology. Similar to acute care, clients receive 24-hour care. Other reasons for residential treatment may include substance abuse and eating disorders. One huge issue with this includes financial responsibility because most residential centers are expensive.

Now that we have gone over the different modalities of treatment, you may be asking yourself, "How do I decide which level of treatment my client needs (i.e., outpatient, short-term inpatient, or residential)?" There is no simple answer to this, and there are two main things to consider: (a) severity of symptomatology and (b) history of treatment. Generally speaking, you can think of treatment in terms of levels, with level 1 being low severity (e.g., well-functioning; manages everyday activities with perhaps an adjustment disorder; little to no distress) and 5 being high severity (e.g., suicidal; homicidal, active hallucinations). Additionally, clinicians should consider history of mental illness and history of treatment.

Juvenile Justice

Juvenile justice at its simplest is an area of the legal system designated for those individuals younger than 18 who cannot be held criminally responsible. Laws set for juveniles are governed mostly by states, with each having its own code. For example, in Texas, the juvenile justice system "emphasizes treatment and rehabilitation" (TJJD, 2022) rather than penalty. In addition, the age limits for juveniles in Texas are "at least 10 years old but not yet 17" (TJJD, 2022). Clinicians should refer to their state's code on this information.

There are clear problems with the juvenile justice system. Studies have shown that incarceration actually increases recidivism and is not related to the safety of communities. In fact, there are far more unfavorable individual outcomes from incarceration than there are positive results.

The Models for Change initiative reports on the main issues with the juvenile justice system specifically in the United States. One of the major issues with the juvenile justice system is the large quantity of youth entering the system. For instance, approximately 31 million youth were in the juvenile justice system, and there were about 1.4 million delinquency cases in 2010 (Puzzanchera & Hockenberry, 2013). Additionally, in 2019, there were 36,479 children in juvenile justice residential facilities (Office of Juvenile Justice and Delinquency Prevention [OJJDP], 2019). While these numbers have decreased since the 1990s, they are still considered fairly high, especially given the deleterious effects that detention has on youth. Especially alarming is the statistic that minority juveniles are 2.3 times more likely to be placed into residential facilities than their White peers (Sickmund et al., 2021). A high majority of the youth involved with juvenile justice (i.e., 70%) experience a mental health disorder (Shufelt & Cocozza, 2006). In addition to this, many youths transfer from the welfare system to the juvenile justice system. Furthermore, many youth offenses are activities that are illegal only because of their age (e.g., truancy curfew laws).

One last systemic issue is related to childhood and adolescent development. Given that the largest sector of juveniles in the justice system are adolescents (15–17 years old), it would seem crucial for anyone working with these youth be educated about adolescent development. Adolescent experience is unique from childhood and adulthood. This is the age range when individuals experience much transition and change. Physical, sexual, cognitive, and social changes all happen within adolescence and can be difficult to navigate. Because of this, it would appear crucial for those working with adolescents to be knowledgeable of adolescent development and the role this normal stage of life can have on decision-making. However, this does not appear to be true in most cases. In fact, the US Department of Justice's Expert Working Group Report (US Department of Justice, 2011) disclosed that most defenders do not have the appropriate knowledge of or experience in working with minors. No matter one's personal thoughts on the justice system itself, it is clear that juvenile justice needs a major reform effort.

At this point, it would be good for clinicians to become knowledgeable on how youth may enter the juvenile justice system. Just like adults, a minor may have an encounter with police, be arrested, and then go to court to determine a ruling. As a result of adjudication, the minor may be sentenced to residential placement or probation, or he may be acquitted and released. All of this should sound familiar if you are familiar with the adult justice system. However, the language used in juvenile justice is not "incarceration" but "residential placement." In other words, the minor is separated from their family and/or guardian and placed in a specific facility for youth who have been determined guilty of a juvenile crime.

Diversion programs have been set up with the goal of addressing minor juvenile justice issues within the community rather than within the typical justice system. Diversion programs are an alternative to residential placement and may decrease recidivism (Wilson et al., 2018) by inhibiting youth from going through the court process or from the incarceration pipeline entirely (Smith et al., 2004).

Evidence-Based Treatments for Youth

Evidence-based treatments (EBTs) are generally referred to as those practices that are backed by scientific evidence or a large body of research. Research studies on treatments that have an extensive amount of studies backing their effectiveness help clinicians to know that what they are doing in therapy is working (and for whom). There are several places to find EBT platforms including

- APA Division 12 (https://div12.org/psychological-treatments/)
- Blueprints (https://www.blueprintsprograms.org/)
- SAMHSA Evidence-Based Practices Resource Center (https://www.samhsa.gov/resource-search/ebp)

We discuss two main treatments here: *family therapy* and *cognitive behavioral therapy* (CBT) because these two are reported in much of the literature as being effective when working with youth.

Family therapy is a type of counseling that includes youth and their family. The purpose is to increase overall family functioning as a whole rather than just focusing on one individual. Goals of family therapy will depend on the specific family's needs. Because we are talking about minors, it is important to include their support system in the counseling room. Examples of evidence-based family therapies include *functional family therapy* (FFT) and *multisystemic therapy* (MST) described below.

FFT (Functional Family Therapy, 2022) is a short-term therapy with five phases that build on each other. Each of the five phases includes goals, a focus, and activities for the family. One of the major tenets of FFT is taking into consideration each family's individual, unique needs when developing the treatment plan. FFT has been proved effective in reducing delinquency.

MST (Zajac et al., 2015) is usually provided in the family's home environment and is focused on ecological impacts on the family itself. One of the key beliefs of MST is that youth do not exist separate from their environment; rather, they are viewed within relation to their system (family, friends, peers, teachers, etc.). MST was originally developed for juvenile offenders and is now used for several other issues (i.e., substance use, psychiatric issues).

Both of these family therapies have several key things in common that a clinician or agency may consider when working with youth; they are

- Considered short-term
- Include youth and their families
- Can be provided in the family's home environment
- Great options for rural areas and families that lack resources

- Shown to be especially effective with at-risk youth in the criminal justice or child welfare system

CBT has the most research in the mental health field when it comes to developing successful outcomes. CBT has been shown to be effective with many different issues that also affect youth, including but not limited to

- anorexia nervosa (McIntosh et al., 2005)
- anxiety (Butler et al., 2006; Mitte, 2005)
- depression (Garber et al., 2009; Hofman et al., 2012)
- substance use (Magill et al., 2019)

CBT takes into consideration thoughts, emotions, and behaviors and how these three are related to each other. For example, a clinician utilizing CBT in practice may focus on helping the client to change their pattern of thinking, thus altering their behaviors. In addition, the clinician may assist clients in understanding how their behavioral patterns are negatively impacting their life and may work on changing those patterns via role-play.

Effective Services for Youth

In this section, instead of focusing on the specific treatments or modalities that a clinician could employ when working with youth, we discuss effective services from a more systemic viewpoint. There is a famous saying by the notable Maya Angelou: "When you know better, do better." At this point in your program, you may have already had a theories course and a techniques course. These two are definitely needed; however, our focus here is on improving the system as a whole. Now that we know some of the failures of and barriers within the system, we can focus on effective services and where we need to go in the future.

One consideration for clinicians is to take a culturally responsive approach to treatment. Ghandour et al. (2019) found that children from lower-income families were more likely to be diagnosed with a mood (i.e., depression or anxiety) or behavioral disorder. Furthermore, Hughes et al. (2020) discovered that children of color are disproportionally referred to the juvenile justice system more so than White children. Even more alarming is that students of color are more likely to enter the juvenile justice system for the same developmentally appropriate behaviors exhibited by White students. Thus, it is crucial for clinicians to play a role in disrupting this oppressive cycle by providing training to teachers, administration, and school resource officers on implicit bias and how that may affect the "school-to-prison pipeline." Alternatives to the punishment viewpoint in schools (through suspensions and expulsions) are important to avoid prosecutions which lead to increased incarceration of students of color. Last, clinicians can support students through teaching conflict resolution and providing family referrals to community resources.

Although incarceration is, in many cases, unnecessary in most cases involving youth, because it is being used, mental health services within juvenile justice are essential to decreasing recidivism. Thus, training in mental health services, EBPs, and suicide prevention is needed by those clinicians working within juvenile justice facilities (Swank & Gagnon, 2016).

Where We Need to Go

Given all of the issues listed above, taking a more integrated approach to care has the potential to reduce stigma related to mental healthcare, decrease family transportation issues, and aid those who live in more rural geographical locations. Integrated care can be defined as a methodical and organized method to physical and behavioral healthcare.

All providers work together in this approach, having shared goals to achieve the best possible health outcome for the client (Substance Abuse and Mental Health Services Administration [SAMHSA]-HRSA, CIHS, n.d.; SAMHSA-HRSA, 2014).

Another improvement that can be made is at the level of clinician advocacy. Research has shown that focusing on certain advocacy efforts related to systemic mental healthcare can help improve access to care (So et al., 2019; Tyler et al., 2017). Advocacy work, including implementing integrated care models, delivering counseling and social-emotional learning in all schools, and pursuing mental health parity in health insurance, has been shown to have a positive impact on the access to necessary services crisis. For example, clinicians may consider serving on school boards or speaking to their local school boards on the importance of including education on mental health and social emotional learning in children. Furthermore, clinicians could provide their specific expertise and speak to pediatrician offices about the importance of integrated care.

Case Study: William

William is a 15-year-old Hispanic boy attending high school in a rural area of the United States. Since he was 7 years old, William has lived alone with his maternal grandparents in their two-bedroom house. He has three younger siblings—one sister and two brothers—who live with their mother in her one-bedroom apartment about an hour away. He has some academic issues in school; however, for the most part, he passes his academic classes with acceptable grades. William mostly keeps to himself and has a few good friends in his small neighborhood. He enjoys playing sports.

One day, William and his new friend Bradley were caught past curfew driving under the influence of marijuana and alcohol. Both boys were arrested that night. Because this was the first time that William has been in any trouble, he was distressed and overwhelmed.

Though William was arrested, the local law enforcement office decided to utilize a diversion program, given that this was the first time he had ever been in trouble with the law. The local police department referred many youth and their families to a program that utilized MST, where a team of mental health professionals provided biweekly therapy to families for 3 months in the hope that this would help the family with their treatment goals and eliminate the need for any future detention issues.

When William's grandparents were told that he would not be charged but would be mandated to a diversion program, they were relieved yet stressed. Their first thoughts were: How can we possibly afford this? Do we have to take William out of school, and how will this affect his grades? Furthermore, as both grandparents are aging, they no longer drive and are worried about transportation issues. These are real issues that many families face.

Because these are issues that many families in rural counties face, the local authorities decided to partner with an agency that provides out-of-office services. In other words, counseling and social work services are provided in the home for families and in school settings for individual youth sessions so many transportation and school issues are no longer relevant.

When thinking about issues with the school, William had a few concerns. Will others know I was arrested and now in counseling? What class will I be missing? Will the counselor tell my business to my teachers?

These were all very real worries to William, and many were addressed during the first session with William, his grandparents, and the clinician who spoke about the importance of confidentiality as well as the collaborative development of a treatment plan and goals. The principal and teachers at William's school were very aware of the MST program and already knew what to expect. The school's policy in these situations was to have children receive their services either during a physical education (PE) class or during their study hall for those who had one. Because William was in the 10th grade, he attended PE class. William was worried about missing PE every week because this was the one class he really enjoyed, where he was able to get out some of his energy. Collaboratively, William, his grandparents, and the clinician decided that their treatment schedule would look like the following:

- Every Monday at 3–4 PM family session in the home
- Every other Thursday, individual youth session at school during PE, 10–11 AM
- Every other Thursday, individual youth session in-home, 3–4 PM

This schedule allowed the family to meet the requirements of the program while taking into consideration the family's schedule and William's preferences.

Through the program's objectives, William was first able to take accountability for his actions. He was able to discuss responsible behaviors and irresponsible behaviors that could lead to recidivism in the future. In addition to this, during their individual sessions, William and his clinician discussed and processed healthy versus unhealthy peer relationships, the importance of academic achievement on William's future goals, and coping skills for stress.

In addition to these topics, and including William's grandparents in those discussions, during the family sessions they all discussed family factors, strengths of their family, and positive family interaction. Together William and his grandparents were able to work on better communication between each other. They even committed to eating dinner together to discuss their day. They all reported a higher level of family functioning overall.

Now, at this point, after meeting treatment plan goals, the clinician would likely discharge, evaluate, and follow-up as needed. However, we believe the following could be added to this scenario to increase overall effectiveness and coordination of care:

- Communication with the school counselor and/or psychologist
- Communication with teachers to develop a plan for academic achievement
- The agency potentially providing training to the local schools on social emotional learning
- The agency potentially providing training to the local schools and juvenile justice agency on the mental health needs of adolescents
- Advocacy for further mental health services in rural areas

Summary

In this chapter, we identified the system of care for youth and systemic issues within that system. Specific factors related to working with youth and their families were explored to shed light on the variety of barriers present and where the variety of mental health fields need to go in the future. Furthermore, the overall system of healthcare, from outpatient to residential treatment, was defined. We also highlighted the need for reform within the juvenile justice system. Many experts agree that taking an overall family therapy approach to treatment is helpful when working with youth. Last, advocacy efforts are needed to encourage and support a more integrative healthcare system.

References

Ali, M. M., Sherman, L. J., Lynch, S., Teich, J., & Mutter, R. (2019). Differences in utilization of mental health treatment among children and adolescents with Medicaid or private insurance. *Psychiatric Services, 70*(4), 329–332. doi:10.1176/appi.ps.201800428

American Psychological Association (APA). (2021). Worsening mental health crisis pressures psychologist workforce: 2021 COVID-19 Practitioner Survey. Retrieved from https://www.apa.org/pubs/reports/practitioner/covid-19-2021

Balkin, R. S., & Roland, C. B. (2005). Identification of differences in gender for adolescents in crisis residence. *Journal of Mental Health, 14*(6), 637–646. doi:10.1080/09638230500347707

Bornheimer, L. A., Acri, M. C., Gopalan, G., & McKay, M. M. (2018). Barriers to service utilization and child mental health treatment attendance among poverty-affected families. *Psychiatric Services*, 69(10), 1101–1104. doi:10.1176/appi.ps.201700317

Butler, A. C., Chapman, J. E., Forman, E. M., & Beck, A. T. (2006). The empirical status of cognitive-behavioral therapy: A review of meta-analyses. *Clinical Psychology Review*, 26, 17–31.

Cree, R. A., Bitsko, R. H., Robinson, L. R., Holbrook, J. R., Danielson, M. L., Smith, C., . . . Peacock, G. (2018). Health care, family, and community factors associated with mental, behavioral, and developmental disorders and poverty among children aged 2–8 years: United States, 2016. *Morbidity and Mortality Weekly Report*, 67(50), 1377. doi:10.15585/mmwr.mm6750a1

Functional Family Therapy. (2022). Evidence-based interventions for youth and families. Retrieved from https://www.fftllc.com

Garber, J., Clarke, G. N., Weersing, V. R., Beardslee, W. R., Brent, D. A., Gladstone, T. R., DeBar, L. L., Lynch, F. L., D'Angelo, E., Hollon, S. D., Shamseddeen, W., & Iyengar, S. (2009). Prevention of depression in at-risk adolescents: A randomized controlled trial. *Journal of the American Medical Association*, 1(21), 2215–2224. doi:10.1001/jama.2009.788. PMID: 19491183; PMCID: PMC2737625.

Ghandour, R. M., Sherman, L. J., Vladutiu, C. J., Ali, M. M., Lynch, S. E., Bitsko, R. H., & Blumberg, S. J. (2019). Prevalence and treatment of depression, anxiety, and conduct problems in US children. *Journal of Pediatrics*, 206, 256–267. doi:10.1016/j.jpeds.2018.09.021

Health Resources and Services Administration (HRSA). (October 2020). Mental and behavioral health NSCH data brief. Retrieved from https://mchb.hrsa.gov/sites/default/files/mchb/Data/NSCH-Data-Brief-2019-Mental-BH.pdf

Health Resources and Services Administration (HRSA), Federal Office of Rural Health Policy. (2022). Defining rural populations. Retrieved from https://www.hrsa.gov/rural-health/about-us/definition/index.html

Heath, B., Wise Romero, P., & Reynolds, K. (2013). *A review and proposed standard framework for levels of integrated healthcare*. SAMHSA-HRSA Center for Integrated Health Solutions.

Hofmann, S. G., Asnaani, A., Vonk, I. J., Sawyer, A. T., & Fang, A. (2012). The efficacy of cognitive behavioral therapy: A review of meta-analyses. *Cognitive Therapy Research*, 36(5), 427–440. doi:10.1007/s10608-012-9476-1.

Hughes, T., Raines, T., & Malone, C. (2020). School pathways to the juvenile justice system. *Policy Insights from the Behavioral and Brain Sciences*, 7(1), 72–79. doi:10.177/2372732219897093

Magill, M., Ray, L., Kiluk, B., Hoadley, A., Bernstein, M., Tonigan, J. S., & Carroll, K. (2019). A meta-analysis of cognitive-behavioral therapy for alcohol or other drug use disorders: Treatment efficacy by contrast condition. *Journal of Consulting and Clinical Psychology*, 12, 1093–1105. doi:10.1037/ccp0000447. Epub 2019 Oct 10. PMID: 31599606; PMCID: PMC6856400.

McIntosh, V. V. W., Jordan, J., Carter, F., Luty, S. E., McKenzie, J. M., Bulik, C. M., Frampton, C. M. A., & Joyce, P. R. (2005). Three psychotherapies for anorexia nervosa: A randomized, controlled trial. *American Journal of Psychiatry* 162, 741–747.

Mitte, K. (2005). Meta-analysis of cognitive-behavioral treatments for generalized anxiety disorder: A comparison with pharmacotherapy. *Psychological Bulletin*, 131, 785–795.

National Council for Mental Wellbeing (NCMW). (2020). National Council for Behavioral Health polling presentation. Retrieved from https://www.thenationalcouncil.org/wpcontent/uploads/2020/09/NCBH_Member_Survey_Sept_2020_CTD2.pdf?daf=375ateTbd56

Office of Juvenile Justice and Delinquency Prevention. (2019). Trends and characteristics of youth in residential placement. Retrieved from https://ojjdp.ojp.gov/sites/g/files/xyckuh176/files/media/document/DataSnapshot_UCR2019_0.pdf

Puzzanchera, C., & Hockenberry, S. (2013). Juvenile court statistics 2010. US Department of Justice. Retrieved from https://www.ojp.gov/pdffiles1/ojjdp/grants/244080.pdf

Schmit, M. K., Watson, J. C., & Fernandez, M. A. (2018). Examining the effectiveness of integrated behavioral and primary health care treatment. *Journal of Counseling and Development, 96*, 3–14.

Shufelt, J. L., & Cocozza, J. J. (2006). Youth with mental health disorders in the juvenile justice system: Results from a multi-state prevalence study. Retrieved fromhttps://www.ojp.gov/ncjrs/virtual-library/abstracts/youth-mental-health-disorders-juvenile-justice-system-results-multi

Sickmund, M., Sladky, T. J., Puzzanchera, C., & Kang, W. (2021). Easy Access to the Census of Juveniles in Residential Placement. Retrieved from https://www.ojjdp.gov/ojstatbb/ezacjrp/

Smith, E. P., Wolf, A. M., Cantillon, D. M., Thomas, O., & Davison, W. S. (2004). The adolescent diversion project: 25 years of research on an ecological model of intervention. *Prevention & Intervention in the Community, 27*(2), 29–47.

So, M., McCord, R. F., & Kaminski, J. W. (2019). Policy levers to promote access to and utilization of children's mental health services: A systematic review. *Administration and Policy in Mental Health and Mental Health Services Research, 46*(3), 334–351. doi:10.1007/s10488-018-00916-9

Substance Abuse and Mental Health Services Administration and the Health Resources and Services Administration. (2014). Essential elements of effective integrated primary care and behavioral health teams. Retrieved from https://www.integration.samhsa.gov/workforce/team-members/Essential_Elements_of_an_Integrated_Team.pdf

Substance Abuse and Mental Health Services Administration-Health Resources and Services Administration, Center for Integrated Health Solutions. (n. d.). Six levels of collaboration/integration (core descriptions). Retrieved from https://www.thenationalcouncil.org/wp-content/uploads/2020/01/CIHS_Framework_Final_charts.pdf?daf=375ateTbd56

Swank, J. M., & Gagnon, J. C. (2016). Mental health services in juvenile correctional facilities: A national survey of clinical staff. *Journal of Child and Family Studies, 25*(9), 2862–2872.

Texas Juvenile Justice Department. (2022). The juvenile justice system in Texas. Retrieved from https://www.tjjd.texas.gov/index.php/juvenile-system#introduction

Tyler, E. T., Hulkower, R. L., & Kaminski, J. W. (2017). Behavioral health integration in pediatric primary care. *Milbank Memorial Fund, 15*. Retrieved from: https://www.milbank.org/publications/behavioral-health-integration-in-pediatric-primary-care-considerations-and-opportunities-for-policymakers-planners-and-providers/

US Department of Justice. (2011). Expert working group report: International perspectives on indigent defense. Retrieved from https://www.ojp.gov/pdffiles1/nij/236022.pdf

Wainberg, M. L., Scorza, P., Shultz, J. M., Helpman, L., Mootz, J. J., Johnson, K. A., Yuval, N., Bradford, J. E. Oquendo, M. A., & Arbuckle, M. R. (2017). Challenges and opportunities in global mental health: A research-to-practice perspective. *Current Psychiatry Reports, 19*(28), 1–10. https://doi.org/10.1007/s11920-017-0780-z

Watson, J. C., & Schmit, M. K. (2019). *Introduction to clinical mental health counseling: Contemporary issues.* Sage.

Wilson, D. B., Brennan, I., & Olaghere, A. (2018). Police-initiated diversion for youth to prevent future delinquent behavior: A systematic review. *Campbell Systematic Reviews, 5*, 1–85. https://doi.org/10.4073/csr.2018.5

Zajac, K., Randall, J., & Swenson, C. C. (2015). Multisystemic therapy for externalizing youth. *Child and Adolescent Psychiatric Clinics of North America, 24*(3), 601–616. https://doi.org/10.1016/j.chc.2015.02.007

4
Addressing Youth Interventions in Schools

Overview

In this chapter, the role of schools in addressing mental health among youth is highlighted. This chapter discusses the purpose of the schools in monitoring public health, the policies and limitations of addressing issues affecting youth, and the need to revise policies and processes to ensure the health and well-being of youth.

> **Case Study: David**
>
> During David's school counseling internship in a middle school, his supervisor left to go to an early morning meeting and told him to hold down the fort. As a second-semester intern, he thought "Sure, I've got this." Sitting there listening to the students file into the hallways for the day, he was busy thinking about all of the items he wanted to accomplish when he heard a light tap at the door. David turned around to see a girl with short blond hair. Smiling, she said, "Do you know where Mrs. Gray is?"
>
> David confidently said, "She's in a meeting. Is there something I can help you with?"
>
> She walked in, sat down, and said, "Well, I was just wanting to talk."
>
> The eager intern in him was jumping for joy! Finally, a kid who wants to talk! In middle schools, that can be hard to find some days. So, smiling back at her, he quickly introduced himself and asked her what she'd like to talk about this morning. She started off by telling him she was new to the area and the school. Her mother had recently moved to town to live with her soon-to-be stepdad. After gathering some basic information about her move and former school, David started asking about her home life, what it was like living with her "new family." All seemed to be going well according to his internal intern rubric when, all of a sudden, she got an interesting look on her face and seemed to drift off for a moment. When

he regained her attention, he asked her where her thoughts were. She said "Oh, I was just listening." When he asked her to what, she said "Oh, the voices that tell me what to do sometimes." David asked her to describe the voices if possible. She went on to talk about how these voices gave her instructions, and when he asked her what were the last instructions they gave her, she told him that just this morning they told her to put a knife in her backpack in case she needed protection today at school.

Completely unprepared for this response, he asked her if there was a knife in her backpack, the one she had carried into the counseling office just a few minutes ago. She said very casually, "Yes, I got the biggest one from the kitchen." Immediately, he panicked (luckily it was internal panic). He quickly asked if she'd like to go with him for a walk? She agreed, and they walked together to get Mrs. Gray, to whom he privately recapped the conversation.

Through Mrs. Gray's supervision, they secured the knife, notified school administrators and the school resource officer, consulted with the girl's mother, and immediately referred the girl to the local inpatient mental health facility for an evaluation. Turns out, mom had not notified the school that her daughter had a diagnosis of a major depressive disorder and was on two different types of medications. She said she wanted her daughter to have a clean slate and was going to tell the school once all the paperwork and an individualized education plan (IEP) was transferred. Through consultation with the student's pediatrician, therapist, and former school, the student was referred to an in-treatment day school for the remainder of the school year. The student received the services she needed, and the issue was resolved without a major incident.

This is just one example of how mental health issues present themselves in the school system each day. Luckily, the school district where David was interning had resources available within the district and within the community; not all schools and students are as fortunate.

Schools and Public Health

The debate around schools and public health often centers on a single question: How many roles does the school system have? Is it the school's responsibility to feed, clothe, and tend to the physical and mental health of every student? No matter where your opinions lie, the truth of the matter is that schools play numerous roles, and the majority of public school students annually receive health screenings, mental health services, and social services at school. Students are fed, receive clothing and toiletries (if needed), and are administered daily medications at school between the hours of 8 AM and 3 PM. Schools provide meals and vision, hearing, and scoliosis screenings, just to name a few public health responses. Yet mental health screening, in terms of priority, resources, and procedures, is wholly lacking. As the roles and responsibilities of public education expand, educating students in the United States is becoming an even more complex undertaking that continues to be complicated by shifting populations, academic requirements, and policy changes.

Moreover, the COVID-19 pandemic, beginning in early 2020, left schools scrambling to respond to a public health crisis. School districts all across the country grappled with weighing the public health risks of opening against the educational and other risks of keeping buildings closed. Governors, school superintendents, and educational leaders looked to public health experts to help establish guidelines for reopening schools safely so that students could return to either a virtual or in-person learning environment. While much of the conversation has centered around returning students to school to continue academic instruction, less attention has been focused on returning students who rely on schools for emotional or mental health supports. According to Phelps and Sperry (2020), it appears that mental health is being viewed as secondary or unrelated to academics. The impact of the COVID-19 pandemic created significant stress for families across the country, which made it difficult for students to focus on learning. These authors go on to state that schools and other institutions that serve children must continue to develop a public health framework to understand the various risks and protective factors for COVID-19 and its aftermath (Phelps & Sperry, 2020). The COVID-19 pandemic is certainly a public health crisis that will be impacting students and families in various ways for years to come.

Mental Health in Youth

Mental health issues for adolescents in the United States are outpacing existing services (Brener et al., 2007). Schools and community agencies cannot keep up, and the increase in mental health problems for youth has created a gap between those who need mental health services and the ability to provide adequate services (Adelman & Taylor, 2009). Forness et al. (2012) estimated that 46% of those between the ages of 13 and 18 have experienced a mental illness at some point in their lives, and slightly more than 20% have been diagnosed with a mental disorder. The most common disorders are anxiety, disruptive behavior disorders, attention deficit hyperactivity disorder (ADHD), and depression. However, despite the significant need demonstrated in schools and communities, adolescents have been identified as the group least likely to receive mental health services (Evans et al., 2006).

School services are often underfunded and underresourced, and few professionals working with youth would debate the fundamental role that mental health plays in the development of an adolescent or its potential long-term impact on interpersonal relationships and/or the ability to live a healthy and productive life. Poor mental health can impact several areas of a youth's existence; for example, mental health challenges are associated with lower educational achievement (Breslau et al., 2009; Stagman & Cooper, 2010) and increased health risk behaviors, such as alcohol or drug abuse and aggressive or self-destructive behavior (Al Odhayani et al., 2013). Additional consequences of insufficient mental health services can be seen in the form of low educational attainment, compromised physical health, substance abuse, underemployment, and, ultimately, premature mortality (Brooks et al., 2002; Cicchetti & Rogosch, 2002; Ghandour et al., 2012). Approximately 65–70% of the more than 2 million children and young adults who formally enter the juvenile justice system have at least one diagnosable mental health disorder (Gremli Sanders, 2020). This creates a significant expense for society and future generations. Youth mental illness has been estimated to cost approximately $247 million annually when factors such as healthcare, special education services, juvenile justice services, and decreased productivity are considered (Centers for Disease Control and Prevention, 2013). According to Roehrig (2016), in the United States, mental health disorders rank as the costliest health-related condition to treat (at least $201 billion annually), and, as previously discussed, mental health resources to treat youth are limited and growing more constrained by increasing demand; therefore, the need for cost-effective analysis and cost-utility analysis of treatments and programs is critical to future care.

School-Based Mental Health

Out of 56.6 million students who attend school in the United States (McFarland et al., 2018), almost 3.5 million struggle with anxiety, depression, or a behavior disorder (Centers for Disease Control and Prevention [CDC], 2018). Previous studies indicate that while millions of students struggle, only a small portion (36%) of school-age children and adolescents with mental health disorders receive mental health services (Bains & Diallo, 2016), providing justification for the expansion of school-based mental health (SBMH) services. An estimated 70–80% of students who receive mental health services receive them on school campuses (Borntrager & Lyon, 2015). Thus, for the majority of these children, the school system is their only hope and resource for accessing mental health services.

The establishment of mental health services in schools has evolved over time, from its beginnings in the early 1900s (Flaherty & Osher, 2003), and it has certainly continued to evolve with the passing of federal legislation to address student needs and the creation of more equitable learning environments. A number of factors have influenced the initiation and expansion of mental health services in schools. These factors include school attendance problems, teen pregnancy, sexually transmitted diseases, drug and alcohol abuse, increasing cases of suicide (the second leading cause of death for teenagers) and homicide (the leading cause of death for Black males between the ages of 15 and 24) (CDC, 2015), and, finally, increasing drop-out rates (Bell, 2014).

A key piece of legislation to support the inclusion of mental health services in schools is the American Disability Act (ADA), which mandates that schools be the largest providers of mental healthcare to children and adolescents (Burns et al., 1995; Leaf et al., 1996; Merikangas et al., 2011). Under ADA mandates, public schools are required to provide students with disabilities equal opportunities to attain the same achievements as students without disabilities (Americans with Disabilities Act of 1990, pub. L. no. 101-336, 104 stat. 328, 1990). Despite federal and state funding, since the economic downturn in 2007–2008, many states have been faced with sharp budget cuts, which have negatively impacted mental health programs (Oliff et al., 2012).

The delivery of mental health services in the schools is key to the achievement of the schools' directive to educate all students, and although schools are clearly providing such services (Ali et al., 2019), it is not known whether the programs being implemented are evidenced-based interventions or are simply built into the curriculum because of a common practice or haphazard decision. However, the good news is that there is evidence that demonstrates that when mental health services are available at schools, these services are successful in reaching children and students who may have otherwise gone without these much-needed services (Amaral et al., 2011).

The methods used in providing mental health services are often diverse, conflicting, and differ significantly across states and school districts. Broadly, there are two approaches to providing mental health services in schools and these are classified into two systems: *school-based services* and *community-based services* that are provided in collaboration or partnership with schools (Fazel et al., 2014). Both are responsive services, provided within schools that are working to meet the existing needs of students; very little programming is preventative. Services typically provided include crisis intervention, comprehensive individual evaluation and treatment, case management, classroom behavior and learning support, substance abuse counseling, assessment and treatment of learning problems, peer mediation and prescription, and management of behavioral health medications (Lofink et al., 2013).

Trauma-Informed Schools

Trauma-informed schools are educational environments that are responsive to the needs of trauma-exposed youth through the application of evidenced-based interventions and system-changing strategies (Chafouleas et al., 2015). A key element in trauma-informed schools is that all personnel have a basic understanding of trauma and how trauma affects learning and behavior in the academic setting (Abuse, 2014; Cole et al., 2013). The importance of employing trauma-informed schools is great: Perfect et al. (2016) estimated that approximately two out of every three school-age children are likely to have experienced at least one traumatic event by age 17.

Trauma-informed schools respond to the needs of students by integrating evidenced-based practices, programs, and protocols into all facets of the school and culture. Professional development and training are a key component of building a trauma-informed school. As school personnel increase their understanding of trauma and implement universal screening to identify the needs of students, they are able to work toward prevention and intervention programs to address documented needs. Numerous evidence-based interventions have been identified for use at the upper tiers (Tiers 2 and 3) within a multitiered framework (Chafouleas et al., 2015); however, fewer options exist at the Tier 1 or universal level. (For more details on tiered inventions, see the section "Promoting Mental Health and Prevention" below.) Curriculum focused on social-emotional learning is often utilized in trauma-informed schools and offers an opportunity for students to learn about and build resilience. However, when a common trauma occurs within the school setting, such as a school shooting, the school may want to take a more global approach to building coping skills around that specific experience or event (Nastasi et al., 2011).

Research on trauma-informed schools is still in its early stages, but recently interest has increased since public policy has mandated trauma-related training in schools. In 2015, the Every Student Succeeds Act provided school districts with guidelines to offer trauma-informed programming to support safe educational environments. Since that time, trauma-informed programming has been shown to reduce discipline referrals and have a positive impact when school districts make changes to their climate and culture (Dorado et al., 2016). The design of this type of programming certainly has the possibility to reach more students than traditional methods such as community mental health responsive services. Similarly, school personnel such as school teachers, school counselors, and administrators are already involved in their students' lives, have existing relationships with them, and are a substantial source of support to their students and community. Offering trauma-informed practices inside the schools should be seen as a practical approach with the potential to reduce office referrals and classroom disruptions, serve the whole child, and offer a more understanding and accepting learning environment which ultimately is going to offer benefits to the entire school community.

Adverse Childhood Experiences and School Services

Adverse childhood experiences were first examined through the Adverse Childhood Experiences Study, a longitudinal study of adults conducted by the Centers for Disease Control and Prevention (CDC) and Felitti et al. (1998). Experiences assessed in the study were exposure to violence; emotional, physical, or sexual abuse; deprivation; neglect; family discord and divorce; parental substance abuse and mental health problems; parental death or incarceration; and social discrimination. Research has linked adverse childhood experiences with increased chronic disease and higher costs of care across a person's life course (Bellis et al., 2019). These results emphasize the importance of addressing a history of childhood trauma relevant to the individual and their treatment. Unfortunately, adverse childhood experiences can have a long-lasting impact both mentally and physically, and, according to researchers, these negative impacts can be transferred from one generation to the next (Murphey & Sacks, 2019). When trauma impacts a student or their family, it can manifest differently in each student (Phifer & Hull, 2016). Adverse childhood experiences have an impact not only on overall mental health but can significantly impact the educational environment and student experience (Murphey & Sacks, 2019). Children who experience trauma are more likely to struggle in school and are vulnerable for low scores on standardized tests, higher dropout rates, engaging in poor behaviors, and being referred to special education (Craig, 2015). According to Blodgett and Lanigan (2018), the more adverse childhood experiences a student has significantly increases the risk of retention and poor academic achievement.

Mental Health Services and Special Education

Children with disabilities have been shown to be at increased risk for mental illness (Witt et al., 2003) and to have an increased need for mental health services. However, a complex relationship exists between special education and mental health services. There is a history of confusion and blurring of symptoms between common special education diagnosis such as autism spectrum disorder (ASD) or ADHD and indicators of a mental health disorder. According to Fergusson and Lacey (2007), the boundaries are often unclear between the characteristics of diagnosed conditions and possible mental health issues. It is extremely challenging to tease out behaviors that are separate from the diagnosed condition; Kim and Turnbull (2004) suggest monitoring behaviors, assessing qualitatively for changes, and monitoring third-party observations of moods, attitudes, and engagement.

Literature documents the level of confusion that surrounds awareness of the differentiation of special conditions and mental health in youth and adolescents (Rose et al., 2013). Students with complex needs often overwhelm underprepared school staff who already operate on underfunded budgets and with bulging caseloads. Lack of resources and access to adequate testing and services complicates schools' abilities to accurately assess, identify, and serve the needs of students. School counselors, who typically serve as the school's mental health experts, unfortunately often lack special education training (Dekruyf et al., 2013) and therefore might be less capable of distinguishing normal or expected from problematic behaviors being exhibited by students with special needs.

Efficacy of School-Based Mental Health Services

Over the past decade, there has been considerable interest in searching for effective and universal interventions that could improve mental health from adolescence to adulthood. Since the majority of adolescents spend most of their time in schools, school-based programs have received increasing attention in these efforts. Yet there is still a great deal to understand about how students experience mental health services in the schools. While there has been some focus on the importance of assessing academic and social emotional indicators in evidence-based intervention research (Shernoff & Kratochwill, 2003), the impacts of mental health interventions on academics and of academic interventions on mental health outcomes are rarely examined. The majority of studies involving school mental health interventions fail to include even basic measures of school-related outcomes (Hoagwood & Johnson, 2013). Unfortunately, the impact of school-based mental health interventions on both mental health and educationally relevant behaviors is largely unknown.

Promoting Mental Health and Prevention

Schools have the unique opportunity to promote positivity using a strengths-based approach to improve mental health and create resilience, providing the student(s) with additional skills to succeed in adverse conditions and cope by safeguarding against stressors. For students who are particularly vulnerable, interventions in the school can be a unique opportunity for many children with few other supports or options (Gross, 2008). While prevention works to promote wellness, the primary focus should be centered around intervening to reduce risks through programs designed for all students.

School interventions are often implemented at three levels (Fuchs & Fuchs, 2017). *Universal interventions* (also called Tier 1 interventions) are applied to the entire student body and *targeted interventions* (also called Tier 2 interventions) are delivered to a subgroup of students who do not adequately respond to universal intervention. *Indicated interventions* (also called Tier 3 interventions) are intensive interventions that are delivered to students one on one who do not respond adequately to universal and targeted interventions. Preventative programming for mental health, according to the Response to Intervention model, is considered a Tier 1 or universal intervention. For those students already known to be at risk and needing interventions to prevent further negative development, the preventive programming is usually offered in smaller groups or individually at the Tier 2 or Tier 3 level for more focused or individualized intervention.

When considering student risk factors, interventions should expand beyond the student and focus on conditions at home, in the community, and at school. This broader focus helps us to recognize that contributing factors to students emotional, behavioral, and academic challenges are often external (e.g., related to community, family, school, friends or factors such as poverty, migrant status, violence, drugs, parental attachment, poor quality schools, or bullying). School leaders and public health professionals should unite to work together to encourage students and their families to take advantage of opportunities in the schools and community to prevent problems and enhance protective factors. Examples of services offered might include enrollment in (1) classes that are designed to enhance knowledge, skills, and attitudes on mental health issues; (2) service learning opportunities at school and/or community; and (3) after-school programs.

Of course, promoting wellness in the schools is not singular to students. The well-being of teachers and other school staff members should also be assessed and promoted with resources and programming. Like students, all school stakeholders require support that encourages healthy habits, reduces risks, and promotes mental health. School districts need to commit to creating environments that encourages respect, integrity, care, and community for all. Despite increasing preventive programs for students, few intervention studies have specifically targeted teachers' wellness. The few studies that do exist were designed to reduce stress and risk of burnout by introducing cognitive-behavioral techniques (CBT) or mindfulness strategies (Curry & O'Brien, 2012). School stakeholders (teachers, staff, counselors, administrators) must be in a position of wellness and feel positively about their school community if they are to proactively work with the challenges presented by our current climate. Otherwise, school staff and personnel will find themselves on a rotating cycle of crisis response which can lead to high levels burnout, teacher turnover, and compassion fatigue.

Mental Health Screening in Schools

There is some argument in the literature that an important factor to providing school-based prevention and/or interventions is the implementation of a student-based approach supported by a universal mental health screening system (Glover & Albers, 2007). This model recommends that all students undergo a general assessment, which may be administered by school stakeholders such as teachers, school counselors, or parent volunteers designed to identify students at risk (Dowdy et al. 2010). According to Williams (2013), the logic behind this model is fairly simple: before intervention can occur in schools, mental health problems must be identified prior to developing strategies and programming. TheAmerican Medical Association's Guidelines for Adolescent Preventative Services (Elster & Kuznets, 1994)recommends screening for behavioral and social/emotional issues such as substance abuse, eating disorders, depression, suicide risk, and learning problems. Previous efforts to screen youth have proved feasible and effective in curbing mental health problems, but this is contingent upon being carried out appropriately and followed by treatment for those found to need mental health services (Marsh & Mathur, 2020).

Formal mental health screening to identify students who are at risk can be accomplished through individual, small-group, or classroom assessments. However, universal screeners are generally known to overidentify issues (Wood & McDaniel, 2020). Specifically, they have the potential to identify students who do not really have significant issues. False positives are higher with elementary school age students, but errors are not uncommon with middle or high school students. Errors or false positives can be greatly reduced by follow-up assessments. Because of this high rate of overidentification there are some concerns and debate about using screening data to label students with a diagnosis or treatment without repeated assessment (Kilgus et al., 2014).

Due to these concerns (among others), schools typically opt out of employing these measures to identify potential student issues. There are numerous barriers to schools utilizing assessments in meaningful ways, such as leadership buy-in, cost, teacher training, and mental health stigma. Misunderstandings about student mental health also serve as a significant barrier to early detection and treatment of youth with mental health issues (Gleason et al., 2012). The misguided belief still exists that suicide-specific screening questions increase suicidal thoughts and behaviors (Joe & Bryant, 2007). For this reason, some schools opt not to use mental health screenings at all. Concerns about privacy and consent also fuel resistance in many school districts.

Public Policies and Legislation

Public policy outlines key issues for school-based mental health services. These specific policies and pieces of legislation determine answers to questions such as: Who pays for it? Who receives it? Who's responsible for it? What does it include? A critical issue within these policies is funding, and this issue will continue to play a key role in the choices most states make regarding services. In 1963, the Community Mental Health Centers Act emphasized the significance of providing services in the local community; specifically, schools were seen as the ideal setting for preventive programming of mental illness for youth and adolescents (Caplan, 1970). Also, during this time period (the 1960s), funding of child mental health services was altered by the development of Medicaid, and these policies have continued to support services to those with the greatest needs. Medicaid funds a significant portion of mental health services, and it also represents almost half of state and local mental health spending (Kenny et al., 2002). Decades later, Medicaid is still the primary payer for mental health services received by children living in poverty, and the role of the State Children's Health Insurance Program (SCHIP) is still evolving and fluctuates based on funding (Howell et al., 2014).

Most recently, the authorization of the Elementary and Secondary Education Act (federal legislation now referred to as the Every Student Succeeds Act [Pub.L. 114–95]) makes explicit provisions for trauma-informed approaches in student support and academic enrichment and in preparing and training school personnel (Prewitt, 2016). This legislation was largely driven by the uptick in school shootings but also due to the increasing number of tragic occurrences nationwide. Recently, the world has experienced civil unrest, public health pandemics, and economic disparities that have shattered family systems in varying ways. The need for policies to support the implementation and funding for school-wide mental health services is more important than ever. While it will be several years before researchers and educators will truly be able to grasp the full impact of recent occurrences, an immediate response is needed from local and national bodies to support our children. The country is truly at a crossroad and needs to both repair and prepare our teens for the complexities of today's world. Our current situation requires attention and resolve to combat the decline of our education system. The response cannot be solved only by politics or legislation but needs also to be based on evidence and research. While additional studies are needed on the effectiveness of school-based mental health services and prevention, "model programs using school-based mental health and student service providers have reduced school suspensions, reduced referrals to the principal's office, reduced the use of weapons, force, and threats, and increased students' feelings of safety" (American Counseling Association, 2013, p. 1). Policymakers and legislators should focus on such results and continue to help support what is producing positive outcomes in teens and adolescents across the country.

Limitations of Services in Schools

Stigma. Recently, a song performed by Marshmello and Demi Lovato "It's OK, to Not Be OK" made headlines regarding mental health. Artist, writers, and social media influencers made pledges to help change the conversation regarding the stigma surrounding mental illness. Despite recent national and local efforts, the stigma of mental health is still prevalent. This is particularly concerning because when stigma prevents teens and adolescents from seeking help, the situation can become dangerous. There are certainly numerous factors that contribute to stigma in youth populations. According to Davidson and Manion (1996), three of the most common factors reported by young people are stigma associated with seeking help, not recognizing one has an illness, and not knowing where to go for help. Teens are particularly susceptible to stigma and less willing to access mental health services because, according to Kranke et al. (2010), they tend to be more concerned with social interaction and peer acceptance in school. Gender also plays a role with stigma: adolescent males are significantly less likely to seek help than females (Chandra & Minkovitz, 2006). Research also indicates that stigma within the family system greatly influences youth (Kranke et al., 2010). Parents who have a stigma toward mental health are more likely to deny their child's illness and be slow and/or resistant to seeking help for their teen. Schools also have biases when it comes to mental health, and many schools are reluctant to even screen for services because they are afraid of what identification means. As you can see, the barriers and factors contributing to stigma come from various sources. But, regardless of the source of stigma, one can assume that if something is done to reduce the stigma it would positively impact youth. Programming centered around universal curriculum and community-based outreach is essential to changing the conversation around mental health. Connecting students with similar experiences, creating safe school environments, training school personnel, empowering students, and opening platforms where adults who have worked to overcome their mental health struggles can serve as mentors are all potential ways to combat the issue of mental health stigma. Increasing research to better understand programming in schools to help reduce stigma will be imperative to helping students and ensuring that what is offered will most likely do the greatest good.

Capacity. Preparedness, supports, and infrastructure as hurdles that are battled each and every day by educators and therapists when working to meet the mental health needs of today's youth. There are also a number of challenges in effectively implementing and maintaining mental health practices in schools. For example, while educators and policymakers recognize that good mental health is vital to achieving academic success, schools are not established or organized to facilitate and deliver mental health services (Hoover & Bostic, 2021). School stakeholders routinely operate within a system of multiple and sometimes competing demands. With the implementation of high-stakes testing and increased academic standards, schools often shift mental health services to the back burner, especially when funding is directly tied to factors such as test scores.

Funding. Federal and state governments are a significant funding source of school-based mental health programs. Two sources of funding come from the Healthy Schools, Healthy Communities program administered by the Health Resources and Services Administration along with the Safe Schools/Healthy Students initiative, which was established in the late 1990s as a national response to school violence, particularly school shootings (Evans et al., 2003). Other sources of federal support for school mental health programs include the Title V Maternal and Child Health Block grant, Title XI funds for disadvantaged youth, the Title XX Social Services block grant, and the Preventive Health and Health Services block grant. States also provide a significant portion of funding; in particular, state taxes provide substantial support for school-based mental health services. For example, tobacco taxes in states such as Arizona, Massachusetts, Florida, and Louisiana provid funding for services (Brener et al., 2007). There are also local and private funds that work to contribute to the mission of providing school-based services. But funds from these varying sources are often limited and variable from year to year. Therefore, in order for school-based programs to be accessible and offer stable programming, other avenues for funding must be pursued. Grants, contracts, and other sources should be explored annually through mental health advocates to ensure adequate funding (Weist et al., 2014).

Privacy and Confidentiality. A significant challenge facing schools when providing mental health services is ensuring students' and families' privacy. Organizations such as the Citizens Commission on Human Rights (1995) state that schools often lack safeguards to protect privacy. This group also states that school-based mental health services can encroach on the educational system and that they are often forced on parents (such as services rendered on the universal or Tier 1 level), thereby potentially compromising parental rights. Fundamentally, students under the age of 18 cannot be treated without parental consent except in certain situations, such as dealing with or responding to a crisis. Schools have an obligation to provide parents with information about accessing the school's mental health services or resources and to inform them that they have the right to decline that their child/student participates. However, students can come from certain situations that can complicate consent, such as divorced parents, children in foster care, parents who disagree about consenting to mental health services, or simply parents/caregivers who refuse to acknowledge or respond to school communications. (Getting some parents to even respond can feel like passing an act of Congress some days.) This brings up the relevant question of active versus passive consent. *Passive consent* occurs when parents are provided with information or notified that they have access to information about a service and have the right to object if they choose (Evans, 1999); if parents do not explicitly "opt-out" of such services, the child can participate. In *active consent* procedures, this same behavior results in a lack of consent and the child cannot participate in the school-based programming. Evans suggested that passive consent is probably sufficient to protect the rights of most, but not all, and should be used cautiously.

Collaboration and Consultation. A significant challenge for joint efforts between schools and community mental health agencies, especially in low or underfunded settings, is how to create a system to support the development of mental health professionals who can then implement and oversee the delivery of programming and services. Barriers related to therapeutic services include several contributing factors such as staffing, training, and coordination of services. Since schools and clinical mental health agencies operate under different missions and schedules, just maintaining communication and collaborating across caseloads can be challenging. According to Herschel et al. (2010), internal supervision and case assessment/management can also be tenuous if there is not adequate coordination across parties. Confidentiality laws also present potential challenges to partnerships. Laws such as the Health Insurance Portability and Accountability Act (HIPAA) and the Family Educational Rights and Privacy Act (FERPA), affect when and how student health information can be shared. While several challenges are pervasive in the current system, if change is to occur in future systems, vision, leadership, and coordination can provide a reciprocal link between providers.

Partnerships for Serving Youth in Schools

No man is an island. . . . It takes a village. . . . There is a reason that these sayings have been passed from one generation to the next. There is a poetic truth in these words. When we work in schools, we see certain students snowballing. They move from one set of issues to another, collecting and gathering emotional, academic, and physical challenges along the way. Most of the time these issues are complicated and require a response that considers the complexities of their situation. Student issues present due to an array of factors and require a multifaceted approach. Schools are organized to work together within their district to respond to the needs of students, but they are less equipped to step outside of the district and collaborate with community partners.

For integrated services to be effective, leadership and coordination is key to offering consistent care. Integrated services are recommended to improve the mental health issues of students facing academic or behavior problems

(Ross & Reichle, 2007). Integrated services mirror the concept of *wraparound services*, which is a structured and well-defined approach toward interagency consultation and collaboration. Quinn and Lee (2007) stated that wraparound service is an individualized, team-based approach that is built on trusting and respectful partnerships with families to create strengths- and evidenced-based interventions that utilize all school stakeholders. Building this type of systemic approach can be a complicated process, but schools are familiar with the structure and concept of wraparound services. In public health, this type of approach is typically referred to as *team-based care*. Team-based care is a collaboration of professionals working together from their different specialties, collaborating in the best interest of the patient, client, or student. This type of network is exactly what we mean when we talk about "integration of services" or "wraparound approaches." To transcend beyond the frames of the school district and work through institutional constraints, this type of approach requires three key elements: leadership roles, financial resources, and agencies' missions. Leadership is key to defining and working through these issues. Once team members' roles have been clearly established, they can begin to evaluate what resources are available and define the overarching goals and mission of the team. Of course, family involvement is key to the team's ability to be productive and achieve positive outcomes. The cooperation of students, parents, and all team stakeholders is imperative to the process, and each person's contributions must be valued. Establishing an environment that recognizes and supports each other's role and work is instrumental for success.

Summary

Many adolescents have concerns and challenges that create troubling and problematic situations in their lives. These issues are not contained to their homes and neighborhoods. This chapter has highlighted many of the benefits and challenges to offering mental health services in schools. While most school districts across the country are supportive of the idea of offering preventative and responsive services, funding, training, and resources are often fluid and scarce. Viewing the mental health of youth as a public health crisis that deserves funding, staffing, and public support through revised policies, federal and state initiatives, and parent–community partnerships is necessary if schools are to be able to fully support the needs of all students.

Case Study: Bryan

Bryan is a 14-year-old boy who is in the ninth grade. Since middle school, Bryan has had escalating difficulties in regards to both academics and his behavior at school. He currently holds a 1.6 GPA and is failing both math and science. He lives with his mother and grandmother. His parents are divorced, and his mother has full custody. His mother, Brenda, works full time at the local hospital as a nurse. Bryan is an only child.

Socially, Bryan has several friends. He is athletic and is currently involved in both baseball and track. But his involvement in both is being threatened due to his low academic performance. Bryan has a strong circle of friends, which includes both boys and girls. He is well liked by most teachers, although this year his behavior has stretched many of those relationships. He is a frequent visitor to the office to see the school counselors and administrators.

In the classroom, teachers report that Bryan talks an excessive amount and often has a hard time staying focused and on task. About a year ago, his mom sought out the school counselor to discuss mood changes that she had begun to see in Bryan. She reported that one day Bryan would be on top of the world and then he'd be grumpy, irritable, and depressed. During his "sad days," Bryan would sleep for long periods of time and refuse to eat or interact with her or her mother. Since the onset of puberty, these symptoms and mood swings have increased. This increase of behavior and mood changes has also been observed at school. Late spring, just after Bryan's 14th birthday he began to periodically smoke marijuana and drink alcohol. Unfortunately, this behavior quickly advanced, and Bryan's risky behaviors have continued to increase. Bryan was arrested at a local party for being a minor in possession of alcohol.

Bryan was referred to a therapist, local AA meeting for teens, and 40 hours of community service as a first-time offender through the Juvenile Court System. At the therapist's urging, meetings between Bryan, Bryan's parents, and school stakeholders were also held to discuss what is being observed at school and what modifications can be made to help support Bryan. Confidentiality releases were signed so that information between the school and community mental health agency and Bryan's pediatrician could be shared to help with collaboration and support. Through individual counseling and an annual checkup, Bryan was referred for a full psychological evaluation. Based on his wellness visit and full psychological evaluation, a diagnosis of bipolar disorder was rendered. Medication was prescribed, along with continued counseling.

Based on the severity of Bryan's diagnosis, a team approach was utilized to support Bryan's health management and function at school and home. Monthly meetings and communication were established between the community mental health agency, school counselor, IEP team leader, school administrator, and parent. These monthly briefings help to update each stakeholder of Bryan's engagement and function. These meetings helped to support communication and any modifications that needed to take place at home or school. While these meetings took effort to coordinate, a virtual platform was used to help alleviate travel time and give more flexibility to each member involved. Meetings were also recorded in the event a team member could not attend, and the files were securely stored according to HIPPAA-compliant software. The ability to maintain communication and support between parties significantly impacted Bryan's function at home and school. The ability to stay abreast of occurrences also positively impacted the school and its ability to work with Bryan in the classroom and socially with his peers. Teachers were updated as needed and were interviewed biweekly to check grades and see how Bryan was operating within the classroom. With the support of consistently managed medication, individual counseling, and modifications based on his IEP at school, Bryan saw improvements in his grades and a reduction in office referrals. Bryan was able to maintain his involvement in sports and school, and his mother has reported less mood swings and decreased episodes of depression and withdrawal.

References

Adelman, H. S., & Taylor, L. (Eds.). (2009). *Mental health in schools: Engaging learners, preventing problems, and improving schools.* Corwin Press.

Al Odhayani, A., Watson, W. J., & Watson, L. (2013). Behavioral consequences of child abuse. *Canadian Family Physician, 59*(8), 831–836.

Ali, M. M., West, K., Teich, J. L., Lynch, S., Mutter, R., & Dubenitz, J. (2019). Utilization of mental health services in educational setting by adolescents in the United States. *Journal of School Health, 89*(5), 393–401.

Amaral, G., Geierstanger, S., Soleimanpour, S., & Brindis, C. (2011). Mental health characteristics and health-seeking behaviors of adolescent school-based health center users and nonusers. *Journal of School Health, 81*(3), 138–145.

American Counseling Association. (2013). Student Support Act: Reducing the student to counselor ratio. Retrieved from https://www.counseling.org/gove rnment-affairs/public-policy/public-policy-newsview/position-papersstudent-supportact-reducing-the-student-to-counselor-ratio

Americans with Disabilities Act (ADA). (1990). Pub. L. No. 101–336, 104 Stat. 328.

Bains, R. M., & Diallo, A. F. (2016). Mental health services in school-based health centers: Systematic review. *Journal of School Nursing, 32* (1), 8–19. doi:10.1177/1059840515590607

Bell, E. E. (2014). Graduating black males: A generic qualitative study. *Qualitative Report, 19*, 13.

Bellis, M. A., Hughes, K., Ford, K., Rodriguez, G. R., Sethi, D., & Passmore, J. (2019). Life course health consequences and associated annual costs of adverse childhood experiences across Europe and North America: A systematic review and meta-analysis. *The Lancet Public Health, 4*(10), e517–e528.

Bernshausen, D., & Cunningham, C. (2001). The role of resiliency in teacher preparation and retention. Paper presented at the American Association of Colleges for Teacher Education 53" Annual Meeting, Dallas, TX.

Blodgett, C., & Lanigan, J. D. (2018). The association between adverse childhood experience (ACE) and school success in elementary school children. *School Psychology Quarterly, 33*(1), 137.

Borntrager, C., & Lyon, A. R. (2015). Client progress monitoring and feedback in school-based mental health. *Cognitive and Behavioral Practice, 22*(1), 74–86. doi:10.1016/j.cbpra.2014.03.007

Brener, N. D., Weist, M., Adelman, H., Taylor, L., & Vernon-Smiley, M. (2007). Mental health and social services: Results from the school health policies and programs study 2006. *Journal of School Health, 77*(8), 486–499.

Breslau, J., Miller, E., Breslau, N., Bohnert, K., Lucia, V., & Schweitzer, J. (2009). The impact of early behavior disturbances on academic achievement in high school. *Pediatrics, 123*(6), 1472–1476.

Brooks, T. L., Harris, S. K., Thrall, J. S., & Woods, E. R. (2002). Association of adolescent risk behaviors with mental health symptoms in high school students. *Journal of Adolescent Health, 313*, 240–246. doi:10.1016/S1054-139X(02)00385-3

Burns, B. J., Costello, E. J., Angold, A., Tweed, D., Stangl, D., Farmer, E. M., & Erkanli, A. (1995). Children's mental health service use across service sectors. *Health Affairs, 14*(3), 147–159.

Caplan, G. (1970). *The theory and practice of mental health consultation.* Tavistock.

Centers for Disease Control and Prevention. (2013). Mental health surveillance among children–United States, 2005–2011. *Morbidity and Mortality Weekly Report, 62*(2), 1–35. Retrieved fromhttp://www.cdc.gov/mmwr/preview/ mmwrhtml/su6202a1.htm?s_cid=su6202a1_w

Centers for Disease Control and Prevention. (2018). Injury prevention and control: Division of violence prevention: Major findings by publication year. Retrieved from http://www.cdc.gov/violence

CDC Prevention Checklist. (2015). Centers for Disease Control and Prevention. Web site. https://www.cdc.gov/prevention/.

Chafouleas, S. M., Riley-Tillman, T. C., Jaffery, R., Miller, F. G., & Harrison, S. E. (2015). Preliminary investigation of the impact of a web-based module on Direct Behavior Rating accuracy. *School Mental Health, 7*(2), 92–104.

Chandra, A., & Minkovitz, C. S. (2006). Stigma starts early: Gender differences in teen willingness to use mental health services. *Journal of Adolescent Health*, 38(6), 754-e1.

Cicchetti, D., & Rogosch, F. A. (2002). A developmental psychopathology perspective on adolescence. *Journal of Consulting and Clinical Psychology*, 70, 6-20. doi:10.1037/0022-006X.70.1.6

Citizens Commission on Human Rights. (1995). *Psychiatry: Education's ruin*. Author.

Cole, S. F., Eisner, A., Gregory, M., & Ristuccia, J. (2013). Creating and advocating for trauma-sensitive schools. Massachusetts Advocates for Children. Retrieved from http://www.traumasensitiveschools.com

Craig, S. E. (2015). *Trauma-sensitive schools: Learning communities transforming children's lives, K 5*. Teachers College Press.

Curry, J. R., & O'Brien, E. R. (2012). Shifting to a wellness paradigm in teacher education: A promising practice for fostering teacher stress reduction, burnout resilience, and promoting retention. *Ethical Human Psychology and Psychiatry*, 14(3), 178-191.

Davidson, S., & Manion, I. G. (1996). Facing the challenge: Mental health and illness in Canadian youth. *Psychology, Health & Medicine*, 1(1), 41-56.

DeKruyf, L., Auger, R. W., & Trice-Black, S. (2013). The role of school counselors in meeting students' mental health needs: Examining issues of professional identity. *Professional School Counseling*, 16(5), 2156759X0001600502.

Dorado, J. S., Martinez, M., McArthur, L. E., & Leibovitz, T. (2016). Healthy Environments and Response to Trauma in Schools (HEARTS): A whole-school, multi-level, prevention and intervention program for creating trauma-informed, safe and supportive schools. *School Mental Health*, 8(1), 163-176.

Dowdy, E., Ritchey, K., & Kamphaus. R. (2010). School-based screening: A population-based approach to inform and monitor children's mental health needs. *School Mental Health*, 2, 1-11. doi:10.1007/s12310-010-9036-3

Elster, A. B., & Kuznets, N. J. (1994). *Guidelines for adolescent preventive services*. Baltimore: Williams and Wilkins.

Evans, S. W. (1999). Mental health services in schools: Utilization, effectiveness, and consent. *Clinical Psychology Review*, 19, 165-178.

Evans, S., Glass-Siegel, M., Frank, A., et al. (2003). Overcoming the challenges of funding school mental health programs. In M. Weist, S. Evans, & N. Lever (Eds.), *Handbook of school mental health: Advancing practice and research* (pp. 73-86). Kluwer Academic/Plenum.

Evans, S. W., Timmins, B., Sibley, M., White, L. C., Serpell, Z. N., & Schultz, B. (2006). Developing coordinated, multimodal, school-based treatment for young adolescents with ADHD. *Education and Treatment of Children*, 29, 359-378.

Fazel, M., Hoagwood, K., Stephan, S., & Ford, T. (2014). Mental health interventions in schools 1: Mental health interventions in schools in high-income countries. *Lancet Psychiatry*, 1(5), 377-387. doi:10.1016/S2215-0366(14)70312-8

Felitti, V. J., Anda, R. F., Nordenberg, D., Williamson, D. F., Spitz, A. M., Edwards, V., et al. (1998). Relationship of childhood abuse and household dysfunction to many of the leading causes of death in adults: The Adverse Childhood Experiences (ACE) Study. *American Journal of Preventive Medicine*, 14(4), 245-258.

Fergusson, A., & Lacey, P. (2007). Guest editorial. *Support for Learning*, 22(3), 106-110.

Flaherty, L. T., & Osher, D. (2003). History of school-based mental health services in the United States. In M. D. Weist, S. W. Evans, & N. A. Lever (Eds.), *Handbook of school mental health: Advancing practice and research* (pp. 11-22). Boston: Springer.

Forness, S. R., Kim, J., & Walker, H. M. (2012). Prevalence of students with EBD: Impact on general education. *Beyond Behavior*, 21(2), 3-10.

Fuchs, D., & Fuchs, L. S. (2017). Critique of the National Evaluation of Response to Intervention: A case for simpler frameworks. *Exceptional Children, 83*(3), 255–268. https://doi.org/10.1177/0014402917693580.

Gleason, M. M., Heller, S. S., Nagle, G. A., Boothe, A., Keyes, A., & Rice, J. (2012). Mental health screening in child care: Impact of a statewide training session. *Early Childhood Research & Practice, 14*(2), n2.

Ghandour, R. M., Kogan, M. D., Blumberg, S. J., Jones, J. R., & Perrin, J. M. (2012). Mental health conditions among school-aged children: Geographic and sociodemographic patterns in prevalence and treatment. *Journal of Developmental and Behavioral Pediatrics, 33*, 42–54. doi:10.1097/DBP.0b013e31823e18fd

Glover, T. A., & Albers, C. A. (2007). Considerations for evaluating universal screening assessments. *Journal of School Psychology, 45*, 117–135. doi:10.1016/j.jsp.2006.05.005.

Gremli Sanders, M. (2020). Gaps in the Mental Health System Justice System and the Transition to Adulthood: An Analysis of Unmet Needs. *Dissertations*, 479. https://digitalcommons.nl.edu/diss/479

Gross, J. J. (2008). Emotion regulation. In M. Lewis, J. M. Haviland-Jones, & L. F. Barrett (Eds.), *Handbook of emotions* (pp. 497–512). New York, NY: Guilford.

Herschell, A. D., Kolko, D. J., Baumann, B. L., & Davis, A. C. (2010). The role of therapist training in the implementation of psychosocial treatments: A review and critique with recommendations. *Clinical Psychology Review, 30*(4), 448–466.

Hoagwood, K., & Johnson, J. (2013). School psychology: A public health framework: I. From evidence-based practices to evidence-based policies. *Journal of School Psychology, 41*, 3–21

Hoover, S., & Bostic, J. (2021). Schools as a vital component of the child and adolescent mental health system. *Psychiatric Services, 72*(1), 37–48.

Howell, E., Palmer, A., Benatar, S., & Garrett, B. (2014). Potential Medicaid cost savings from maternity care based at a freestanding birth center. *Medicare & Medicaid Research Review, 4*(3), 1–13.

Joe, S., & Bryant, H. (2007). Evidence-based suicide prevention screening in schools. *Children & Schools, 29*(4), 219–227.

Kang-Yi, C. D., Mandell, D. S., & Hadley, T. (2013). School-based mental health program evaluation: Children's school outcomes and acute mental health service use. *Journal of School Health, 83*, 463–472. doi:10.1111/josh.12053

Kenny, H., Oliver, L., & Poppe, J. (2002). *Mental health services for children: An overview.* National Conference of State Legislatures. http://www.ncsl.org/programs/cyf/CPI.pdf

Kilgus, S. P., Riley-Tillman, T. C., Chafouleas, S. M., Christ, T. J., & Welsh, M. E. (2014). Direct behavior rating as a school-based behavior universal screener: Replication across sites. *Journal of School Psychology, 52*(1), 63–82.

Kim, K., & Turnbull, A. (2004). Transition to adulthood for students with severe intellectual disabilities: Shifting toward person-family interdependent planning. *Research and Practice for Persons With Severe Disabilities, 29*, 53–57.

Kranke, D., Floersch, J., Townsend, L., & Munson, M. (2010). Stigma experience among adolescents taking psychiatric medication. *Children and Youth Services Review, 32*(4), 496–505.

Leaf, P. J., Bruce, M. L., Tischler, G. L., Freeman, D. H., Weissman, M. M., & Myers, J. K. (1996). Factors affecting the utilization of specialty and general medical mental health services. *Medical Care, 26*, 9–26.

Lofink, H., Kuebler, J., & Juszczak, L. (2013). 2011 *School-Based Health Alliance census report*. School-Based Health Alliance.

Marsh, R. J., & Mathur, S. R. (2020). Mental health in schools: An overview of multitiered systems of support. *Intervention in School and Clinic, 56*(2), 67–73.

McFarland, J., Hussar, B., Wang, X., Zhang, J., Wang, K., Rathbun, A., Barmer, A., Forrest Cataldi, E., & Bullock Mann, F. (2018). The Condition of Education 2018 (NCES 2018-144). U.S. Department of Education. Washington, DC: National Center for Education Statistics. Retrieved from https://nces.ed.gov/pubsearch/pubsinfo. asp?pubid=2018144.

Merikangas, K. R., He, J. P., Burstein, M., Swendsen, J., Avenevoli, S., Case, B., ... Olfson, M. (2011). Service utilization for lifetime mental disorders in US adolescents: Results of the National Comorbidity Survey–Adolescent Supplement (NCS-A). *Journal of the American Academy of Child & Adolescent Psychiatry, 50*(1), 32–45.

Murphey, D., & Sacks, V. (2019). Supporting students with adverse childhood experiences: How educators and schools can help. *American Educator, 43*(2), 8–11.

Nastasi, B. K., Overstreet, S., & Summerville, M. (2011). School-based mental health services in post-disaster contexts: A public health framework. *School Psychology International, 32*(5), 533–552.

Oliff, P., Mai, C., & Leachman, M. (2012). New school year brings more cuts in state funding for schools. *Center on Budget and Policy Priorities, 4*(1). Website: www.cbpp.org.

Perfect, M., Turley, M., Carlson, J. S., Yohannan, J., & Gilles, M. S. (2016). School-related outcomes of traumatic event exposure and traumatic stress symptoms in students: A systematic review of research from 1990 to 2015. *School Mental Health*. doi:10.1007/s12310-016-9175-2.

Phelps, C., & Sperry, L. L. (2020). Children and the COVID-19 pandemic. *Psychological Trauma: Theory, Research, Practice, and Policy, 12*(S1), S73–S75. http://dx.doi.org/10.1037/tra0000861

Phifer, L. W., & Hull, R. (2016). Helping students heal: Observations of trauma-informed practices in the schools. *School Mental Health, 8*(1), 201–205.

Prewitt, E. (2016). New elementary and secondary education law includes specific "trauma-informed practices" provisions. Retrieved from http://www.acesconnection.com/g/aces-in-education/blog/new-elementary-and-secondary-education-law-inclu desspecific-trauma-informed-practices-provisions

Quinn, K. P., & Lee, V. (2007). The wraparound approach for students with emotional and behavioral disorders: Opportunities for school psychologists. *Psychology in the Schools, 44*, 101–111.

Roehrig, C. (2016). Mental disorders top the list of the most costly conditions in the United States: $201 billion. *Health Affairs, 35*(6), 1130–1135. doi:10.1377/hlthaff.2015.1659

Rose, C. A., Forber-Pratt, A. J., Espelage, D. L., & Aragon, S. R. (2013). The influence of psychosocial factors on bullying involvement of students with disabilities. *Theory Into Practice, 52*(4), 272–279.

Ross, R., & Reichle, J. (2007). Forming interagency partnerships. In C. L. Betz & W. M. Nehring (Eds.), *Promoting health care transitions for adolescents with special needs and disabilities* (pp. 235–254). Brooks.

Substance Abuse and Mental Health Services Administration. (2014). SAMHSA's Concept of Trauma and Guidance for a Trauma-Informed Approach. HHS Publication No. (SMA) 14-4884. Rockville, MD.

Shernoff, E. S., Kratochwill, T. R., & Stoiber, K. C. (2003). Training in evidence-based interventions (EBIs): What are school psychology programs teaching?. *Journal of School Psychology, 41*(6), 467–483.

Snyder, T. D., De Brey, C., & Dillow, S. A. (2019). Digest of Education Statistics 2017, NCES 2018-070. *National Center for Education Statistics.*

Stagman, S., & Cooper, J. L. (2010). *Children's mental health: What every policymaker should know.* New York, NY: National Center for Children in Poverty.

Weist, M. D., Lever, N. A., Bradshaw, C. P., & Owens, J. S. (Eds.). (2014). *Handbook of school mental health: Research, training, practice, and policy* (pp. 1–14). Springer US.

Williams, S. (2013). Bring in universal mental health checks in schools. *British Medical Journal 5478,* 24–26. doi:10.1136/5478.

Witt, W. P., Riley, A. W., & Coiro, M. J. (2003). Childhood functional status, family stressors, and psychosocial adjustment among school-aged children with disabilities in the United States. *Archives of Pediatrics & Adolescent Medicine, 157*(7), 687–695.

Wood, B. J., & McDaniel, T. (2020). A preliminary investigation of universal mental health screening practices in schools. *Children and Youth Services Review, 112,* 104943.

5
Immigrant and Refugee Youth

Overview

This chapter provides a framework to guide mental health providers who work with refugees and immigrants. We examine the complex ways in which culture impacts the refugee experience, barriers to engaging in mental health practice and strategies for overcoming them, collaborative and integrated mental health interventions, and efforts to increase resilience in children, families, and communities.

Introduction

The US foreign-born population reached a record 44.8 million in 2018 (US Census Bureau). Depending on the legal determination made related to the circumstances of migration, immigrants may be refugees, asylum seekers, asylees, undocumented immigrants, unaccompanied children, unaccompanied refugee minors, or authorized immigrants. Understanding the legal standing of the child or family with whom a clinician works is important to recognizing what benefits they have access to and the stability of their residency. Some immigrants are voluntary migrants who migrate for reasons such as educational or professional opportunity or for family connection (American Psychological Association [APA] Presidential Task Force on Immigration, 2012). In contrast, some immigrants—including refugees, asylum seekers, and many undocumented immigrants—migrate in search of humanitarian refuge (APA Presidential Task Force on Immigration, 2012).

Within the past decade, the United States has seen a large increase in the number of unaccompanied immigrant minors (UIMs; immigrants under the age of 18 who are not accompanied by a parent or legal guardian) detained at the border (United Nations High Commissioner for Refugees; UNHCR, 2014). Under long-standing law and policy, migrants under the age of 18 who present themselves at the border without their biological parents must

Counseling Youth. Richard S. Balkin, Amanda Winburn, Erika L. Schmit, and Samantha M. Mendoza, Oxford University Press. © Oxford University Press 2023. DOI: 10.1093/oso/9780197586761.003.0005

be admitted into the United States. Most are released to relatives already living in the United States, while others are sent to youth shelters or foster homes. Approximately 81,000 UIMs were released to adult sponsors across the United States between October 2013 and December 2015 (US Customs and Border Protection, 2016).

UIMs, because of their unique needs, represent a complex service population, particularly within the counseling field. Almost half (48%) report leaving their home country because of experiences of violence (including gang violence, violence perpetrated by organized crime or government, and sexual violence), 22% report abuse at home, and many report wanting to reunite with parents or other family members living in the United States (UNHCR, 2014).

Mental health professionals and advocates are in a position to improve the lives of these youth at the clinical and systems levels, which makes it increasingly important to improve our understanding and address the needs of UIM.

How Culture Impacts the Refugee Experience

The refugee experience for the UIM population is shaped by unique histories that likely included one or more of the following:

- Trauma in their country of origin
- Trauma during the journey to United States
- Trafficking or potential for exploitation while in the United States
- Culture shock upon arrival to the United States

Trauma in Country of Origin

For many UIMs, particularly those within the refugee population, life in their respective countries of origin included a dangerous past of cartel or gang violence, drugs, sexual abuse, etc. For other children, the responsibility of caring for younger siblings or acting as head of household is a stark reality. Guatemala, Honduras, and El Salvador, known as the Northern Triangle of Central America, have been plagued with increasing gang and cartel violence, declining governmental and educational infrastructures, and increased corruption among law enforcement (Restrepo & Garcia, 2014). Currently their homicide rates are among the highest in the world (Gagne, 2017; UNODC Statistics and Surveys Section, 2014). Children and adolescents are often deliberate targets, particularly if they decline gang recruitment efforts (Jones & Podkul, 2012). In response to these rising levels of violence, migration out of these countries dramatically increased starting in 2014 (Schmidt & Somers, 2014), and more than 120,000 unaccompanied immigrant youth and another 120,000 family units with young children have come to the United States from Central America since then (Restrepo & Mathema, 2016).

Case Study: Yasmin

Yasmin is a 15-year-old UIM from El Salvador. She disclosed being physically abused by her father from age 9 to 14. She categorizes the incidents as discipline and states that her father would hit her with a cord or stick when she failed to complete household chores, when she didn't do well in school, or when she got home after dark. Yasmin reports that this often resulted in a visible mark or scratch on her body—usually her back, shoulders, or legs, but sometimes her face or hands. The minor also reported having been shot in the leg by gang members at the age of 12. She denies being gang affiliated and notes that area gang members would often threaten her in an effort to coerce her into joining the gang. On one occasion, there was a shooting next door and Yasmin was harmed, though she was not a direct target. Yasmin also reports having had a sexual relationship with an 18-year-old man when she was 13 years of age. This resulted in a pregnancy and miscarriage just before Yasmin's 15th birthday.

Trauma During Journey to United States

The journey to the United States is not an easy one. Minors report a great deal of time and money that goes into planning one's journey. Many hire a "coyote," or a foot guide, to aid in navigating the road from the home country to the United States. While this is sometimes a relatively uneventful journey, more often than not it involves trauma. UIMs have reported physical assault, sexual assault, robbing, exploitation, etc. in their weeks' long journey.

> **Case Study: Jessica**
>
> Jessica is a 17-year-old UIM from Guatemala. She was sexually assaulted by another migrant on the journey to United States. After many months of severe anxiety attacks and depression, Jessica's mental health progressively improved during her length of stay due to her diligent work and commitment to getting better. Jessica's mother is her proposed sponsor. Jessica has been separated from her mother for the past 3 years. Her mother lives with a recent boyfriend, with whom she has a strained relationship. While there is no record of domestic violence, the case manager feels that the mother might be in a psychologically abusive relationship due to comments that the mother has made, including needing to make sure Jessica follows the boyfriend's rules. Jessica will turn 18 in 4 months. The mother is the only viable sponsor at this time as there are no other relatives or family friends in a position to sponsor Jessica at this time.

Trafficking or Potential Risk of Exploitation While in the United States

While any child can be vulnerable to human trafficking, UIMs are at increased risk of being trafficked or exploited once they arrive in the United States. These children are particularly vulnerable due to prior abuse or neglect, poverty, unfamiliarity in a new country, etc. These minors are sometimes told they have a debt to pay upon their arrival to the United States. This may be from the financial cost to make the journey, or it could be that their prospective sponsor has agreed to house them provided they repay the debt with labor. Though illegal, this often includes unpaid labor, childcare duties, housekeeping, etc. Others are at risk of human trafficking or sexual slavery (minors being forced into sex work, child pornography, exotic dancing, etc.).

Culture Shock when Transitioning to the United States

"Culture shock" is a term used to describe the anxiety and feelings of surprise, disorientation, and confusion felt when individuals have to operate within an entirely different cultural or social environment (such as a foreign country).

Upon arrival to the United States, UIMs find themselves removed from everything that is familiar. Language, family life, cultural norms and traditions (including food, living arrangements, education, etc.) are often very different from their country of origin. These experiences as UIMs attempt to adapt to life in the United States can be uniquely challenging to minors and contribute to an increase in their overall stress levels.

The following list includes experiences of trauma that may be more prevalent in immigrant and refugee families (Miller et al., 2019):

- Anxiety about the possibility of parental deportation or safety of family members in the country or origin
- Family separation, either planned separation due to immigration logistics or separation as a result of immigration policy or detention
- Bullying or victimization at school
- Physical or sexual abuse
- Dangerous conditions during migration
- Family conflict or intrafamilial violence
- Unsafe neighborhoods or gun violence (in country of origin and after relocation)
- Racism and microaggressions (both in country of origin and after relocation)

Parental deportation can be traumatic for children in multiple ways, including witnessing the forced removal of the parent, the sudden and unexplained absence of a parent, and the ensuing instability in housing or family functioning (Brabeck et al., 2014).

Postmigration

Arrival in the United States does not signal the end of a minor's adversity. Conversely, substantial stressors remain, such as stays in detention centers, immigration proceedings, and adaption to a foreign environment as a UIM. The length of stay in detention impacts psychological symptoms for immigrant and refugee youth (Fazel et al., 2012). Youth may then find themselves resettled in areas where they continue to be exposed to community violence and economic deprivation. For example, in the Boston area, Salvadoran youth describe migrating to the United States to flee gang violence only to be recruited by local members of Salvadoran gangs (Ransom, 2016).

> **Case Study: Wilmer**
>
> Wilmer, a 12-year-old from Honduras, reports having been sexually assaulted by a distant relative in his home country. Wilmer eventually reported this to his aunt, who was his caregiver, and she reported it to local authorities. Because the perpetrator was a city official, charges were not brought against the perpetrator, nor was he arrested or fined—there were simply no consequences. Wilmer now states that he doesn't see the point in being honest or reporting things if no one is going to believe him or protect him. Consequently, Wilmer is unenthused about participating in counseling or disclosing any of his past to his therapist.
>
> Wilmer's example is just one of many possible scenarios involving a UIM who has difficulty trusting authoritative figures. For other youth, there is confusion or fear about the overall refugee experience. UIM wonder if they have the right to speak at all, or to whom? Others may experience abuse during their journey or upon their arrival to the United States and wonder, "Is this normal? Do I tolerate abuse because it gets me to America?"

Barriers to Engagement in Mental Health Practice

Interviews with young adults who had received Deferred Action for Childhood Arrivals (DACA) indicated that the largest unmet need was for mental health services (Raymond-Flesch et al., 2014). With regard to the UIM population, there are many barriers to engagement in mental health practice. Most obvious, a language barrier typically exists between UIM and most counselors. While technology for translation services does exist, the language barrier is just the first of many obstacles in place when working with this population of youth. For a number of UIMs, there is a lack of established trust between the therapist and the minor. This can simply be due to the therapist being an American, or it could be exacerbated by negative experiences with Immigration and Custom Enforcement (ICE) officers, the

Border Patrol, or other authorities. For other minors, there is a level of difficulty trusting authoritative figures because often trauma or abuse was reported in their country of origin and nothing was done about it.

Financial access to care for undocumented immigrants has been limited in Northern Europe and North America (Ruiz-Casares et al., 2010), and immigrant families may limit their own use of healthcare even when offered in a low-cost setting. Furthermore, fear of deportation may prevent families from enrolling in and using available services even when they possess valid immigration documents, especially in areas with increased proportions of deportations (Watson, 2010). Families may be reluctant to enter their own information into health center records, even if their children are US-born, for fear of having this information shared with law enforcement agencies (Page & Polk, 2017). In addition to fear, isolation and lack of awareness may limit access to healthcare, as has been noted even in long-time Guatemalan immigrants (Zhen-Duang et al., 2017). Given the increased mental health burden of undocumented status and fear of deportation, as well as a lack of trust in healthcare services, an effective system of care for immigrants might combine both medical and legal services in one location. Such collaborative and integrated mental health interventions might include the following:

- Multidisciplinary approach (CM/social workers, medical/nursing, educational staff, child care workers)
- Cognitive behavioral therapy at the shelter level (prior to a minor's release from care)
- Creating a safe space, developing cultural competence

Socioecological Model

One approach to navigating the refugee or immigrant child's experience is using a socioecological model (Bronfenbrenner, 1979; Figure 5.1). Through this lens, the developing child is seen as being at the heart of a series of concentric circles that make up the social ecology: he or she lives in a family, attends school, is part of a neighborhood and larger society, and all of this is embedded in a culture—for immigrants, both their culture of origin and the culture of their resettlement community. Disruptions in any one layer of this social ecology can have profound consequences for the developing child at its core. So, too, can assets—the gifts of family bonds, a teacher's warmth, a place on the town's baseball team.

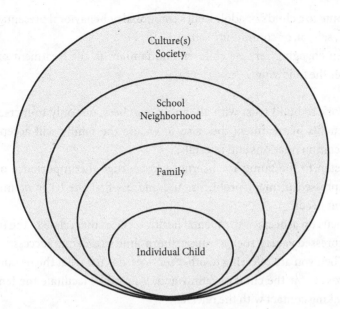

Figure 5.1 Socioecological model showing how the individual child is nested within layers of the social ecology.

Different levels of the social ecology interact such that disruptions or interventions within one level of the ecology may affect the functioning and stability of another level.

Trauma-Informed Care

The National Child Traumatic Stress Network has developed trauma-informed resources related to refugees and focused on the traumatic exposures that many refugee children have sustained related to war, persecution, displacement, and resettlement in the United States. Trauma can affect a refugee child's emotional and behavioral development. Mental health providers should consider how the refugee experience (e.g., exposure to hunger, thirst, and lack of shelter; injury and illness; serving as a material witness, victim, or perpetrator of violence; fleeing your home and country; separating from family; living in a refugee camp; resettling in a new country; and navigating between the new culture and the culture of origin) may contribute to a child's or adolescent's emotional or behavioral presentation in a clinic, school, or community setting.

When engaging refugee children and families in the treatment process, consider the following:

- Work to build trust with all family members, not only to increase the benefits of treatment, but also to ensure the family will accept your recommendations and referrals.
- Listen to the family's concerns, acknowledge the importance of their expressed primary problems, and address first the basic or most urgent needs.
- Focus on aspects of the mental health services that relate to the family's expressed values, such as supporting a child's academic success.
- When you are referring to other services, discuss what the resource can provide for the child or family and, if possible, facilitate the family in making contact with the referral.

Trauma Systems Therapy (TST; Saxe et al., 2007, 2016) is an evidence-based model of care for youth who have experienced trauma. TST addresses the needs of the (1) individual youth and (2) the social environment (i.e., family, school, and neighborhood) in which the youth lives.

TST is both a clinical model for the efficient and effective treatment of traumatized youth and an organizational model for the integration of services for agencies and programs that provide treatment to traumatized youth and families. TST is a framework for organizing interventions that addresses the real-world needs of youth facing considerable adversity. TST is designed to help youth and families where there is ongoing stress in the social environment by addressing the trauma system.

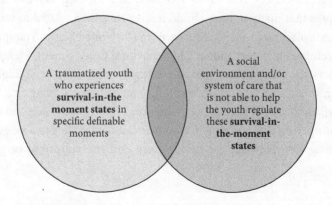

Trauma Systems Therapy for Refugees (TST-R) is a comprehensive method for treating traumatic stress in children and adolescents that adds to individually based approaches by specifically addressing social environmental/system-of-care factors that are believed to be driving a child's traumatic stress problems (National Child Traumatic Stress Network [NCTSN], 2016). TST-R is adapted for refugee youth and families who have experienced war and violence prior to resettlement and continue to face ongoing acculturation and resettlement stress. It consists of three components of prevention and intervention. TST-R has been adapted for, and implemented with, various refugee communities. TST-R was adapted from TST to address the specific needs of refugee youth. In addition to the TST model of care, TST-R includes new components such as skills-based groups focused on acculturative stress and community outreach. TST-R is a comprehensive method for treating traumatic stress in children and adolescents by specifically addressing social environmental/system-of-care factors that are believed to be driving a child's traumatic stress problems. In TST-R, TST was adapted to address the experience of war and violence prior to resettlement, and the ongoing acculturative and resettlement stressors that refugee families experience. TST-R specifically seeks to improve engagement of refugee youth and their families by offering services along a continuum of care, and treatment is embedded within systems of care (e.g., schools) (NCTSN, 2016). TST-R was developed to provide culturally appropriate trauma-informed mental healthcare for refugee youth and their families who may not seek services otherwise. TST was inspired in part by Bronfenbrenner's Social-Ecological Model (Bronfenbrenner, 1979), which acknowledges the complexity of the social environment that surrounds an individual and how disruptions in one area of the social ecology may create problems in another. Interventions in TST-R/TST are designed to work in two dimensions: strategies that operate through and in the social environment to promote change and strategies that enhance the child's capacity to self-regulate. The TST model involves a phase-based approach to intervention that corresponds to the fit between the traumatized child's own emotional regulation capacities and the ability of the child's social environment and system-of-care to help them manage emotions or protect them from threat. Targeted population for TST-R includes youth between 10 and 18 years of age; both males and females; newly arriving, recently resettled, and established refugee youth and communities. Three key prevention and intervention components necessary for TST-R implementation are community engagement, prevention/early intervention, and intensive intervention.

Community Engagement

Refugee and immigrant community engagement. Parent education forums help families understand how mental health problems affect children's functioning and ability to learn and how parents are critical partners in promoting their children's health. This component also elicits feedback from parents about the specific challenges and needs they perceive for children within their particular ethnic community.

School and community engagement. Teacher trainings and student and teacher resources to promote understanding of cultural diversity and a more inclusive school community will be developed and delivered.

Prevention/Early Intervention

Within the school, prevention/early intervention skill-building groups are conducted with school-based clinicians and cultural brokers to help refugee students with acculturation and socialization. These groups also serve to help identify youth who are in need of more intensive mental health services. Teacher trainings and consultations further minimize acculturative stress within the school setting and help teachers understand how learning and behavior may be affected by trauma and stress.

Intensive Intervention

Individuals who demonstrate significant mental health needs receive community-based, linguistically and culturally sensitive care under the TST model. Intensive treatment may include home-based care, office- or school-based care, pharmacology, and/or advocacy and include the following four critical elements for the implementation of a TST-R program:

- All TST-R programs must partner with the community of interest;
- All TST-R teams must include a cultural provider or a cultural broker;

- TST-R teams must include a combination of home-based clinicians, an outpatient clinician, school-based clinicians, a clinical supervisor, and organizational support persons; and
- The capacity for the delivery of services to occur in home, school, or community settings.

Cultural Humility

Cultural humility is the bedrock of developing a strong multicultural orientation (Hook et al., 2013). Cultural humility involves an awareness of one's limitations in understanding a client's cultural background and experience. Cultural humility also involves an interpersonal stance that is other-oriented rather than self-focused in regard to the cultural background and experience of the client. The culturally humble therapist is interested in and open to exploring the client's cultural background and experiences. The culturally humble therapist does not assume their cultural perspective is "the correct one"; rather, the culturally humble therapist recognizes that there are several valid ways of viewing the world and developing a sense of one's beliefs and values (Hook et al., 2017). Humility encourages therapists to approach their work with culturally diverse clients with an attitude of openness, being engaged in a dynamic process of growth (Hook et al., 2013). This process is characterized by acknowledging and owning limitations and striving to express openness and interest in the client's salient cultural identities. There is no end-state of competence. There is only humility and continued growth and development over time. The next aspect of multicultural orientation involves attending to and eliciting cultural opportunities in one's work with clients (Owen, 2013; Owen et al., 2016). This is also a specific expression of cultural humility. Therapists have several decision points during therapy, and many of these decisions involve whether to engage a discussion about the client's cultural background and identities. These choice points, which are guided by the therapist's multicultural orientation, can directly or indirectly communicate to the client that the therapist views the client's culture as an important aspect of the client's life that should be addressed in therapy. However, avoiding or moving away from a cultural opportunity can communicate that the client's cultural identity is unimportant or invalid. The final aspect of multicultural orientation involves *cultural comfort*. This is an expression of cultural humility that involves the therapist's sense of ease when addressing cultural topics and engaging the client in cultural discussion (Owen, 2013; Owen et al., 2017). Cultural comfort is expected to directly influence a therapist's likelihood of initiating cultural dialogue with a client, and it is also expected to relate positively to the quality of a discussion with a client about culture. Cultural comfort can be developed through experiences both inside and outside the therapy room (Hook et al., 2017).

A summary of the definitions of various legal statuses for immigrants is presented in Table 5.1, along with their clinical implications.

Summary

In this chapter, we discussed foreign-born youth and the unique driving forces that lead youth to make the journey to the United States. We learned that some minors make a voluntary journey due to professional or educational ambitions or family connection, while others, including refugees and asylum seekers, migrate in search of humanitarian refuge. We explored case studies in an effort to highlight the many traumas that are unique to this population of youth. The case study examples also identified some of the increased risks that undocumented youth often face as newcomers to a society and culture that is unfamiliar to them. We touched on trafficking, post-migration struggles, and barriers to youth engaging in mental health practice. We identified useful approaches and frameworks, such as incorporating a socioecological model and trauma-informed care, including TST, which are especially helpful when working with immigrant or refugee youth. We addressed the importance of cultural humility and maintaining a strong multicultural orientation when working with this special population. We also provided useful definitions of legal statuses and cultural implications for each group, along with suggestions for increasing resilience within immigrant or refugee youth, their families, and the communities in which they reside.

Approaches to addressing the multitude of challenges of UIM include being knowledgeable about resources available, including English lessons; provision and monitoring of services (post-release service providers); and counseling/therapy. Keep in mind that the caregivers/parents of UIMs may require parenting classes because they may lack experience due to minors being raised by other family members in the child's country of origin. Children may be living with adults they are not related to. Not only should

Table 5.1 Definitions of legal statuses and clinical implications

	Definition	Clinical implications
Refugees	A legal status provided to individuals who are recognized by the 1951 Convention definition as persons who have crossed an international boundary because they are "unable or unwilling to avail themselves of the protection of their former country due to a well-founded fear of persecution based on race; religion; nationality; membership of a particular social group; or political opinion" (UNHCR, 1951).	Knowing the rights and benefits that refugees can claim in their state or country will allow providers to best serve these individuals. Refugees are eligible to work immediately upon arrival and may apply for a green card 1 year after arrival.
Asylum seekers	Individuals who have applied for international protection but whose refugee-status claims have not been verified. Asylum seekers may have similar experiences as refugees but have not been afforded the same legal protections and benefits.	Understanding that these individuals face additional uncertainty around legal status and deportation can help providers address the unique challenges they may face.
Unaccompanied children (UAC)	Children under the age of 18 "who have been separated from both parents and other relatives and are not being cared for by an adult who, by law or custom, is responsible for doing so" (UNHCR, 1951).	A UAC's age and lack of legal status may make them particularly vulnerable to exploitation or victimization during their journey. UACs may also be accustomed to assuming adult responsibilities. A UAC may seek to remain in the country legally through applying for asylum or a Special Immigrant Juvenile Status visa. During the application process, UACs are housed under the auspices of the Office of Refugee Resettlement (ORR) in foster homes, residential centers, detention centers, or other care facilities.

(*continued*)

Table 5.1 Continued

	Definition	Clinical implications
Unaccompanied refugee minor (URM)	Children who enter the United States legally as refugees through the US refugee admissions program, or children referred from the UAC program who have received Special Immigrant Juvenile Status. URMs typically are placed in foster care until age 21, with some benefits extending to age 23.	A URM may be placed with families whose ethnicity and associated customs differ from their own. Older children or adolescents may have functioned independently for many years and may be unaccustomed to being within a family system where they lose independence and autonomy.
Undocumented immigrant	An undocumented immigrant enters the United States without proper authorization documents or enters legally but then overstays his or her visa.	Undocumented immigrants may not access needed services out of fear that they will be reported and deported. Federal policies restrict access to federal public benefits such as Food Stamps and Supplemental Social Security Income (SSI), though a small number of states provide access to benefits (Fix & Passel, 2002).

clinicians be concerned with exploitation and maltreatment, but they must also be alert to current treatment within the new environment.

Past experiences in economically disadvantaged countries and the immigration experience may lead to issues of security, competence, and capability among youth. Acknowledging their past while recognizing that it does not define them as a human being is an important intervention. This is especially true for victims of sexual abuse, trafficking, and other trauma.

Crime and violence exposure in the country of origin may not have to carry over into their life in the United States. Youth may need help developing new social circles or a reduced reliance of having to provide for their families. The survivor versus victim mentality may be difficult to teach but not impossible to achieve.

Clinicians, education professionals, and social service agents can help UIMs by pointing out their accomplishments to develop a sense of pride, and this is particularly important in the new educational setting in which youth will participate. Success in the educational realm is pertinent to developing a sense of responsibility for their future and/or the future of their children (breaking the cycle of abuse, poverty, etc.).

References

American Psychological Association, Presidential Task Force on Immigration. (2012). Crossroads: The psychology of immigration in the new century. American Psychological Association. Retrieved from http://www.apa.org/topics/immigration/report.aspx

Brabeck, K. M., Lykes, M. B., & Hunter, C. (2014). The psychosocial impact of detention and deportation on US migrant children and families. *American Journal of Orthopsychiatry, 84*(5), 496–505. https://doi.org/10.1037/ort0000011

Bronfenbrenner, U. (1979). *The ecology of human development: Experiments by nature and design*. Harvard University Press.

Fazel, M., Reed, R. V., Panter-Brick, C., & Stein, A. (2012). Mental health of displaced and refugee children resettled in high-income countries: Risk and protective factors. *The Lancet, 379*(9812), 266–282.

Fix, M., & Passel, J. (2002). The scope and impact of welfare reform's immigrant provisions: *Assessing the New Federalism. Discussion Paper (02-03)*. The Urban Institute.

Gagne, D. (2017). Insight Crime's 2016 Latin America homicide round-up (article). Retrieved December 17, 2020, from http://www.insightcrime.org/news- analysis/insight-crime-2016-homicide-round-up

Hook, J. N., Davis, D. E., Owen, J., Worthington, E. L., Jr., & Utsey, S. O. (2013). Cultural humility: Measuring openness to culturally diverse clients. *Journal of Counseling Psychology, 60*, 353–366. http://dx.doi.org/10.1037/a0032595

Hook, J. N., Davis, D., Owen, J., & DeBlaere, C. (2017). Cultural humility: Engaging diverse identities in therapy. *American Psychological Association*. https://doi.org/10.1037/0000037-000

Jones, J., & Podkul, J. (2012). Forced from home: The lost boys and girls of Central America. Retrieved from http://www.womensrefugeecommission.org/programs/detention/unaccompanied-children

Miller, K., Brown, C., Shramko, M., & Svetaz, M. (2019). Applying trauma-informed practices to the care of refugee and immigrant youth: 10 clinical pearls. *Children, 6*(8), 94.

National Child Traumatic Stress Network. (2016). TST-R: Trauma systems therapy for refugees. Retrieved from https://www.nctsn.org/sites/default/files/interventions/tstr_fact_sheet.pdf

Owen, J. (2013). Early career perspectives on psychotherapy research and practice: Psychotherapist effects, multicultural orientation, and couple interventions. *Psychotherapy, 50*(4), 496–502. https://doi.org/10.1037/a0034617

Owen, J., Drinane, J., Tao, K. W., Adelson, J. L., Hook, J. N., Davis, D., & Fookune, N. (2017). Racial/ethnic disparities in client unilateral termination: The role of therapists' cultural comfort. *Psychotherapy Research, 27*(1), 102–111. https://doi.org/10.1080/10503307.2015.1078517

Owen, J., Tao, K. W., Drinane, J. M., Hook, J., Davis, D. E., & Kune, N. F. (2016). Client perceptions of therapists' multicultural orientation: Cultural (missed) opportunities and cultural humility. *Professional Psychology: Research and Practice, 47*(1), 30–37. https://doi.org/10.1037/pro0000046

Page, K. R., & Polk, S. (2017). Chilling effect? Post-election health care use by undocumented and mixed-status families. *New England Journal of Medicine, 376*(12), e20. http://doi.org/:10.1056/NEJMp1700829

Ransom, J. (2016, Feb. 3). Salvadoran teen recounts threats from gangs. *The Boston Globe.* Retrieved from http://www.bostonglobe.com/metro/2016/02/02/salvadoran-teen-recounts-threats-fromgangs/U7SoEXgVVgWgtWP14XeH7J/story.html?s_campaign=8315

Raymond-Flesch, M., Siemons, R., Pourat, N., Jacobs, K., & Brindis, C. D. (2014). "There is no help out there and if there is, it's really hard to find": A qualitative study of the health concerns and health care access of Latino "DREAMers." *Journal of Adolescent Health, 55*, 323–328. https://doi.org/10.1016/j.jadohealth.2014.05.012

Restrepo, D., & Garcia, A. (2014). The surge of unaccompanied children from Central America: Root causes and policy solutions. Retrieved from http://www.americanprogress.org/issues/immigration/report/2014/07/24/94396/the-surge- of-unaccompanied-children-from-central-america-root-causes-and-policy-solutions/

Restrepo, D., & Mathema, S. (2016). A medium- and long-term plan to address the Central American refugee crisis. Retrieved from https://www.americanprogress.org/issues/immigration/report/2016/05/05/136920/a- medium-and-long-term-plan-to-address-the-central-american-refugee-situation/

Ruiz-Casares, M., Rousseau, C., Derluyn, I., Watters, C., & Crepeau, F. (2010). Right and access to healthcare for undocumented children: Addressing the gap between international conventions and disparate implementations in North America and Europe. *Social Science and Medicine, 70*, 329–336. https://doi.org/10.1016/j.socscimed.2009.10.013

Saxe, G. N., Ellis, B. H., & Brown, A. D. (2016). *Trauma systems therapy for children and teens* (2nd ed.). Guilford.

Saxe, G. N., Ellis, B. H., & Kaplow, J. B. (2007). *Collaborative treatment of traumatized children and teens: The trauma systems therapy approach.* Guilford.

Schmidt, S., & Somers, A. (2014). Children on the run: Unaccompanied children leaving Central America and Mexico and the need for international protection. Retrieved from http://www.unhcr.org/en-us/about-us/background/56fc266f4/children- on-the-run-full-report.html

UN High Commissioner for Refugees (UNHCR), The 1951 Convention Relating to the Status of Refugees and its 1967 Protocol, September 2011, available at: https://www.refworld.org/docid/4ec4a7f02.html [accessed 2 May 2022]

United Nations High Commissioner on Refugees (UNHCR). (2014). *Children on the run: Unaccompanied children leaving Central America and Mexico and the need for international protection.* UNHCR.

UNODC Statistics and Surveys Section. (2014). Global study on homicide 2013: Trends, contexts, data. Retrieved from http://www.unodc.org/documents/data-and- analysis/statistics/Homicide/Globa_study_on_homicide_2011_web.pdf

US Census Bureau (2018). American Community Survey 1-year estimates. https://www.census.gov/programs-surveys/acs

US Customs and Border Protection. (2016). Southwest Border Unaccompanied Alien Children Statistics FY. 2016. https://www.cbp.gov/newsroom/stats/southwest-border-unaccompanied-alien-children-statistics-fy-2016

Watson, T. (2010). Inside the refrigerator: Immigration enforcement and chilling effects in Medicaid participation. Retrieved from http://www.nber.org/papers/w16278.pdf

Zhen-Duan, J., Jacquez, F., & Vaughn, L. (2017). Demographic characteristics associated with barriers to health care among Mexican and Guatemalan immigrants in a non-traditional destination area. *Family Community Health, 40*, 101–111. doi:10.1097/fch.0000000000000141

PART II
ISSUES AFFECTING YOUTH

6
Stress, Depression, and Suicide

Overview

Youth, including childhood and adolescence, can be a stressful time in one's life; however, taking a normalized developmental approach to stress through this transition may be necessary. In some instances, stress may impact an individual's mental health and may lead to a depressed state. Furthermore, depression is a known and well-researched risk factor for suicidal behavior in youth (American Foundation for Suicide Prevention [AFSP], n.d.).

Introduction

At times, clinicians must provide crisis counseling to help their clients reach a safe space. While there has been a considerable amount of research on how stress, depression, and suicide interact, there remains a dearth of literature addressing many of these constructs with youth, particularly those from minority groups. For example, much of what we know generally emphasizes that adverse childhood experiences (ACEs) correlate with mental illness and suicide attempts (Felitti et al., 1998), youth living in disadvantaged areas or distressed environments have a higher likelihood of depression (Cheng, 2014), and LGBT youth have higher levels of depression and suicidal ideation (Baams et al., 2015). More research on what specifically affects children and adolescents' mental health (e.g., depressive symptoms) and, furthermore, what may cause suicidal behaviors is necessary to describe appropriate treatments and aid clinicians who work with mental health populations.

The latest statistics in suicide research show that suicide is the 10th leading cause of death in the United States (American Foundation for Suicide Prevention [AFSP], 2020). In one year, there were 1.4 million suicide attempts. In 2018, more than 48,000 Americans died by suicide, which was an increase from 45,000 in 2016 (Centers for Disease Control and Prevention [CDC], 2022a). Last, in 2015, suicide cost the United States $69 billion.

Counseling Youth. Richard S. Balkin, Amanda Winburn, Erika L. Schmit, and Samantha M. Mendoza,
Oxford University Press. © Oxford University Press 2023. DOI: 10.1093/oso/9780197586761.003.0006

Younger groups tend to have a lower rate of suicide than do adults. However, suicide is the second leading cause of death in children and adolescents (aged 10–14) and the third leading cause for those aged 15–17, only behind unintentional injury (CDC, 2022a). Those aged 15–24 (which is inclusive of adolescents and young adults) have a rate of 14.45 suicides per 100,000. Since 2008, suicide has been steadily increasing in this age category (CDC, 2017) One child per day (ages 5–14) dies by suicide (CDC, 2022a). Although, suicide rates have been on a slight decline the past few years (Ehlman et al., 2022), these rates are still alarming, especially given the unpredictability of reporting.

Clinicians must be knowledgeable about the factors, including stress and depression, that may lead to suicide in order to provide prevention, intervention, and postvention services to clients. Research continues to show us that counselors are uncomfortable with talking about suicide, particularly when it comes to children. Therefore, the purpose of this chapter is to discuss youth stressors, depression, suicide, and how these three interact and impact each other. Protective factors, risk factors, and effective counseling services will be discussed.

Stress in Youth

Stress, simply put, is our body's normal reaction to a circumstance, event, or emotion. To normalize the discussion on stress, we must remember that stress is common and not always a bad thing. For example, remember when you got married, had your first child, or got a promotion at work. These exciting events are sometimes filled with stress-induced feelings because they are new and unknown. Maybe you were stressed before having to complete a presentation for your college class. These types of stress tend to be short-lived and an indicator that your body is working to help you get through that event. But what happens when stress becomes unhealthy for a person or becomes more long term? We will look at this further below.

Generally speaking, individuals come to treatment attempting to eliminate some sort of unhealthy stressor in their life. Something is not working for them, whether that be a lack of coping, feeling down, or the inability to fix a problem.

Common stressors in youth generally include either academic or interpersonal issues. Academic issues are related to meeting demands in school.

Youth spend much of their life and time in academic settings, acquiring information, developing skills, and experiencing new social relationships. There are many mutual sources of stress that children go through. For example, many children will have feelings of being overwhelmed when preparing for their first academic test. Children are also learning how to interact with social peers in an appropriate way, which, at times, causes conflict. Teenagers may experience additional stressors from having pressure to meet academic standards to prepare for college. Additionally, peer pressure is common at this stage as teenagers need to fit in with their peers. Last, technology has made major advancements in the past 10 years, particularly with social media platforms (e.g., YouTube, Snapchat). While utilizing these platforms has benefits (i.e., social connectedness), cyberbullying and indecent, improper exposure (e.g., early sexual content) have become serious issues in this age group. Because childhood years are important for healthy adult development, it is crucial for clinicians to be aware of some of these common personal stressors and how they might impact mental well-being.

Stress and Mental Health

When stress is not appropriately addressed, it may lead to longer-term problems in physical or mental health (e.g., depression). Although depression has no single known cause, myriad factors may trigger a depressive state in an individual. Examples include genetics, illness or medical issues, or trauma. Among these common examples, chronic stress, particularly in minors, can increase a person's likelihood for developing depression. Chronic stress can be defined as being in a constant state of feeling stressed through repeated exposure to stress hormones (i.e., cortisol). For example, imagine your client, a 10-year-old girl is being bullied at school. This in itself may not be enough to trigger depression. However, you also know that this client just moved to your city due to her parent's divorce and is having issues adjusting to such a major life change while keeping up with school work. All of these stressors together may impact that client's mental health and trigger a trauma response.

Childhood trauma can have a lasting impact on the health of individuals, particularly in adulthood (Mandelli et al., 2015). Some examples that clinicians may see in their work with minor clients include abuse, neglect, divorce of parents, family death, parental health issues, and bullying. In their meta-analysis, Mandelli (2015) showed that emotional abuse and neglect were the strongest predictors of depression. On some occasions, clients you see may have been diagnosed with posttraumatic stress disorder (PTSD). (Chapter 11 will further discuss abuse and trauma and their impact on youths' development.)

In some cases, childhood trauma or abuse may lead to mental health diagnoses such as depression. Furthermore, while mood disorders such as depression are risk factors for suicidal behavior, they are not necessarily the cause. Depression may be mostly linked to suicidal ideation and less likely to suicidal attempts, with approximately 25% of those experiencing depression making a nonfatal suicide attempt (i.e., an attempt that does not end in death; Verona et al., 2004). Depression may be one factor in a multifaceted health issue. Thinking that depression automatically means death by suicide plays into the stigma related to mental health and suicide. Clinicians must be cautious with thinking that depression equals death by suicide (Foiles, 2018).

The Impact of Stress, Depression, and Suicide on Society

These aforementioned issues in youth not only impact the individual person but also have the potential to impact society as a whole. You will likely read or have read many texts that focus on this one individual area. In fact, this chapter focuses mostly on the minor client, as an individual. However, it is a disservice to the helping fields when we do not take a systemic approach and consider all facets of an issue and how each impacts the others.

Mental health in youth is a public health concern and must be viewed as such, especially by mental health providers. According to the Centers for Disease Control and Prevention (CDC, 2021; 2022b), mental illness is a global burden and the leading cause for injury and disease. The World Health Organization reports that 20% of children and adolescents experience mental illness. Furthermore, mental illness in youth can have a negative effect on the family, friends, peers, and others who interact with youth. The latest statistic shows that, in 2010, depression cost the United States $200 billion, which is a substantial economic burden.

One example of how mental health is a concern systemically and perhaps long term: you begin seeing a client experiencing depression symptoms and suicidal ideation. He expresses a desire to "never wake up again." After further assessment, you determine a need for inpatient hospitalization (further on this topic later in the chapter). The client misses 4 days of school; this is in addition to other days in the school year he has missed due to both physical and mental health concerns. This will likely lead to a negative effect on his academics. In addition, depending on communication and continuity of care, this child may be labeled as "truant," and, in some states, his parent(s)/guardian may be forced to participate in community programs or face jail time or pay fines. These consequences on the parent(s) may lead to lower income or loss of a job. Globally, this impacts society as a whole through lower productivity and/or future economic earning power.

Funding is one such systemic failure that can affect mental health and crisis-effective counseling services at every stage. To put it plainly, the more funding, the more efforts and strategies to be implemented at all levels. Given the critical need for clinicians to not only be aware of and comfortable with but also competent in addressing suicide with clients, the remaining sections of this chapter will address suicide in youth by including topics such as definitions, risk factors, protective factors, theories, and appropriate counseling services.

Suicide in Youth

Generally speaking, suicide can be defined as ending or taking one's own life (i.e., the act is self-initiated; National Institute of Mental Health, 2020). However, this is a simplistic definition for a complex issue. Let's focus on four terms: suicidal behaviors, suicidal thoughts, suicidal ideation, and suicidal attempts. It is important for clinicians to know the nuances of these terms in order to correctly assess for them in young clients.

Suicidal behaviors, also known as *suicidality*, is inclusive of ideation (i.e., thoughts), plans, and attempts. Did you know that a person can have an absence of intent to die and still be considered in the category of suicide-related behaviors? Intent to die and physical injury can be present or absent in children: the point is that suicidality is a multifaceted issue, and clinicians working with youth should be knowledgeable of the factors influencing suicidality. For example, self-harm or self-injury can be commonly experienced in adolescents. Common types of self-harm are cutting, burning, pulling hair, and picking. The main intent of self-harm is emotion regulation with an absence of intent to die (NAMI, 2020).

Suicidal ideation is often used interchangeably with *suicidal thoughts*. *Suicidal attempts* are self-initiated and potentially injurious behavior. An individual attempting suicide has the presence of intent to die but has a nonfatal outcome. A fatal outcome is described using the terms *suicided* or *death by suicide*.

Given the dire nature of suicide in youth, clinicians should be prepared to provide education and advocacy efforts. Prevention is one such solution. One large issue with suicide prevention is that it is still a newer phenomenon in our society. The field of suicidology has only a 60-year history: first suicide prevention center opened in 1958. Currently and throughout these 60 years, more mental health clinicians have become aware of and educated on this topic. Because of this, we are slowly increasing research and evidence on suicide and prevention efforts.

Suicide in Children

There is an extant amount of research on suicide in youth, particularly children. One of the largest myths is that children cannot experience suicidal behaviors. In fact, they can; however, they may present differently than in adults or even older adolescents. The first thing to note is that children who are suicidal are not seeking attention. In fact, there has been a debate among some researchers on whether children actually understand suicide. This is where the clinical judgment of counselors really comes into play. Furthermore, there is also debate over the possible age of death by suicide. Ruch et al. (2021) discussed deaths by suicide occuring as early as 5, while some researchers discussed 3 years as being the earliest occurrence. This is difficult to determine because suicide deaths in children may be labeled as accidents. "If the data on suicidal adolescents are similarly representative of younger children, the implication is that 250 to 1,000 children are likely to attempt suicide every year, thousands more will engage in suicidal behaviors or make plans to injure themselves, and tens of thousands may experience suicidal ideation" (Shirley, 2020, p. 49). Thus, even if we have some statistics for suicide in minors, the actual numbers are likely larger than previously found.

Risk Factors
A risk factor, generally speaking, can be defined as a factor that increases your chances of getting something, doing something, or developing a disease. You will see this term used a lot in the medical field. However, it is

important to note that risk factors are not a direct cause. Rather, suicidal risk factors are associated with suicide and correlate with suicidal behaviors. There are many common risk factors related to suicide (e.g., family history, previous attempts, isolation, etc.; CDC, 2022b). Bilsen (2018) discussed several risk factors directly related to suicide in youth. These may include mental disorders (with depression and substance use being the most common); previous suicide attempts; personality characteristics; family factors; life events common in youth such as break-ups, academic stress, and bullying; imitation; and availability of suicide means. Keep in mind that suicidal thoughts are not the same as suicidal attempts, and youth need a means to attempt suicide (which is why we discuss taking away the means).

Lesbian, gay, bisexual, transgender, and questioning or queer (LGBTQ) youth are particularly vulnerable to mental health issues including suicidality. Furthermore, suicide rates among LGBTQ youth are higher than in the general population (thoughts of suicide are three times more common than in heterosexual youth and attempts are five times as common). Additionally, transgender and gender-nonconforming youth have higher rates of suicidal thoughts and behaviors. Rejection after "coming out" to family increases the suicide attempt likelihood by 8.4 times. The Trevor Project (2019) estimated "that at least 1.2 million LGBTQ youth aged 13–18 in the U.S. seriously consider suicide each year" (findings; para. 3).

Protective Factors

A protective factor is something that lowers your chances of an outcome and helps to protect against a situation, event, or result. Examples of protective factors related to youth suicide include effective healthcare, family support, and coping skills. Other protective factors may include cultural or religious influences, community connection, and peer support. Protective factors are especially crucial in the lives of youth in decreasing suicidal behaviors. Note that protective factors may be related to an overall relational system rather than just to individual influences (e.g., a youth's mental health status). While research on protective factors is not as extensive as that on risk factors, what is known is the need for connectedness in some form. For example, Lambert, Boyd, and Ialongo (2022) discovered that social support was an important aspect in mitigating suicidal risk. Furthermore, Fraser, Geoffroy, Chachamovich, and Kirmayer (2015) found that community programs and culturally relevant experiences aided in suicide prevention. Thus, taking a social or community approach to suicide prevention in which all contexts are considered may be necessary (Standley & Foster-Fishman, 2021). It is clear that we must strengthen protective factors in order to reduce suicidal behaviors and overall suicidal risk in youth.

Imagine you have two clients, both around the same age and both experiencing suicidal thoughts. One client has a supportive family system and attends a safe school while another client lacks any family or social support. Think about which of these clients may be more likely to transition from having suicidal thoughts (i.e., "I don't want to be here anymore") to making a suicide attempt and why. Knowing that a support system and community are critical protective factors, it may be more likely that the client with minimal support has a higher risk of suicide.

Precipitating Factors Versus Warning Signs

In addition to risk and protective factors, clinicians need to be aware of the difference between precipitating factors and warning signs. *Precipitating factors* are crisis triggers for an individual. These may include the sudden death of a loved one or an arrest. Furthermore, precipitating factors specific for children include childhood abuse, separation from a parent, or sudden physical illness (Shirley, 2020). On the other hand, *warning signs* provide clinicians with causes for immediate action. In other words, if a client exhibits a warning sign, you, as the clinician, must act now. Below is a list of potential warning signs, and these signs do not act in isolation of each other. For instance, a client can be isolated yet not suicidal. Furthermore, a client could be suicidal and not isolated from others. This is why it is extremely important for clinicians to have knowledge of suicidal behaviors and have appropriate steps to take when doing a suicide assessment.

- Stating that they want to die
- Searching for a means to kill themselves
- Feeling a deep sense of burden to others
- Increasing their use of alcohol or illicit substances
- Appearing extremely anxious or distressed during a session
- Increasing reckless behavior
- Changing daily patterns (e.g., sleep habits)
- Isolating themselves from others

Interpersonal Theory of Suicide

For the purpose of this chapter, we will not be extensively covering suicide theories. There have been many proposed theories attempting to explain suicidal behavior. Some of these perspectives are based on biological, psychological, and sociological mechanisms, but all theories leave unexplained facts about suicide. Each has a different, extremely important focus point while ignoring other factors (e.g., culture). Thus, these theories may not give clinicians a holistic picture of suicide. Given this, here we present an overview of the Interpersonal Theory of Suicide (ITS).

The ITS, developed by Van Orden and Joiner and colleagues (2010), is the most comprehensive theory related to conceptualizing suicide. It is continuously researched, and clinicians can find articles in several suicide-related journals (e.g., *Suicide and Life-Threatening Behavior*). At the center of the ITS is the belief that "people die by suicide because they can and because they want to" (Van Orden et al., 2010, p. 8). However, few people attempt suicide and even fewer die by suicide. Let's look a bit closer at the main constructs of the ITS.

The ITS includes two primary concepts of suicidal desire (thwarted belongingness and perceived burdensomeness) and one concept of capability (acquired capability). *Thwarted belongingness* is a feeling of being alone. For instance, youth may feel a lack of support from family and friends. *Perceived burdensomeness* is this idea that the individual is a burden to others. For example, youth may think that the world is better off without them. When these two constructs are found, a person may be likely to have a desire for suicide. Having an *acquired capability* for suicide is seen when an individual either has an increased level for pain (e.g., past suicide attempts) or a decreased fear of dying (e.g., combat experience). The ITS posits that when these three assumptions are met, a person is more likely to make a lethal suicide attempt (i.e., potential death).

In summary, experiencing thwarted belongingness and perceived burdensomeness contributes to passive suicidal ideation (i.e., suicide thoughts). This, in addition to a desire for suicide, may indicate intent for suicide (i.e., active suicidal ideation). These, combined with an acquired capability for suicide, may lead to a lethal suicide attempt.

An Integrative Approach to Effectively Work with Children and Adolescents in Crisis

Awareness, Education, and Prevention

Here, we present an integrative approach that may help to bridge the gap that exists when viewing youth services as distinctive entities (i.e., healthcare, community resources, mental health). These systems often fail youth by offering insufficient healthcare and a lack of continuity of care (see Chapter 3). For example, many youth and families do not have access to prevention services in their communities. Furthermore, there is a lack of resources to even provide said services.

The first thing to always think about in terms of providing effective services is prevention. Suicide prevention efforts include clinicians and the greater community's help in reducing the risk of suicide and can occur at many different levels (i.e., individual, family, community, society, global). Furthermore, prevention can be ongoing in the counseling relationship. For example, instead of only providing suicide assessment when absolutely necessary, clinicians should be asking clients throughout their professional relationship about any past and/or current suicidal behaviors and providing education on suicide.

> **Case Study: Stan**
>
> Stan is a 16-year-old boy who has talked to his therapist about his depression, which has been ongoing for the past 2 years. Stan's therapist administers the Kutcher Adolescent Depression Scale (Brooks et al., 2003); Stan scored 31, indicating very severe symptoms. Stan's therapist was very concerned and addressed the scores during the session.
>
> THERAPIST: Stan, I got to tell you, this one of the highest scores I have ever seen. You sure you are doing ok?
> STAN: Yeah, I am fine.
> THERAPIST: I hear you. I know you say you are depressed. But sometimes when people score this high, they are considering other things. Any thoughts of harming yourself?
> STAN: No. I feel bad a lot. But I am not thinking of that.

> THERAPIST: Would you tell me if you were? Or at least tell someone?
> STAN: Yes. I would tell you if I was that bad off.
>
> In this case, even though Stan was not endorsing any suicidal ideations, Stan's therapist was concerned due to other indicators and broached the topic as a preventative measure. Standardized assessments can be one way to obtain additional, objective information to address prevention and early intervention with youth.

From an individual perspective to prevention, there are some strategies that clinicians can take to provide an effective approach to suicide prevention. First, those working with clients should educate themselves on biases, myths, and stigma related to suicide. How clinicians talk about suicide matters and can perpetuate stigma if not done carefully. An individual's bias is their personal viewpoint for or against something and is usually one-sided. Your own internal bias can have an effect on your clients. Many times, the term "bias" can be triggering; however, I encourage readers to think of bias as a part of the human experience. So, now you know this, what do you do with it? Awareness of your biases is the first step. Think about the following statement: *Suicide is wrong.* Take a moment to write down some reasons why you believe this is true or false. Now think about how those statements or feelings may inadvertently harm a client. Other examples of common biased statements related to suicide include

- How could they do that to their loved ones?
- That person is weak.
- You have so much to live for.
- Those who think of suicide are mentally ill.
- Dying by suicide is shameful.

These statements are biased because they only show one side of a multifaceted issue. It is important for clinicians to be aware of these biases because they play into the negative stigma related to suicide, particularly in the Western culture. Even though awareness is key, to stop there would be a disservice to clients. Clinicians should also challenge those biases and determine where they came from and why they are there. Last, communicating respect and listening to different viewpoints are always crucial skills and even more so when speaking about suicide. The Teaching Tolerance website (2020) is a great resource for those wanting more education on social justice issues and bias (https://www.tolerance.org).

There are also common myths related to suicide that clinicians should be aware of. I will discuss four main ones here. The most common and detrimental to the person's life is the idea that asking about suicide leads to suicide. You must ask. One of the best things you can do is ask. Research shows that talking about suicide decreases the actual risk. Another common myth is that people who die by suicide do not seek help or reach out. In reality, 90% of individuals show warning signs, 80% tell someone, and 75% see a physician. A third common myth is that those who express suicidal ideation just want attention. Those who talk about suicide want help, and a high majority tell someone about their plans in the week prior to their death. Furthermore, those not speaking are afraid of being silenced, ridiculed, or minimized. The last myth is that the person expressing suicidal behavior wants to die. Many people experiencing these behaviors are facing ambivalence between wanting the pain to stop and not knowing what to do to make the pain stop. A great example of ambivalence in suicide is found in a study of survivors who jumped from the Golden Gate Bridge in a suicide attempt. More than 3,000 people have leaped to their death from San Francisco's Golden Gate Bridge, but of the 26 people who survived the jump, all reported that the moment they leaped from the bridge, they regretted their action and wanted to live.

One important consideration to note is that language matters. We caution against the use of the phrase "committed suicide" as this implies a criminal offense and plays into stigma related to suicide. The appropriate terms to use when talking about suicide are "suicided" or "died by suicide."

The important takeaway here is that your own biases (or lack of awareness surrounding your biases) can lead to a missed opportunity to talk about suicide when it matters most. Furthermore, stigma toward suicide and toward seeking help (as from a counselor) is a negative barrier to preventing suicide. Thus, we encourage anyone working with clients to do some work related to personal bias throughout your professional career.

Other individual counseling strategies for clinicians to consider:

- Taking a proactive stance on suicide is key.
- Perform suicide check-ins during sessions.
- Work with the family.

- Normalize help-seeking for the youth and the family.
- Find positive coping strategies.
- Work on social connectedness and belongingness with the client.

Prevention in Schools

Because youth spend much of their time in school (7 hours a day; National Center on Education and the Economy, 2018), the easiest system through which to gain the most access to youth is their schools. The main strategy discussed here is mental health and suicide education within schools.

Other prevention strategies may include

- Media campaigns
- Social media
- Technology
- Crisis hotlines
- Crisis chat rooms

Mental Health Education

Historically, schools in the United States have only offered physical health education in schools. This usually includes information related to overall physical health, sex education, and tobacco, drug, and alcohol use. While these topics certainly warrant youth education, schools are missing an enormous opportunity to not only educate but also to check in with students' mental health needs. Many states have delegated more funding in recent years to add more school counselors and school psychologists on campuses. This undoubtedly deserves attention because it shows we are going in a positive direction toward holistic programming for our children. However, these improvements only draw attention to the few children that these mental health providers serve and focuses on intervention rather than prevention. Recently, two states began requiring mental health education within schools due to increased numbers of suicides and mental illness in children and adolescents. The state of New York is now requiring mental health education in kindergarten through 12th grade, while Virginia requires this in 9th and 10th grade (NAMI, 2018). Several mental health organizations have been advocating for years for more comprehensive mental health services and education programming in their schools (see Mental Health Liaison Group).

Although mental health and/or suicide screening may be insufficient in addressing the comprehensive approach needed, it is a necessary step for schools to implement. Suicide education in schools is crucial. As stated above, suicide is a highly stigmatized subject. Much of this is due to the detrimental bias and myths related to suicide. This is where educating communities is important because, remember: talking about suicide does not lead to suicide; instead it decreases stigma and saves lives.

Community Approach to Prevention

Taking a community approach to prevention is important. Here we discuss some things mental health professionals can easily do. First, stay up to date on your state- and federal-level legislation. The American Foundation for Suicide Prevention (AFSP; https://afsp.org) is a great place to start. Not being "political" is not an option when lives are on the line (you cannot have education or programs without politics and vice versa). Second, become an advocate. Advocacy efforts are an important part of being a mental health professional. Third, discuss suicide in society and have others (nonprofessionals) become trained in suicide prevention. The biggest source of help a society has is each other. Last, collaborate with other helping professionals (i.e., mental health, public health, medical). Helping fields have a similar end goal and can benefit each other.

Intervention

Suicide intervention happens when you, as the mental health professional, intervene with a client expressing suicidal behaviors. You may have read about suicide intervention as suicide assessment. That's because any suicide intervention must include the clinician's assessment of their client's suicidality. Generally speaking, assessment will go through these phases: (1) notice a client is having signs of being suicidal, (2) ask the question, (3) determine specifics of a suicide plan, (4) dismantle the plan, (5) check in with the client, and (6) always follow-up. There are also many screening tools available to clinicians (e.g., ASQ, C-SSRS).

Several assessment tools and mnemonic devices are used to assess for suicidality. Three common ones are: IS PATH WARM (Juhnke et al., 2007), SADPERSONS (Juhnke, 1996), and SIMPLE STEPS (McGlothin et al., 2016). These are used when clinicians are assessing for a client's suicide risk. Some mnemonic devices are used for assessing risk factors, while others are used to assess intent. The SADPERSONS mnemonic device measures risk factors and has an older and modified version. The modified version of this device (SADPERSONAS) added availability for lethal means, a very crucial aspect, to risk factors. The IS PATH WARM mnemonic device is used to assess for immediate suicide risk. Each of the letters represents a specific risk factor. Last, the SIMPLE STEPS mnemonic device is used to assess suicide lethality. Uniquely, this device takes a holistic and clinical approach while exploring protective factors and coping skills.

One specific suicide intervention approach to pay particular attention to is the LivingWorks Applied Suicide Intervention Skills Training (ASIST) because it has been proved to be effective as an intervention program (Gould et al., 2013; Shannonhouse et al., 2017). ASIST is an empirically supported, in-person training developed by LivingWorks (https://www.livingworks.net). ASIST takes a community approach to suicide intervention with the belief that anyone can save a life. In fact, anyone aged 16 years or older can be trained under ASIST. The organization's 2-day workshop includes an interactive learning approach where members are actively involved in the process (i.e., practicing skills). In addition to the ASIST program, there has been some research on the use of dialectical behavior therapy, cognitive behavioral therapy, and family therapy as interventions for suicide.

Inpatient Hospitalization

Given the crisis nature of suicidal behaviors, youth may require hospitalization in inpatient psychiatric settings. Youth may require hospitalization if they are a danger to self or others. Suicidal ideation is the leading cause of psychiatric hospitalization. Other reasons you may find include homicidal ideation, experiencing psychotic symptoms, severe behavioral issues, or substance use.

Hospitalization generally ranges from acute to subacute, depending on client symptom severity. Clients are under 24-hour supervision from hospital staff when receiving treatment in an inpatient setting. There are two main types of psychiatric care: residential, which is a longer-term stay (i.e., 30 days) and acute, which is short-term (i.e., 5–7 days). The focus of inpatient care is on stabilization (i.e., no longer a danger to self or others). Individuals are admitted to hospitals either on a voluntary or involuntary basis and usually experience the following:

- A mental status exam
- A psychosocial assessment
- Medication evaluation
- Treatment groups

It is important for all mental health providers to be aware that most inpatient care works from a medical model and has employees from a variety of fields such as psychiatrists, registered nurses, licensed professional counselors, social workers, chemical dependency counselors, activity therapists, medical doctors, mental health technicians, and discharge planners.

Given that a medical model is utilized in most psychiatric care hospitals, there are important considerations for clinicians working in these settings. *Therapeutic alliance*, also called *therapeutic relationship* or *working alliance*, is still key yet may come with some challenges. Research has found that having many treatment providers (Dinger et al., 2008; Munder et al., 2010) can affect alliance outcomes (Blais et al., 2010) and that severity of symptoms can also affect alliance outcomes (Bettmann & Jasperson, 2009; Munder et al., 2010). In addition, the ability to communicate empathy is a crucial skill to embody when working with youth in hospitals. Given the chaotic, multidisciplinary, short-term (i.e., short time to effect change) nature on hospitalization, the ability of a clinician to experience and demonstrate empathy may affect the overall treatment of youth in crises. Last, advocating for your clients in these settings will be imperative. Much of this may be educating medical professionals (i.e., psychiatrists, nurses) on mental healthcare and how to best incorporate the client's developmental needs within a medical framework.

The Aftermath of Suicide and Postvention Services

Postvention, simply put, is your response to the aftermath, after a suicide (fatal or nonfatal) has occurred. There is less known about postvention and, generally speaking, less support for those who have lost someone to suicide. Some of the themes found from research on those who are survivors of suicide include stigma, shame, and isolation. The time after suicide can also be traumatizing for family members and loved ones due to (a) suicide being sudden and/or unexpected, (b) suicide being violent, and (c) survivors having reoccurring thoughts of the suicide. Support from others (i.e., family, friends, counselors) is crucial yet scarce, especially since society as a whole is unaware of how to be supportive. Let's look at some of the strategies that clinicians can employ to provide postvention support.

Three main strategies are discussed here: (1) support groups, (2) family counseling, and (3) advocacy and education. Support groups may be difficult to find, and family members may not be ready to share outside of their family system due to stigma. However, support groups may help families who have lost someone from suicide feel less isolated. James and Gilliland (2017) discussed three main themes for group. First, it is important for survivors to discuss reactions and experiences related to the suicide. Some of these harsh realities include the incapability of understanding from the family member's social network, extreme isolation, and questioning the ability to parent. Second, survivors move toward grief work when group members can provide support and the focus is on coping skills. Last, by reminiscing about their suicide loss and coming to terms with it, the group moves toward its termination phase (James & Gilliland, 2017).

Family counseling is important to help a family process stigmatized grief and trauma, address common suicidality in the family, and provide family resources for coping (Jaques, 2000).

The last piece for clinicians to consider in the postvention phase is advocating for resources where needed and educating the general public on suicide in order to decrease stigma. The main takeaway from the literature on postvention is that it requires support in all forms. The Suicide Prevention Resource Center (2017) provides resources for individuals who have lost someone to suicide (http://www.sprc.org/sites/default/files/resource-program/Survivors.pdf).

Summary

This chapter highlighted stress, depression, and suicide as separate yet related constructs. Stressors are common during childhood and adolescence but, when not given attention, may create further mental health symptoms. Depression, for example, is a common mental health diagnosis in youth who experience chronic stress (e.g., bullying, pressure to achieve, difficult emotional experiences) or live in distressful environments (e.g., violence, abuse, trauma). Furthermore, youth in these situations may experience suicidal behaviors such as ideations or attempts. Clinicians may consider solutions for these youth issues through education, prevention efforts, and advocacy for a community approach to mental healthcare.

References

American Foundation for Suicide Prevention (AFSP). (n.d.). Risk factors, protective factors, and warning signs. Retrieved from https://afsp.org/risk-factors-protective-factors-and-warning-signs

American Foundation for Suicide Prevention (AFSP). (2020). Suicide statistics. Retrieved from https://afsp.org/suicide-statistics/

Baams, G., Grossman, A. H., Russell, S. T., & Eccles, J. S. (2015). Minority stress and mechanisms of risk for depression and suicidal ideation among lesbian, gay, and bisexual youth. *Developmental Psychology, 51*(5), 688–696.

Bettmann, J. E., & Jasperson, R. A. (2009). Adolescents in residential and inpatient treatment: A review of the outcome literature. *Child Youth Care Forum, 38*, 161–183.

Bilsen, J. (2018). Suicide and youth: Risk factors. *Front. Psychiatry, 9*(540). doi.org/10.3389/fpsyt.2018.00540

Blais, M. A., Jacobo, M. C., & Smith, S. R. (2010). Exploring therapeutic alliance in brief inpatient psychotherapy: A preliminary study. *Clinical Psychology and Psychotherapy, 17*, 386–394.

Brooks, S. J., Krulewicz, S. P., & Kutcher, S. (2003). The Kutcher Adolescent Depression Scale: Assessment of its evaluative properties over the course of an 8-week pediatric pharmacotherapy trial. *Journal of Child and Adolescent Psychopharmacology, 13*(3), 337–349.

Centers for Disease Control and Prevention (CDC). (2021). About mental health. Retrieved from https://www.cdc.gov/mentalhealth/learn/

Centers for Disease Control and Prevention (CDC). (2022a). Facts about suicide. Retrieved from https://www.cdc.gov/suicide/facts/index.html

Centers for Disease Control and Prevention (CDC). (2022b). Global burden of mental illness. Retrieved from https://blogs.cdc.gov/global/2014/02/10/global-burden-of-mental-illness/

Centers for Disease Control and Prevention (CDC). (2017). Health, United States-Data Finder. Retrieved from https://www.cdc.gov/nchs/hus/data-finder.htm?year=2017&table=Figure%20023#citation

Centers for Disease Control and Prevention (CDC). (2022c). Risk and protective factors. Retrieved fromhttps://www.cdc.gov/violenceprevention/suicide/riskprotectivefactors.html

Cheng, L. (2014). The association between social support and mental health among vulnerable adolescents in five cities: Findings from the study of the well-being of adolescents in vulnerable environments. *Journal of Adolescent Health, 55*(6), S31–S38.

Dinger, U., Strack, M., Leichsenring, F., Wilmers, F., & Schauenburg, H. (2008). Therapist effects on outcome and alliance in inpatient psychotherapy. *Journal of Clinical Psychology, 64*(3), 344–354.

Ehlman D. C., Yard E., Stone D. M., Jones C. M., & Mack K. A. (2022). Changes in suicide rates—United States, 2019 and 2020. *Morbidity and Mortality Weekly Report, 71*(8), 306–312. doi:http://dx.doi.org/10.15585/mmwr.mm7108a5external icon.

Felitti, V. J., Anda, R. F., Nordenberg, D., Williamson, D. F., Spitz, A. M., Edwards, V., & Marks, J. S. (1998). Relationship of childhood abuse and household dysfunction to many of the leading causes of death in adults: The Adverse Childhood Experiences (ACE) Study. *American Journal of Preventive Medicine, 14*(4), 245–258.

Foiles, J. (2018). Ending the stigma surrounding suicide. *Psychology Today.* https://www.psychologytoday.com/us/blog/the-thing-feathers/201806/ending-the-stigma-surrounding-suicide

Fraser, S. L., Geoffroy, D., Chachamovich, E., & Kirmayer, L. J. (2015). Changing rates of suicide ideation attempts among Inuit youth: A gender-based analysis of risk and protective factors. *Suicide and Life-Threatening Behavior, 45*(2), 141–156.

Gould, M. S., Cross, W., Pisani, A. R., Munfakh, J. L., & Kleinman, M. (2013). Impact of applied suicide intervention skills training on the National Suicide Prevention Lifeline. *Suicide & Life-Threatening Behavior, 43*(6), 676–691.

James, R. K., & Gilliland, B. E. (2017). *Crisis intervention strategies* (8th ed.). Cengage Learning.

Jaques, J. D. (2000). Surviving suicide: The impact on the family. *Family Journal, 8,* 376–379.

Juhnke, G. A. (1996). The adapted-SAD PERSONS: A suicide assessment scale designed for use with children. *Elementary School Guidance & Counseling, 30,* 252–258.

Juhnke, G. A., Granello, P. F., & Lebrón-Striker, M. (2007). *IS PATH WARM? A suicide assessment mnemonic for counselors (ACAPCD-03).* American Counseling Association.

Lambert, S. F., Boyd, R. C., & Ialongo, N. S. (2022). Protective factors for suicidal ideation among Black adolescents indirectly exposed to community violence. *Suicide and Life-Threatening Behavior, 52*(3), 1–12. https://doi.org/10.1111/sltb.12839

Mandelli, P., Petrelli, C., & Serretti, A. (2015). The role of specific early trauma in adult depression: A meta-analysis of published literature. Childhood trauma and adult depression. *European Psychiatry, 30*(6), 665–680. https://doi.org/10.1016/j.eurpsy.2015.04.007

McGlothlin, J., Page, B., & Jager, K. (2016). Validation of the SIMPLE STEPS model of suicide assessment. *Journal of Mental Health Counseling, 38*(4), 298–307.

Munder, T., Wilmers, F., Leonhart, R., Linster, H. W., & Barth, J. (2010). Working alliance inventory-short revised (WAI-SR): Psychometric properties in outpatients and inpatients. *Clinical Psychology and Psychotherapy, 17,* 231–239.

National Alliance on Mental Illness (NAMI). (2018). States begin requiring mental health education in schools. Retrieved December 8, 2020, from https://namivirginia.org/states-begin-requiring-mental-health-education-schools/

National Alliance on Mental Illness (NAMI). (2020). Self-harm. Retrieved from https://www.nami.org/About-Mental-Illness/Common-with-Mental-Illness/Risk-of-Suicide

National Center on Education and the Economy (2018). How much time do students spend in school? Retrieved December 8, 2020, from http://ncee.org/2018/02/statistic-of-the-month-how-much-time-do-students-spend-in-school/

National Institute of Mental Health. (2020). Suicide. Retrieved November 13, 2020, from https://www.nimh.nih.gov/health/statistics/suicide.shtml

Ruch, D. A., Heck, K. M., Sheftall, A. H., Fontanella, C. A., Stevens, J., Zhu, M., Horowitz, L. M., Campo, J. V., & Bridge, J. A. (2021). Characteristics and precipitating circumstances of suicide among children aged 5 to 11 years in the United States, 2013–2017. *JAMA Network Open, 4*(7), e2115683–e2115683.

Shannonhouse, L., Lin, Y. D., Shaw, K., & Porter, M. (2017). Suicide intervention training for K-12 schools: A quasi-experimental study on ASIST. *Journal of Counseling & Development, 95*(1), 3–13.

Shirley, K. A. (2020). Reported trends in suicidality in children 10 and younger. *Journal of Mental Health Counseling, 42*(1), 47–62.

Standley, C. J., & Foster-Fishman, P. (2021). Intersectionality, social support, and youth suicidality: A socioecological approach to prevention. *Suicide & Life Threatening Behavior, 51,* 203–211. https://doi.org/10.1111/sltb.12695

Suicide Prevention Resource Center. (2017). Suicide prevention resources for survivors of suicide loss. Retrieved November 19, 2020, from http://www.sprc.org/sites/default/files/resource-program/Survivors.pdf

Teaching Tolerance. (2020). Retrieved November 13, 2020, from https://www.tolerance.org

The Trevor Project. (2019). National estimate of LGBTQ youth seriously considering suicide. Retrieved November 19, 2020 from https://www.thetrevorproject.org/2020/04/03/implications-of-covid-19-for-lgbtq-youth-mental-health-and-suicide-prevention/

Van Orden, K. A., Witte, T. K., Cukrowicz, K. C., Braithwaite, S., Selby, E. A., & Joiner Jr., T. E. (2010). The interpersonal theory of suicide. *Psychology Reviews, 117*(2), 575–600. doi:10.1037/a0018697

Verona E., Sachs-Ericsson N., & Joiner T. E. (2004). Suicide attempts associated with externalizing psychopathology in an epidemiological sample. *American Journal of Psychiatry, 161,* 444–451.

7

Sex and Sexuality

Overview

In this chapter, we discuss some of the many issues in sexuality which affect today's youth: sexual activity, sex trafficking, and teen pregnancy and parenthood. In addition, we discuss the diverse and complex issues involved in counseling LGBT teens and adolescents. While we recognize that this chapter covers material that may be uncomfortable for some, we must also acknowledge that these complex issues are just a few of the many presenting issues that youth bring to session.

Issues Pertaining to Sex and Sexuality

As therapists, it may be difficult to consider issues of sex and sexuality as they relate to youth. We may not want to think of our students, nieces, nephews, children, or grandchildren as individuals who engage in sexual behaviors or maintain their own sexual identities. Nonetheless, therapists will benefit from becoming well-versed in the complexities that surround adolescent sexuality and in recognizing the skillset and effective strategies required to successfully explore these topics in session. The following list contains statistics from the Centers for Disease Control (2019) National Youth Risk Behavior Survey regarding sexual activity among high school students in the United States.

- 38% had ever had sexual intercourse.
- 9% had four or more sexual partners.
- 7% had been physically forced to have sexual intercourse when they did not want to.
- 27% had had sexual intercourse during the previous 3 months, and, of these,
    o 46% did not use a condom the last time they had sex.

- 12% did not use any method to prevent pregnancy.
- 21% had drunk alcohol or used drugs before last sexual intercourse.

These data provide a snapshot of some risks, concerns, and issues associated with adolescent sex and sexuality. More accurately, therapists can connect some of these occurrences to the presenting and related problems identified by their teen clients.

Sexual Activity: Trends, Social Media, Sexting

Technology continues to have a tremendous influence on societal norms, relationships, human interaction, marketing, and communication. Social media, cellular phones, and internet access are relatively accessible to nearly anyone, including today's youth. In fact, adolescents in the 2020s likely cannot recall a time in their lives when social media did not exist. Facebook (first appeared in 2004), Instagram (in 2010), Snapchat (in 2011), and TikTok (in 2016) have formed a permanent and lasting impact on our society. Specific social platforms may evolve, but, as an entity, it appears that social media is here to stay. With the increase in variety of social media platforms comes an increased desire among adolescents for public presence, presenting a ripple effect related to adolescent sexuality. Topics of concern include but are not limited to cyberbullying, exploitation, identity crisis, pressure to conform, lack of boundaries, risky or unsafe behavior, and grooming (see Table 7.1).

In addition to social media platforms, the mere accessibility and prevalence of cellular phones and internet access has facilitated the sharing of photos and messages in an instant and in a way that cannot be reversed. *Sexting*, or the practice of sending sexually explicit content (including messages, photos, videos), has become increasingly common with adolescents who often do not grasp the permanency of information submitted electronically, nor do they fully understand the severity of risk associated with this practice.

Potential Interventions

Therapists will consider differential diagnoses and look holistically at the adolescent and their network. Each assessment is unique, and treatment decisions are made on a case-by-case basis aiming for the least restrictive

Table 7.1 Terms related to adolescent use of social media

Term	Definition
Cyberbullying	Online bullying of adolescents based on sexual identity or sexual activity. This includes "slut-shaming."
Exploitation	Particularly, the risk of minors being exploited by adults. This includes child pornography, child sex trafficking, sextortion, the live streaming of child sexual abuse, and child sex tourism.
Identity crisis	Includes sexual identity and gender identity issues, confusion, and struggles.
Pressure to conform	The pressure to express nudity, sexually suggestive content, or to participate in sexual activities of any sort.
Lack of boundaries	Oversharing, inability to appropriately identify private moments and information, false sense of entitlement regarding knowledge of other's intimate life details.
Risky or unsafe behaviors	Engagement in behaviors seen "trending" on social media platforms. Engagement in sexual activities or utilization of products in such a manner that they pose a risk of physical harm to one's body or to one's health, wellness, or safety. This includes risk of infection, pregnancy, or sexual violence.
Grooming	Manipulative behavior used to gain access to a potential child/adolescent victim, coerce them to agree to abuse, and reduce the risk of getting caught.

treatment option (Martin, 2019). Two research-based practices for sexual behavior challenges are trauma-focused–cognitive behavioral therapy (TF–CBT) and problematic sexual behavior–cognitive behavioral therapy (PSB–CBT).

TF–CBT is used by therapists for children and adolescents recovering from trauma by addressing the components of trauma in the forms of depression, anxiety, and cognitive and behavioral problems. Clinicians will often focus on improving the participating parent's or caregiver's personal distress about the child's traumatic experience as well. Hence, TF–CBT may include effective parenting skills and supportive interactions with the child (National Therapist Certification Program, 2019).

PSB–CBT is a lesser-known model, but the approach from the clinician is more specific to youth who experience or exhibit sexual behavior challenges. Throughout the course of counseling, the clinician will focus on developmentally appropriate sex education, explaining rules about sexual behavior, and setting boundaries that include abuse prevention skills and safety planning.

For clients who experience sexual trauma, clinicians using PSB–CBT address emotional regulation and coping skills, impulse control and problem-solving skills, and social skills and peer relationship.

The link between exposure to trauma and engagement in sexual violence is well-established. Ybarra and Thompson (2018) surveyed 752 youth between 14 and 21 years of age and found that aggressive behaviors, exposure to spousal abuse (between caregivers), and exposure to violent pornography were strong predictors of sexual harassment and sexual assault. Furthermore, youth who were victims of psychological abuse and females who felt pressure to have sex also predicted sexual assault. PSB–CBT includes psychoeducation and a focus on acknowledgment of sexual behavior, apology, and making amends. Because of the role of caregiver violence in increasing the likelihood of sexual assault and harassment in youth, additional key clinical components of PSB-CBT include parent behavior training to prevent and respond to problematic sexual behavior and other behavior problems. Parents are educated on child and adolescent development with an emphasis on psychological and emotional changes, dispelling misconceptions regarding problematic sexual behavior and implications for the child, communicating with children and adolescents about sexual behavior and development, and supporting the use of coping and decision-making skills for children.

Adolescents and the LGBTQIA+ Community: Terms, Sexual Identity, Gender Identity, Sexual Orientation

Widespread access to information about sexual orientation, gender identity, and LGBTQIA+ resources through the internet has contributed to significant changes in how young people learn about LGBTQIA+ people and their lives. Consequently, this has helped young people "come out" at much earlier ages than in prior generations. Coming out at an earlier age has important implications for how therapists work with children, youth, and families; how they educate parents, families, and caregivers about sexual orientation and gender identity; and how services are provided to LGBTQIA+ adolescents. Table 7.2 contains a glossary of some relevant LGBTQIA+ terminology provided by the Human Rights Campaign.

Just as today's adolescents face societal pressures related to sexual activity, there is also a tremendous level of perceived pressure to label oneself and identify with a particular group of individuals. As listed in Table 7.2, there

Table 7.2 Terminology related to LGBTQIA+ populations

LGBTQIA+ terminology	Definition
Ally	A term used to describe someone who is actively supportive of LGBTQ+ people. It encompasses straight and cisgender allies, as well as those within the LGBTQ+ community who support each other (e.g., a lesbian who is an ally to the bisexual community).
Asexual	Often called "ace" for short, asexual refers to a complete or partial lack of sexual attraction or lack of interest in sexual activity with others. Asexuality exists on a spectrum, and asexual people may experience no, little, or conditional sexual attraction.
Biphobia	The fear and hatred of or discomfort with people who love and are sexually attracted to more than one gender.
Bisexual	A person emotionally, romantically, or sexually attracted to more than one sex, gender, or gender identity though not necessarily simultaneously or in the same way or to the same degree. Sometimes used interchangeably with *pansexual*.
Cisgender	A term used to describe a person whose gender identity aligns with those typically associated with the sex assigned to them at birth.
Coming out	The process by which a person first acknowledges, accepts, and appreciates their sexual orientation or gender identity and begins to share that with others.
Gay	A person who is emotionally, romantically, or sexually attracted to members of the same gender. Men, women, and nonbinary people may use this term to describe themselves.
Gender binary	A system in which gender is constructed into two strict categories of male or female. Gender identity is expected to align with the sex assigned at birth, and gender expressions and roles fit traditional expectations.
Gender dysphoria	Clinically significant distress caused when a person's assigned birth gender is not the same as the one with which they identify.
Gender-expansive	A person with a wider, more flexible range of gender identity and/or expression than typically associated with the binary gender system. Often used as an umbrella term when referring to young people still exploring the possibilities of their gender expression and/or gender identity.
Gender expression	External appearance of one's gender identity, usually expressed through behavior, clothing, body characteristics, or voice, and which may or may not conform to socially defined behaviors and characteristics typically associated with being either masculine or feminine.

(continued)

Table 7.2 Continued

LGBTQIA+ terminology	Definition
Gender-fluid	A person who does not identify with a single fixed gender or has a fluid or unfixed gender identity.
Gender identity	One's innermost concept of self as male, female, a blend of both or neither: how individuals perceive themselves and what they call themselves. One's gender identity can be the same or different from one's sex assigned at birth.
Gender nonconforming	A broad term referring to people who do not behave in a way that conforms to the traditional expectations of their gender or whose gender expression does not fit neatly into a category. While many also identify as transgender, not all gender nonconforming people do.
Genderqueer	Genderqueer people typically reject notions of static categories of gender and embrace a fluidity of gender identity and often, though not always, sexual orientation. People who identify as "genderqueer" may see themselves as being both male and female, neither male nor female, or as falling completely outside these categories.
Homophobia	The fear and hatred of or discomfort with people who are attracted to members of the same sex.
Intersex	Intersex people are born with a variety of differences in their sex traits and reproductive anatomy. There is a wide variety of difference among intersex variations, including differences in genitalia, chromosomes, gonads, internal sex organs, hormone production, hormone response, and/or secondary sex traits.
Lesbian	A woman who is emotionally, romantically, or sexually attracted to other women. Women and nonbinary people may use this term to describe themselves.
LGBTQ+	An acronym for "lesbian, gay, bisexual, transgender and queer" with a "+" sign to recognize the limitless sexual orientations and gender identities used by members of the community.
Nonbinary	An adjective describing a person who does not identify exclusively as a man or a woman. Nonbinary people may identify as being both a man and a woman, somewhere in between, or as falling completely outside these categories. While many also identify as transgender, not all nonbinary people do. Nonbinary can also be used as an umbrella term encompassing identities such as agender, bigender, genderqueer or gender-fluid.
Outing	Exposing someone's lesbian, gay, bisexual transgender or gender nonbinary identity to others without their permission. Outing someone can have serious repercussions on employment, economic stability, personal safety, and religious or family situations.

SEX AND SEXUALITY 127

Table 7.2 Continued

LGBTQIA+ terminology	Definition
Pansexual	Describes someone who has the potential for emotional, romantic, or sexual attraction to people of any gender though not necessarily simultaneously, in the same way, or to the same degree. Sometimes used interchangeably with bisexual.
Queer	A term people often use to express a spectrum of identities and orientations that are counter to the mainstream. "Queer" is often used as a catch-all to include many people, including those who do not identify as exclusively straight and/or those who have nonbinary or gender-expansive identities. This term was previously used as a slur but has been reclaimed by many parts of the LGBTQ+ movement.
Questioning	A term used to describe people who are in the process of exploring their sexual orientation or gender identity.
Same-gender loving	A term some prefer to use instead of lesbian, gay, or bisexual to express attraction to and love of people of the same gender.
Sex assigned at birth	The sex—male, female, or intersex—that a doctor or midwife uses to describe a child at birth based on their external anatomy.
Sexual orientation	An inherent or immutable enduring emotional, romantic, or sexual attraction to other people. Note: an individual's sexual orientation is independent of their gender identity.
Transgender	An umbrella term for people whose gender identity and/or expression is different from cultural expectations based on the sex they were assigned at birth. Being transgender does not imply any specific sexual orientation. Therefore, transgender people may identify as straight, gay, lesbian, bisexual, etc.
Transitioning	A series of processes that some transgender people may undergo in order to live more fully as their true gender. This typically includes social transition, such as changing name and pronouns; medical transition, which may include hormone therapy or gender-affirming surgeries; and legal transition, which may include changing legal name and sex on government identity documents. Transgender people may choose to undergo some, all, or none of these processes.

are numerous *gender and sexual identity classifications* with which an individual can identify. Gender and sexual identity can be especially problematic for teens and adolescents due to internal struggles; fear of rejection; societal, religious, or family system pressures; or confusion. *Gender dysphoria* is a diagnosis identified by the American Psychiatric Association (APA) under the *Diagnostic and Statistical Manual of Mental Disorders* (DSM-5; APA,

2013) and defined as a feeling of distress or discomfort in individuals who have gender identity confusion and feel uncomfortable with or uncertain about their assigned gender at birth, leading to feelings of distress. Multiple treatment modalities may be utilized to treat gender dysphoria. Individual psychotherapy works well for adolescents who struggle with gender identity, anxiety, and depression. Family therapy can be especially beneficial when acceptance or understanding is lacking within the family system. Family therapy may be helpful in providing a safe space in which to facilitate dialogue for families who are not comfortable speaking on the subject of gender identity or sexuality on their own.

Keep in mind that gender dysphoria is related to confusion and distress over gender identity. This disorder does not apply to individuals who accept their identity. Reactions and distress as a result of discrimination and oppression toward those who identify as LGBTQIA+ are not gender dysphoria.

Sexual minority adolescents have a higher lifetime risk of suicide ideation (26.1% vs. 13.0%), plan (16.6% vs. 5.4%), and attempt (12.0% vs. 5.4%) than do heterosexual adolescents (Luk et al., 2021). Similarly, the Trevor Project Survey data reveal many of the serious challenges experienced by LGBTQIA+ youth over the past year. These data also speak to the diversity and resiliency of LGBTQIA+ youth and provide valuable insights into their unique struggles. Key findings from the Trevor Project's National Survey on LGBTQ Youth Mental Health (2021) are listed here.

- 42% of LGBTQ youth seriously considered attempting suicide in the past year, including more than half of transgender and nonbinary youth.
- More than 80% of LGBTQ youth stated that COVID-19 made their living situation more stressful—and only 1 in 3 LGBTQ youth found their home to be LGBTQ-affirming.
- 70% of LGBTQ youth stated that their mental health was "poor" most of the time or always during COVID-19.
- 48% of LGBTQ youth reported they wanted counseling from a mental health professional but were unable to receive it in the past year.
- 75% of LGBTQ youth reported that they had experienced discrimination based on their sexual orientation or gender identity at least once in their lifetime.
- Half of all LGBTQ youth of color reported discrimination based on their race/ethnicity in the past year, including 67% of Black LGBTQ youth and 60% of Asian/Pacific Islander LGBTQ youth.

- 13% of LGBTQ youth reported being subjected to conversion therapy, with 83% reporting it occurred when they were under age 18.
- Transgender and nonbinary youth who reported having pronouns respected by all of the people they lived with attempted suicide at half the rate of those who did not have their pronouns respected by anyone with whom they lived.
- Transgender and nonbinary youth who were able to change their name and/or gender marker on legal documents, such as driver's licenses and birth certificates, reported lower rates of attempting suicide.
- LGBTQ youth who had access to spaces that affirmed their sexual orientation and gender identity reported lower rates of attempting suicide.
- An overwhelming majority of LGBTQ youth said that social media has both positive (96%) and negative (88%) impacts on their mental health and well-being.
- 72% of LGBTQ youth reported symptoms of generalized anxiety disorder in the past 2 weeks, including more than 3 in 4 transgender and nonbinary youth.
- 62% of LGBTQ youth reported symptoms of major depressive disorder in the past 2 weeks, including more than 2 in 3 transgender and nonbinary youth.

LGBTQIA+ youth encounter a higher number of stressors compared to their heterosexual peers. These stressors, combined with a real or perceived lack of support, set the stage for an increase in potential mental health challenges. The Family Acceptance Project's (FAP) family support model uses a strengths-based and harm reduction framework to help parents, families, and caregivers understand sexual orientation and gender identity as components of child development. Clinicians provide education and direction to parents/caregivers on how specific reactions to sexual and gender minority (SGM) children affect youth well-being and impact their child's risk for suicide, depression, illegal drug use, and HIV. The FAP utilizes a comprehensive systemic perspective to assess, educate, provide counseling, and integrate a culturally sensitive approach to SGM youth and family (see Table 7.3; Ryan, 2019).

The Trevor Project is the world's largest suicide prevention and crisis intervention organization for LGBTQ+ youth. Research provided by the Project stated that a lack of family support helps to explain the higher rates of suicidal ideation that LGBTQ+ young people face.

Table 7.3 Family Acceptance Project (FAP) model

Assessment Integrate FAP assessment questions and measures into intake process, individually for parent and child/youth.	Assessment occurs individually with the parent and child. Assess family strengths, identify cultural and religious values and beliefs. Assess knowledge and attitudes about sexual orientation and gender identity. Identify family behaviors toward LGBTQ/gender diverse child (rejecting + accepting behaviors) and underlying issues that affect capacity for family support.
Psychoeducation Psychoeducation should be ongoing to reframe parent's perceptions of child/youth's identity and to support positive behavioral change and affirmative parenting.	Provide accurate information about sexual orientation, gender identity, and child development. Educate parents on the impact of family accepting/rejecting behaviors on their child's risk and well-being, aligned with the family's cultural foundation. Educate child/youth to identify rejecting and accepting behaviors and impact on their risk behaviors and relationships. Family rejecting behaviors contribute to suicidality, self-harming behaviors, depression, drug use, and risky sexual behaviors. Family accepting behaviors protect against suicide, depression, and substance abuse, and promote overall health, self-esteem, and positive development.
Counseling and skill-building Counseling is provided individually and for the parent and child together.	Address underlying issues that impact family support. Provide counseling and family therapy that builds self-observation skills, increases empathy and communication, develops advocacy skills, and increases affirmative parenting and connectedness between parent and child. Continue to assess growth and change.
Provide access to culturally relevant peer support Decrease isolation, increase peer support and reframe perceptions of child's LGBTQ identity and life course	Connect caregivers with other caregivers who are learning to support their SGM children, particularly parents who share language, cultures, and faith traditions to decrease the parent's isolation and build a positive new reference group.

From Ryan (2019).

Compared to their straight, cisgender peers, LGBTQ youth are significantly more likely to experience discrimination, rejection, bullying, violence, and harassment—which can compound and produce negative mental health outcomes. (The Trevor Project, 2021)

Clinicians working collaboratively with schools and parents may improve suicide interventions and support for young people who fall within the greater LGBTQIA+ community by increasing acceptance and providing a support network to "create affirming spaces and support systems for LGBTQ young people," which may save lives. LGBTQ+ youth who have access to LGBTQ-affirming spaces at home, in school, or online report lower rates of attempted suicide. Also, having at least one accepting adult in a young LGBTQ+ person's life can reduce the risk of a suicide attempt by 40%. Creating a safe, supportive environment for this population of youth begins in session with nonjudgmental acceptance and unconditional positive regard and aims to create a network of support for the youth comprised of trusted adults and family members (Green et al., 2022).

Sex Trafficking

Sex trafficking is defined by the US Department of Justice Office for Victims of Crime (2015) as the recruitment, harboring, transportation, provision, obtaining, patronizing, or soliciting of a person for the purpose of a commercial sex act, in which a commercial sex act is induced by force, fraud, or coercion, or in which the person induced to perform such act has not attained 18 years of age. The existence of a social media account, mental health issues such as depression and anxiety, or prior abuse or neglect history are just a few of the items that make youth especially vulnerable to sex trafficking. Individuals from any class or religious, cultural, or ethnic group can be targeted for human trafficking. The following groups, however, are especially vulnerable:

- Individuals who have experienced childhood abuse or neglect
- Children and youth involved in the foster care and juvenile justice systems
- People experiencing homelessness
- LGBTQ+ individuals

- Migrant workers
- Undocumented immigrants
- Racial and ethnic minorities
- People with disabilities
- People with low incomes
- People with a history of substance abuse
- Communities exposed to intergenerational trauma

It is important for therapists and school counselors to be aware of sex trafficking and mindful of the signs and indicators that a minor may be experiencing trafficking. Figure 7.1 shows the physical, behavioral, and social signs of human trafficking that one might observe in a youth victim.

While accurate estimates are notoriously difficult to obtain, more than half (51.6%) of US sex trafficking cases in 2018 involved children (Human Trafficking Institute, 2018). Victim identification represents one of the most challenging aspects of working with child sex trafficking survivors (Litam, 2017). Educating counselors on strategies that promote victim identification, improve trauma-informed practices (Gonzalez-Pons et al., 2020; Litam 2017, 2019; Litam & Lam, 2020), and challenge human trafficking myths (Cunningham & Cromer, 2016; Houston-Kolnik et al., 2020; Litam & Lam, 2020) is an important strategy to remove barriers to working with this vulnerable population. Therapists can use human trafficking tools to aid in identifying sex trafficking victims. The Comprehensive Human Trafficking

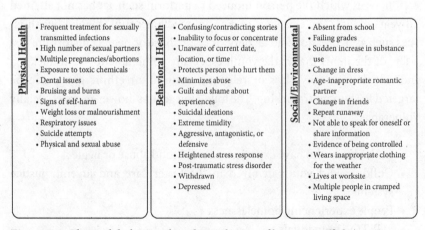

Figure 7.1 Physical, behavioral, and social signs of human trafficking.

Assessment Tool and Trafficking Victim Identification Tool (TVIT) are available at no cost and can help identify survivors of trafficking.

Comprehensive Human Trafficking Assessment Tool

The Comprehensive Human Trafficking Assessment Tool (National Human Trafficking Resource Center, 2011) is used to identify and assist potential victims of both labor and sex trafficking. The tool consists of general trafficking, sex trafficking-specific, labor trafficking-specific, and network-specific assessment questions and outlines important assessment tips and questions necessary to conduct comprehensive safety checks in person or over the phone. The sex trafficking-specific questions consist of nine open- and closed-ended questions that assess general areas related to sex trafficking including whether individuals have ever felt pressured to engage in sex acts against their will, whether they were required to meet a nightly quota of sex acts, and whether they felt forced to engage in sex acts with friends or business associates for money, safety, resources, or favors (National Human Trafficking Resource Center, 2011).

Therapists who work with trauma survivors hold legal and ethical responsibilities to provide effective treatment services (American Counseling Association [ACA], 2014). Although evidence-based interventions specifically developed for sex trafficking survivors are lacking (Jordan et al., 2013), treatments for sex trafficking survivors have been borrowed from clients who suffer from posttraumatic stress disorder (PTSD), domestic violence, slavery, and other forms of trauma (Jordan et al., 2013; Litam, 2017; Williamson et al., 2008). For instance, *motivational interviewing* can be used to assess clients' readiness to change (Osilla et al., 2015). After survivors develop change talk, professional counselors can use trauma-focused cognitive behavioral therapy (TF–CBT) to promote continued progress (Williamson et al., 2008).

Trafficking Victim Identification Tool

Created by the Vera Institute of Justice (2014), the TVIT yields valid and reliable scores for identifying victims of sex and labor trafficking. The TVIT is offered in both long and short versions in a binary format with opportunities for clarification and follow-up throughout the assessment process. The TVIT is the first validated instrument to screen human trafficking victims across a variety of clinical and forensic settings. Therapists must have preliminary knowledge of human trafficking to most effectively assess responses.

Clinicians may combine items from the TVIT into their existing intake processes to assess for child sex trafficking. While the TVIT was not validated with youth populations, the instrument may serve as a tool for collecting relevant information (Vera Institute of Justice, 2014). Professional counselors must adjust the TVIT items to meet the individual needs of survivors, including adopting the usage of colloquial language or slang terms.

The effectiveness of TF–CBT when working with survivors of childhood abuse, trauma, and sex trafficking has been preliminarily established (Wolf et al., 2014). TF–CBT principles emphasize creating a safe, trustworthy, collaborative, empowering, and client-centered approach, which remains crucial when working with survivors of trauma (Litam, 2017; Wolf et al., 2014). In one study, a 12-week TF–CBT psychoeducational group with adolescent sex trafficking survivors was linked to a significant increase in peer support validation, engagement in self-discovery, and improvement in life skills, self-care, and overall wellness (Hickle & Roe-Sepowitz, 2014). Indeed, TF–CBT appears to represent an efficacious evidence-based intervention for counseling survivors of child sex trafficking.

Teen Pregnancy and Parenthood

Parenting at any age can be challenging, but it can be particularly difficult for adolescent parents. In 2019, just over 171,600 babies were born to females ages 15–19 (Martin et al., 2021). Some challenges adolescents face when they have babies before they turn 20 compared to older parents include being

- Less likely to finish high school
- More likely to need public assistance
- More likely to have low income as adults, and, as a result,
- More likely to have children who face challenges like poorer educational, behavioral, and health outcomes (Hoffman & Maynard, 2008)

From peaks in 1991 and 2019, the teen birth rate decreased by more than 73% in the United States (from 61.8 to 16.7 births per 1,000 females ages 15–19) (Martin et al., 2021). Despite this decline, the US teen birth rate is still highest among industrialized nations (Kearney & Levine, 2012). Many issues surround teen pregnancies, all of which should be considered when working with adolescents; these include

- Disclosure
- Loss of friendships in peer group
- Bullying
- Self-care healthy pregnancy
- Body image
- Teen parenting

Limits to client–therapist confidentiality affect clients of all ages, and there are several gray areas that are specific to counseling and therapy with youth. In general, if a client discloses information about the abuse of a child, an elderly person, or someone who is vulnerable due to a disability, the therapist is required by law to report the abuse. Of course, therapists are also required to report threats to personal safety, including clients' threats or intentions to harm themselves or others. Additionally, because adolescents are considered minors until the age of 18, therapists who work with them should always discuss confidentiality issues with teens and parents together prior to the beginning of treatment. One of the most important determinants in the success of teen therapy is the confidential and trusting relationship created between the teen and his or her therapist. In order for a teenager to trust his or her therapist, he or she must know that the therapist will keep what he or she shares in confidence. Given the uniqueness of each teenager and the difficulties they face—not to mention the variance in local, state, and national laws regarding confidentiality and disclosure—there are often differences in the confidentiality arrangements that are mutually agreed upon by a therapist, teen, and parents.

Even school counselors are not required to report an instance of teen pregnancy unless the student displays any potential for self-harm or harm to others. The American School Counseling Association (ASCA) 2012 Ethical Code provides guidelines for school counselors to keep student information confidential. Some teens may request that their therapist aid in disclosing the pregnancy to a parent or guardian. It is important to inquire about and assess the minor's safety prior to helping them with such a disclosure.

Many of the obstacles that arise with a pregnancy can also impede one's social interactions. Social connectedness is an important factor in retaining teens in schools (Rumberger, 2011). As a population more at risk of drop-out, pregnant teens may particularly benefit from school-based social support networks that encourage educational persistence. Indeed, a teen's level of connectedness prior to pregnancy has been found to relate to her post-pregnancy educational attainment (Humberstone, 2018). Following pregnancy, teens may experience stigmatization, new educational environments, and added responsibilities—all of which can alter the friendships they held prior to pregnancy. Pregnant teens have been found to have less reciprocated friendships and are less likely to be considered a friend by their peers than are nonpregnant girls (Humberstone, 2019). Pregnant teens also report facing stigma, ostracization, or bullying by their peer group (Bermea et al., 2018; Cherry et al., 2015), which can be defined as loss of social standing or discrimination as a result of a distinguishing characteristic (Link & Phelan, 2001). Peers may avoid forming or continuing relationships with stigmatized individuals, and, in turn, stigmatized teens may avoid settings where they face stigmatization (school being one such setting). These factors are also likely to vary depending on a pregnant teen's school environment. For example, pregnant teens may face less social disruption if they attend schools without alternate educational placement options because this would mean they could avoid having to transfer schools. Alternatively, a pregnant student may find herself better supported through school resources available in a location with a high prevalence of teen pregnancies.

A unique component of working with pregnant teens is working in conjunction with a larger interdisciplinary team; for this population, such a team might consist of school staff, social worker, and medical team in addition to the teen's parents or other familial support. Together, this collaboration would help ensure that the pregnant teen is receiving the medical, mental health, and social support required to best suit her needs. While body image issues, self-esteem, and a focus on physical appearance are common concerns with many adolescents, these can be elevated in the pregnant teen population. The current research exploring the relationship between body image and pregnancy in adolescence is limited both in quality and quantity. Some studies show an increase in body image disturbance and dissatisfaction during pregnancy in adolescents (Zaltzman et al., 2015). Therapists can be instrumental in helping pregnant teens form and maintain a healthy, positive body image. When possible, a group approach can be very beneficial to pregnant adolescents. This group approach may vary from an open support group setting to a more structured group intervention with a didactic approach.

While pregnant teens have a subset of vulnerabilities all their own, it is important to consider adolescent concerns beyond the pregnancy stage. Teen parenting presents its own set of challenges from the moment teens become aware of impending parenthood, on to the birth and upbringing of their children. Teen parents, regardless of gender, often face many adversities related to their newfound responsibilities; these include

- Concerns regarding stability (shelter, employment, financial resources, transportation)
- Training, coaching, or education on how to parent
- Academic endeavors (finishing high school, attending trade school or college)
- Child care
- Navigating personal relationships and/or co-parenting

Teens who live in communities with higher rates of substance abuse, violence, and hunger are more likely to start having sex early and to have a child (Kirby & Lepore, 2007). The links between teen childbearing and family planning and socioeconomic characteristics, as well as the relatively high rates of adolescent childbearing among Black and Hispanic teens, can be attributed largely to inequities in access to family planning services and information; differences in attitudes about contraception, teen pregnancy, and teen childbearing; and distrust of medical professionals due to experiences with providers and some groups' history of mistreatment by the medical field (Dehlendorf et al., 2010). Therapists working with youth should be aware of and acknowledge the historical reasons that disparities in adolescent reproductive health and childbearing exist in the United States.

Summary

The content in this chapter provides a closer look into an area that most adults are unfamiliar with. Due to the very sensitive and intimate nature of the topic, many are understandably uncomfortable exploring the complexities related to adolescent sexuality. Even as therapists, we acknowledge the objectivity required to dive into this subject. In this chapter, we examined the complexities involved in counseling LGBTQ+ teens and adolescents. We identified issues related to adolescent sexuality which affect today's youth:

- Sexual activity, influences, and related concerns
- Sex trafficking
- Teen pregnancy and parenthood

This chapter also included an overview of the adolescent LGBTQIA+ community, which included review of terms, sexual identity, gender identity, and sexual orientation. Suggested therapeutic interventions and strategies were outlined for these multifaceted issues related to teen sex and sexuality. Although self-harm and suicide are not the focus of this particular chapter, we deemed it necessary to include an honest acknowledgment of suicidal ideation related to adolescent sexuality.

References

American Counseling Association (ACA). (2014). ACA code of ethics. http://www.counseling.org/docs/ethics/2014-aca-code-of-ethics.pdf?sfvrsn=4

American Psychiatric Association. (2013). *Diagnostic and statistical manual of mental disorders: DSM-5* (5th ed.). American Psychiatric Association.

American School Counseling Association (ASCA). (2012). *District policy and student pregnancy*. American School Counselor Association.

Bermea, A. M., Toews, M. L., & Wood, L. G. (2018). "Students getting pregnant are not gonna go nowhere": Manifestations of stigma in adolescent mothers' educational environment. *Youth & Society, 50*(3), 423–436. https://doi.org/10.1177/0044118X16661734

Centers for Disease Control and Prevention. (2019). Youth risk behavior survey data. Retrieved from www.cdc.gov/yrbs

Cherry, C. O., Chumbler, N., Bute, J., & Huff, A. (2015). Building a "better life." *SAGE Open, 5*. https://doi.org/10.1177/2158244015571638

Cunningham, K. C., & Cromer, L. D. (2016). Attitudes about human trafficking: Individual differences related to belief and victim blame. *Journal of Interpersonal Violence, 31*(2), 228–244. https://doi.org/10.1177/0886260514555369

Dehlendorf, C., Rodriguez, M. I., Levy, K., Borrero, S., & Steinauer, J. (2010). Disparities in family planning. *American Journal of Obstetrics and Gynecology, 202*(3), 214–220. https://ovc.ojp.gov/sites/g/files/xyckuh226/files/media/document/HT_Intro_to_HT_fact_sheet-508.pdf

Gonzalez-Pons, K. M., Gezinski, L., Morzenti, H., Hendrix, E., & Graves, S. (2020). Exploring the relationship between domestic minor sex trafficking myths, victim identification, and service provision. *Child Abuse & Neglect, 100*, 104093–104093. https://doi.org/10.1016/j.chiabu.2019.104093

Green, A. E., Price, M. N., & Dorison, S. H. (2022). Cumulative minority stress and suicide risk among LGBTQ youth. *American Journal of Community Psychology, 69*(1-2), 157-168. https://doi.org/10.1002/ajcp.12553

Hickle, K. E., & Roe-Sepowitz, D. E. (2014). Putting the pieces back together: A group intervention for sexually exploited adolescent girls. *Social Work with Groups (New York. 1978), 37*(2), 99-113. https://doi.org/10.1080/01609513.2013.823838

Hoffman, S. D., & Maynard, R. A. (Eds.). (2008). *Kids having kids: Economic costs and social consequences of teen pregnancy* (2nd ed.). Urban Institute Press.

Houston-Kolnik, J. D., Soibatian, C., & Shattell, M. M. (2020). Advocates' experiences with media and the impact of media on human trafficking advocacy. *Journal of Interpersonal Violence, 35*(5-6), 1108-1132. https://doi.org/10.1177/0886260517692337

Human Trafficking Institute. (2018). Federal human trafficking report. Retrieved from https://www.traffickingmatters.com/wp-content/uploads/2019/04/2018-Federal-Human-Trafficking-Report-Low-Res.pdf

Humberstone, E. (2018). Social networks and educational attainment among adolescents experiencing pregnancy. *Socius: Sociological Research for a Dynamic World, 4*, 237802311880380. https://doi.org/10.1177/2378023118803803

Humberstone, E. (2019). Friendship networks and adolescent pregnancy: Examining the potential stigmatization of pregnant teens. *Network Science, 7*(4), 523-540. https://doi.org/10.1017/nws.2019.25

Jordan, J., Patel, B., & Rapp, L. (2013). Domestic minor sex trafficking: A social work perspective on misidentification, victims, buyers, traffickers, treatment, and reform of current practice. *Journal of Human Behavior in the Social Environment, 23*(3), 356-369. https://doi.org/10.1080/10911359.2013.764198

Kearney, M. S., & Levine, P. B. (2012). Why is the teen birth rate in the United States so high and why does it matter? *Journal of Economic Perspectives, 26*(2), 141-166.

Kirby, D., & Lepore, G. (2007). *Sexual risk and protective factors: Factors affecting teen sexual behavior, pregnancy, childbearing and sexually transmitted disease: Which are important? Which can you change?* ETR Associates. Retrieved from http://recapp.etr.org/recapp/documents/theories/RiskProtectiveFactors200712.pdf

Link, B. G., & Phelan, J. C. (2001). Conceptualizing stigma. *Annual Review of Sociology, 27*(1), 363-385.

Litam, S. D. A. (2017). Human sex trafficking in America: What counselors need to know. *Professional Counselor (Greensboro, N. C.), 7*(1), 45-61. https://doi.org/10.15241/sdal.7.1.45

Litam, S. D. A. (2019). She's just a prostitute: The effects of labels on counselor attitudes, empathy, and rape myth acceptance. *Professional Counselor (Greensboro, N. C.), 9*(4), 396-415. https://doi.org/10.15241/sdal.9.4.396

Litam, S. D. A., & Lam, E. T. C. (2020). Sex trafficking beliefs in counselors: Establishing the need for human trafficking training in counselor education programs. *International Journal for the Advancement of Counselling, 43*(1), 1-18. https://doi.org/10.1007/s10447-020-09408-8

Luk, J. W., Goldstein, R. B., Yu, J., Haynie, D. L., & Gilman, S. E. (2021). Sexual minority status and age of onset of adolescent suicide ideation and behavior. *Pediatrics (Evanston), 148*(4). https://doi.org/10.1542/peds.2020-034900

Martin, J. A., Hamilton, B. E., Osterman, M. J. K., Driscoll, A. K., Schwartz, S., & Horon, I. (2021). Births: Final data for 2019. *National Vital Statistics Reports, 70*(2), 1. Centers for Disease Control and Prevention https://www.cdc.gov/nchs/data/nvsr/nvsr70/nvsr70-02-508.pdf

Martin, S. (2019). Sexualized behaviors in children and youth. Retrieved fromwww.militaryfamilieslearningnetwork.org/event/29419

National Human Trafficking Resource Center. (2011). Retrieved December 8, 2022 from https://humantraffickinghotline.org/resources/comprehensive-human-trafficking-assessment-tool

National Therapist Certification Program. (2020). About trauma-focused cognitive behavioral therapy (TF-CBT). Retrieved from https://tfcbt.org/about-tfcbt/

Osilla, K. C., Ortiz, J. A., Miles, J. N. V., Pedersen, E. R., Houck, J. M., & D'Amico, E. J. (2015). How group factors affect adolescent change talk and substance use outcomes: Implications for motivational interviewing training. *Journal of Counseling Psychology, 62*(1), 79–86. https://doi.org/10.1037/cou0000049

Rumberger, R. W. (2011). *Dropping out: Why students drop out of high school and what can be done about it.* Harvard University Press. https://doi.org/10.4159/harvard.9780674063167

Ryan, C. (2019). 20.1 the family acceptance project's model for LGBTQ youth. *Journal of the American Academy of Child and Adolescent Psychiatry, 58*(10), S28–S29. https://doi.org/10.1016/j.jaac.2019.07.123

The Trevor Project. (2021). *2021 National Survey on LGBTQ Youth Mental Health.* The Trevor Project.

Vera Institute. (2014). Screening for Human Trafficking: Guidelines for Administering the Trafficking Victim Identification Tool (TVIT). Retrieved December 8, 2022 from https://www.ojp.gov/pdffiles1/nij/grants/246713.pdf

Williamson, E., Dutch, N. M., & Clawson, H. J. (2008). Evidence-based mental health treatment for victims of human trafficking. https://aspe.hhs.gov/system/files/pdf/76116/index.pdf.

Wolf, M. R., Green, S. A., Nochajski, T. H., Mendel, W. E., & Kusmaul, N. S. (2014). "We're civil servants": The status of trauma-informed care in the community. *Journal of Social Service Research, 40*(1), 111–120. https://doi.org/10.1080/01488376.2013.845131

Ybarra, M. L., & Thompson, R. E. (2018). Predicting the emergence of sexual violence in adolescence. *Prevention Science, 19*(4), 403–415. https://doi.org/10.1007/s11121-017-0810-4

Zaltzman, A., Falcon, B., & Harrison, M. E. (2015). Body image in adolescent pregnancy. *Journal of Pediatric & Adolescent Gynecology, 28*(2), 102–108. https://doi.org/10.1016/j.jpag.2014.06.003

8
Bullying and Violence

Overview

In this chapter, we address violent behaviors and their implications for adolescents. Exposure to these behaviors, such as bullying, can certainly hinder academic and social development. Bullying is now documented as the most common form of school violence, and, through technology, bullying has evolved into a complex psychological and social cruelty that is no longer confined to school buildings or playgrounds. Mental health, conflict resolution, coping skills, prevention, and interventions will be discussed.

Introduction

> **Case Study: Jenna**
>
> Jenna was in the fifth grade the first time she experienced bullying behavior. She was sitting in the back row of the classroom, daydreaming again, something she did quite often. The teacher called on her and she didn't hear her, so the boy in front of her turned around and said "Hey, fatso, she's calling your name!" All the kids around him giggled. Jenna was so embarrassed, she didn't know what to say. The teacher asked her later if the boy had said something, but of course she said "No" because she was so embarrassed. How could she repeat what he said? For the rest of fifth grade that was Jenna's nickname, a soft opener to the years of bullying she would have ahead of her. As a child she moved almost yearly and with each new school came new faces, new bullies, and new nicknames. Jenna did her best to keep her head down, operate under the radar, and remain unnoticed if at all possible. This was genuinely pretty easy because most students and teachers didn't know her; she made a friend or two and tried to survive until it was time to move again. This strategy worked until

eighth grade when one day she went to school to find that the few friends she had made "fired her" so to speak without warning and without cause. Again, Jenna was embarrassed, fearful, and felt like it was something she had done. Now, more than three decades later, Jenna can say that she did in fact survive all of these bullying incidents, and she knows now that she was not alone. But in those moments of adolescence, she did not have the kind of perspective she has now as an adult. In those moments, she was mortified, rejected, and quite frankly lonely. These experiences left her insecure and apprehensive to trust others. Today, Jenna still battles feelings of self-doubt and trust in peer relationships. Unfortunately, the lingering impact of bullying is common, and years later some adults are still trying to understand what happened, what was their role, and why they were singled out.

Most youth have experienced bullying on some level, as either the bully, the victim, or the by-stander. Best estimates on the prevalence of bullying is that 30% of youth in the United States are involved in bullying as either perpetrator or victim (Nansel et al., 2001). According to Finkelhor et al. (2015) 16% of 0- to 17-year-olds have experienced assault by a non-sibling peer, 13% have experienced physical intimidation, and 36% have experienced relational aggression in the previous year. So, the question is: What can helping professionals do? Because, for better or worse, adults play a very important role in this process. Often the mishandling of bullying situations starts with very good intentions, so we must work to listen and act with conscious intention based on knowledge. Another question we must ask: What types of collaborations can we join together to best support our youth and adolescents who most desperately need help? Simply put, all of this is easier to say or write and much harder to accomplish in the real world. Bullying isn't monolithic; there is no single bullying experience, and there is no single solution. For future prevention and interventions to be successful, youth and adolescents need to know that when they bring bullying issues to adults (the helpers), things can get better and not worse.

Bullying

Bullying involving children and adolescents has been around as long as school buildings and playgrounds have existed (Sharp & Smith, 2002). Olweus (1978), one of the first researchers to examine bullying, defined bullying as repeated violence or oppression, either mental and/or physical, by one or more peers against another. Olweus (1993) later expanded this definition, stating that bullying occurs when one or more people repeatedly expose another to negative actions, making it difficult for the victim to defend him- or herself due to a power imbalance. As noted earlier, most bullying researchers estimate that roughly 3 in 10 youth in the United States are involved in bullying as either the perpetrator or victim (Nansel et al., 2001). Research has documented for decades that bullying is a persistent and pervasive issue for youth and adolescents, and, while bullying is a much more heavily discussed, debated, and researched topic now than in previous decades (Olweus, 2013), despite this increase in discussion and education on the ill effects of bullying, children and adolescents still experience bullying at the same or increased rates as those in previous generations. However, youth may not experience bullying in the exact same way as their parents did. Traditional face-to-face bullying and victimization have actually declined over the past few decades (Chester et al., 2015; Perlus et al., 2014; Shetgiri et al., 2013), while cyberbullying has increased (Kessel Schneider et al., 2015; Ybarra et al., 2011). Cyberbullying has negated any safe haven for students who experience bullying. Youth once offered respite at home, away from school or playground, now find that, through online forums, they are open to non-stop victimization. Victims of cyberbullying perceive their harassment as inescapable, potentially more severe, and possibly fundamentally different from traditional face-to-face bullying.

The Centers for Disease Control and Prevention (CDC) categorizes bullying according to four principles: (1) unwanted aggressive behavior by youth other than siblings or dating partners; (2) power imbalance, observed or perceived; (3) repeated incidents or high likelihood of repetition; and (4) physical, psychological, social, or educational harm or distress for the victim (Centers for Disease Control and Prevention [CDC], 2017). Anchored within these parameters are four subtypes: face-to-face relational bullying, which is a covert bullying that includes rumor spreading or social isolation; physical bullying, which is overt and includes hitting and fighting; verbal bullying, which is also overt and includes teasing and name calling; and cyberbullying, which is relational bullying that takes place via an electronic device (online, texting, social media platforms, etc.). Approximately 58% of children and adolescents reported being cyberbullied, with more than half of them not telling their parents when bullying occurs (Bullying Statistics, 2013).

Although youth have experienced or perpetuated bullying in varying ways, Greene (2006) compiled a list of behaviors or actions common to bullying. These include (a) the bully intends to cause harm and/or inflict fear, (b) there is repeated aggression, (c) bullying is not provoked by the victim with verbal or physical aggression, (d) behavior occurs in familiar peer groups, and (e) there is a real or perceived difference of power. Bullying behavior can be described as being either overt (e.g., direct physical aggression) or covert (e.g., spreading rumors or social rejection). These behaviors plus technology have opened up a whole new "can of worms" so to speak for youth. Parents, teachers, counselors, and helpers from all different professional backgrounds are struggling with how to protect youth from bullying and cyberbullying while also allowing youth the space to grow and develop into adulthood. This heightened awareness is positive in many ways, allowing adults to recognize the cruelty that children and adolescents experience and just how debilitating bullying can be to an individual. In addition, professionals recognize that certain youth populations require additional support or protections, such as youth who identify as LGBTQ or who may be overweight or belong to a certain religion. This awareness has led to parent education, school programming, and community-based anti-bullying campaigns, along with policy changes at the state and federal levels.

The management of these types of programs, weighing both benefits and cautions, guides us through this chapter. The guiding question is "How do we pull from the available resources the necessary support to help youth who are at risk?" Some may view bullying as pretty simple—there's a bully and the bullied—but as therapists or therapists in training we know this isn't always how it goes; it's usually much more complex. In the following sections we will discuss many of the topics that add to the complexity of bullying.

Implications of Bullying

Research confirms what many have experienced: there are severe and long-lasting consequences to bullying involvement that may persist into adulthood. Victims of bullying may manage to get through and learn to cope with those toxic relationships and social cruelty, but they likely have not forgotten these experiences, which may stay with them, firmly planted, long into middle and late adulthood. Studies indicate there are numerous implications to being involved in the bullying process. Specifically, children and adolescents who have been victims of bullying report increased symptoms of anxiety and depression (Ybarra, 2004), higher levels of stress (Newman et al., 2005), and may engage in delinquent behavior such as skipping school, unhealthy peer relationships, or poor academic performance in school (Hinduja & Patchin, 2007). Additionally, children and adolescents who have bullied others report poor emotional bonds with parents, higher levels of drug or alcohol use, and more delinquent behavior when compared with their non-bully peers (Ybarra & Mitchell, 2004). Youth who bully against or have been the victims of bullying are also more likely to develop conduct disorder later in adolescence. Looking beyond adolescence, victims of bullying are at risk of suffering from internalizing and social problems, such as anxiety, depression, and trouble making or keeping friends; these issues can be present well into early and middle adulthood (18–50 years) (Takizawa et al., 2014).

Bullying and Social Development

In regards to social development, bullying has broadly been associated with parent–child relationships characterized by poor parental involvement (Curtner-Smith, 2000; Dishion, 1990; Flouri & Buchanan, 2003; Olweus, 1978; 1993; Pepler et al., 2008; Ybarra & Mitchell, 2004), high hostility (Olweus, 1980, 1993; Pettit & Bates, 1989; Schwartz et al., 1997; Strassberg et al., 1994), and severe, punitive, and/or inconsistent discipline (Barnow et al., 2001; Curtner-Smith, 2000; Dishion, 1990; Espelage et al., 2000; Loeber & Dishion, 1983; Olweus, 1993; Schwartz et al., 1997). According to Olweus (1978) the learning of aggression in the family happens from very early in the development of the child, and it can persist for up to three generations. These findings are supported by Patterson, DeBaryshe, and Ramsey's (1989) Coercive Family Process Theory, which found that ineffective parenting strategies often lay the foundation for the development of antisocial behavior. Early relationships categorized by these traits can influence development and lead to mistrust and poor relationships later in childhood, adolescence, and adulthood. The importance of healthy, nurturing relationships in early childhood is well-documented and aids the development of a secure ego which will undoubtedly influence the development and maintenance of peer relationships during the school years and beyond.

Bullying and Public Health

Given the complexity of bullying and the severity of symptoms youth and adolescents can experience, bullying has broadened from being a parental or school concern to a public health concern. While there are numerous bullying prevention programs supported by school and community campaigns, their effectiveness is often arguable. Samara and Smith (2008) reported that narrowly focused anti-bullying policies tend to have little effect, and most school- or community-based anti-bullying interventions have had only modest results. Therefore leaders in public health, such as the Society for Adolescent Medicine, encourage healthcare providers to be familiar with the characteristics and behaviors associated with the bullying process, sensitive to signs and symptoms of bullying and victimization, and intervene when necessary (Eisenberg & Aalsma, 2005). The National Center for Mental Health Promotion and Youth Violence Prevention also suggested that bullying is best addressed by a comprehensive approach, which would certainly include public health figures. These professionals play an important role in preventing bullying by taking opportunities (as during wellness checkups) to assess adolescents for signs of bullying (National Research Council and Institute of Medicine, 2009). Due to the association between mental and physical health, Dale, Russell, and Wolke (2014) found bullied youth experience both acute mental and physical health problems; knowing this, it is only to be expected that adolescents with bullying experiences are more likely to encounter healthcare professionals than are their non-bullied peers. Public health providers are unequivocally in a unique position to intervene and support youth and adolescents who might be experiencing the ill consequences of being involved in the bullying process.

Bullying and Mental Health

The mental and emotional impact of the bully experience is distressing; within the literature there is consistent evidence of a significant relationship between bullying and psychological maladjustment in youth. What may be even more disturbing is that youth involved in bullying are at a greater risk for more severe emotional instability than are youth who are diagnosed with a major mental illness, such as bipolar disorder (Schreier et al., 2009). Chronic victimization has also been linked to psychotic-like symptoms in later adolescence as well as an extended impact well into adulthood. These effects are believed to be related to the extended periods of stress associated with victimization (Gladstone et al., 2006; Schreier et al., 2009).

For those who have experienced bullying or worked with someone who has, as therapists we know that youth can experience a variety of side effects such as stress, depression, anxiety, and, in severe victimization, even suicidal ideation (Fekkes et al., 2004). Specifically, anxiety and depression have been closely linked with bullying and bully victimization (Seals & Young, 2003). Saluja et al. (2004) found that youth who are involved in bullying either as bullies or as victims have rates of depressive symptoms at least twice that of non-involved youth. While not all youth involved in the bullying process experience the same severity of symptoms, according to Fitzpatrick et al. (2010) victims of bullying were found to have higher levels of perceived stress, anxiety, and depressive symptoms than bullies and non-involved youth. However, it is important to note that all youth, regardless of role(s) associated with bullying, reported lower life satisfaction compared to non-involved youth.

Others factors that could contribute to low life satisfaction and poor mental health among bullies/bullied youth are social anxiety and loneliness. A teen who suffers from social anxiety may feel scared of being seen as an outsider or a failure, especially in situations involving social skills, physical skills, or intellectual skills or in situations where they stand out due to physical appearance or position in a peer group (Mulder & van Aken, 2014). Social anxiousness can essentially put a target on the back of any adolescent and make them at risk for victimization (Mulder & van Aken, 2014). Acquah et al. (2016) wanted to better understand the connectedness of these factors and examined the relationships among loneliness, social anxiety, and bully victimization. Their findings concluded that adolescents who experienced social loneliness experienced more bully victimization. Most of their participants also indicated feeling social anxiety due to previous experiences of bully victimization. However social anxiety is not isolated to victimization: Pabian and Vandebosch (2016) found that adolescents who were perpetrators of bullying also had higher levels of social anxiety. Regardless of the youth's role in bullying, internalizing problems should be addressed with evidenced-based prevention and intervention programs. Failure to intervene with youth who are experiencing poor mental health due to their role in bullying can lead to serious consequences in the immediate and long terms.

Bullying in Schools

Because students spend a large portion of their day at school, schools have a substantial impact on a student's academic and behavioral development (Bradshaw & Waasdorp, 2009). For some students, bullying creates a serious obstacle to their success in both academic and social settings (Iyer et al., 2013). How students are treated by their peers and classmates goes beyond any one incident: it is how behavior is managed on a day-to-day basis, how students are encouraged to think about and treat each other. These attitudes and management of behaviors create or make up the *school climate*. School climate is a fundamental component of school safety (Barnes et al., 2006). Research indicates that among middle school students, males feel less safe at school in comparison to their female classmates (Birkett et al., 2014). Feelings of insecurity, fear, negative thoughts, and behaviors such as these can affect the student's ability to learn and their overall functioning in school (Boekaerts, 2011). Beyond academic and social development, bullying can also negatively impact postsecondary planning, such as college or vocational aspirations, potentially diminishing the capacity for a student's future growth and development into adulthood (Gladden, 2014).

Over the past two decades, researchers learned that schools are not necessarily safe places for learning and achievement but are instead institutions where a considerable number of students are concerned about "getting beat up" or harassed by their peers/classmates (Juvonen et al., 2013). A safe and healthy school environment is important for supporting students' academic success (Konishi et al., 2010). The challenge is not in getting educator buy-in; the challenge is implementing effective programming and interventions that reduce bullying incidents and academically and emotionally support students who have been involved in bullying in some capacity. As a result of the 1999 Columbine shootings and in response to the growing number of bullying-related suicides, Georgia became the first state to pass bullying legislation that requires schools to implement character education programs that include bullying prevention education (US Department of Education, 2011). These policies and laws have now been passed in some capacity in all 50 states and US territories to support students, schools, and communities; however, entities such as GLSEN argue that these laws and policies do not provide enough support and protections to vulnerable student populations who might be at higher risk for victimization (Kosciw et al., 2015).

Many school districts are falling short of prevention, overwhelmed with high-stakes testing all while being woefully underfunded and understaffed. The No Child Left Behind (NCLB) Act of 2001 was created for the purpose of closing the achievement gap with accountability, flexibility, and choice (No Child Left Behind Act of 2001). This legislation also called for school officials to create a safe learning environment, and training was provided to teachers and administrators to increase awareness of bullying and prevent victimization (Bradshaw et al., 2007). However, critics of NCLB might argue that this increased focus on academic achievement took away from social emotional learning and overly emphasized student performance on standardized tests. In 2015, the Every Student Succeeds Act was passed and appeased many of the critics who pushed against the overreliance on high-stakes testing; however, many feel that the legislation failed to devise a new system and simply broadened state discretion (Black, 2017).

Evidenced-based anti-bullying programs should be implemented in all schools (Lester & Maldonado, 2014). The roles of teachers, school counselors, administrators, and other stakeholders must be clearly defined. Unfortunately, many bullying stories highlight times when teachers or administrators clearly ignored (Watson & Miller, 2012) or even participated in the bullying incident. There is still much work to be done in schools. Training, curriculum, resources, and adequate funding are elements that must be prioritized before statistically significant results will take place.

Bullying and Violent Behaviors

The most publicized bullying events are those that involve violent acts. Risky behaviors associated with bullying vary and can range from harmful to deadly. Most of the times we associate violent bullying behaviors with the perpetrator, but bullied students may be at risk for behavior problems such as displaying signs of aggression, hyperactivity, and inattention (Stanton and Beran, 2009). Victims of bullying are also more likely to be engaged in behaviors such as fighting, heavy drinking, and drug use (Kim et al., 2011). Bullying and being bullied have also been found to be related to higher rates of physical assault and weapon carrying (Glew et al., 2008). Meyer-Adams and Conner (2008) concluded that if youth have an overly negative view of their school, there is a greater chance they will react by cutting class, skipping school, or carrying a weapon. According to Eaton et al. (2012) in the National Overview of the Youth Risk Behavior Survey (YRBS) 16.6% of students carried a weapon on at least one occasion 30 days prior to the survey's distribution (Eaton et al., 2012). These risky behaviors create a scenario that puts youth at risk for long-term criminal engagement; in fact, Peckham (2007) found that adolescents involved in school bullying had a 1 in 4 chance of being found guilty of a crime before the age of 30. These studies clearly demonstrate a connection between bullying and violent behaviors.

School Violence

In response to increasing numbers of violent incidents in schools, specifically increasing incidents involving weapons, school districts have been quick to reassess their safety and crisis response strategies. According to Fox and Harding (2005), schools are particularly vulnerable targets for violent attacks, but they also provide opportunities for prevention and intervention due to the fact that they are an environment in which behaviors and symptoms of trauma become apparent and can be treated. School districts often struggle to identify and evaluate student behaviors, primarily due to a lack of knowledge and training among school faculty and a lack of knowledge around violence-related warning signs and symptoms of psychological crisis (Leuschner et al., 2017).

School culture must be a focus for violence prevention, and this culture must be one that values information sharing and encouraging students to speak out when they have concerns regarding their classmates. School districts must work to strengthen their partnership with local law enforcement agencies because fragmented partnerships can lead to misinformation and lack of structure in programming and supportive services. According to Leuschner et al., there are five crucial goals when it comes to violence prevention: (1) alert teachers to detect issues in adolescents' development, (2) increase communication about students in crisis, (3) use evidence-based assessments to evaluate for student support, (4) hire staff who are trained in case management, and (5) build a professional network to provide counseling and other supportive resources within the school environment. Due to the fact that such a large number of youth and adolescents attend schools each day, millions of students can be assessed with ease, thus making schools a logical choice for violence prevention programs (Farrell et al., 2001). The World Report on Violence and Health has pushed for systemic change in prevention and action (WHO, 2014). Since its publication, programming has been focused on the prevention of violence for children and adolescents, and many of these efforts have been conducted within the K-12 school setting. These types of school-based programming often target skills, knowledge, and social attitudes to reduce violent behaviors before they can occur (Prothrow-Stith & Davis, 2010).

Bullying and Protective Factors

According to the literature, several factors might contribute to or predict that an adolescent is more at risk for being involved in the bullying process. Much of the research in this area is related to parental attachment and early development. Farrington (2011) found that several family factors, such as poor parental supervision, poor monitoring, erratic or harsh parental discipline, inconsistency between parents, parental disharmony, parental rejection, and low parental involvement with the child all correlated with or predicted problematic behavior in youth. According to Mazzone and Camodeca (2019), there is a significant relationship between bullying and poor family functioning, signifying that youth with behavioral problems suffer from poor parenting. Christie-Mizell et al. (2011) state that bullies differs from non-bullies in having punitive and incompatible parents. These youth were more likely to experience harsh punishments such as name calling, yelling, and corporal punishment. Therefore, parents of bullies are in general more violent in their engagement with and punishment of their children (Gómez-Ortiz et al., 2016). These early experiences of violence in the home often predict future aggression in youth peer relationships.

Risk factors for victimization show that these adolescents often have low authoritative parents who often fail to value their children and tend not to give them the opportunity for autonomy (Martínez et al., 2019). These youth are more likely to advance into adulthood with anxiety issues, low levels of self-confidence, and apprehension in self-expression. This reluctance to engage with others and lack of self-confidence could possibly contribute to being identified as a target for bullying.

Coping Skills

To reduce victimization of bullying and its harmful effects, bullied adolescents need to be equipped with coping tools and strategies. Lazarus and Folkman's (1984) pioneering work found that coping is a process that uses either problem-focused (e.g., problem-solving and help-seeking) or emotion-focused (e.g., avoiding) methods. Frydenberg and colleagues (Frydenberg 2008; Frydenberg & Lewis, 1993, 2000) expanded on this research and found that adolescent coping could be classified as productive (e.g., problem-solving and investing in friends), help-seeking (e.g., seeking social support and professional help), or nonproductive (e.g., avoidance and wishful thinking).

Bradbury et al. (2019) found that adolescents actually use a wide variety of coping strategies, not just one of the previously mentioned (problem-focused, emotional, or avoidance) strategies to manage experiences of bullying. Another important note is that gender has a strong influence on the selection(s) of coping skill. According to previous research, girls are more likely use problem-solving or help-seeking strategies as a way of coping with bullying compared with boys (e.g., Dooley, Gradinger, Strohmeier, Cross, & Spiel, 2010; Li, 2006) while nonproductive coping strategies (e.g., retaliation) are more likely used among boys (Machmutow et al., 2012). Since boys and girls experience bullying in different ways, it's logical that they would also respond with contrasting coping strategies. Age also influences coping strategy: the older the child is, the more likely they are to use avoidance strategies; younger children tend to use more emotional strategies (Tenenbaum et al., 2011).

There has also been research to show that coping strategies change through the bullying experience. Olafsen et al. (2000) found a progressive change in the use of coping strategies (from active, assertive, and aggressive to passive, submissive, and appeasing) as the bullying experience increases in severity. I think it's easy for some of us to say what we would or would not do when we encounter a bully: "Stand up for yourself," "Don't be a pushover," "Tell an adult," but is that what we would actually do in the moment when we experience or witness bullying? Maybe . . . maybe not. There has even been research showing a disconnect between what individuals say they would do to address bullying and what they actually do. Rayner (1999) found that a smaller percentage of victims confronted the bully or told a person with authority compared with what non-victims claimed they would do. The same discrepancy was found between victims and non-victims with respect to the use (or expected use) of coping strategies such seeking support from helpers or peers. There is no one right way to cope with being involved in the bullying process. While some strategies are more positive than others, being involved in the bullying experience is tough, and youth need a variety of tools and strategies. While coping strategies have been extensively debated and researched throughout the literature and there are varying results and outcomes in regards to these strategies, much of their utility and efficacies depends on population and external factors.

Responding to Bullying

Unfortunately, bullying often goes unreported. So, how do systems prevent or respond to something when there is no way to know when or how bullying is occurring? As stated early in this chapter, bullying has existed as long as the playground. Even if we do not always witness it directly, we know that, no matter from what perspective we work with children and adolescents, at least 1 in 3 of them are experiencing bullying in some way. According to Petrosino, Guckenburg, DeVoe, and Hanson (2010), 36% of bullying victims (ages 11–17) reported their victimization to a teacher or other adult at school and 64% of victims did not. Overt bullying, such as physical aggression, was generally reported but bullying that involved teasing, exclusion, rumors, or forcing the victim to do things he or she did not want to do were often not reported (Petrosino et al., 2010). Youth may often feel that adults cannot or will not be of assistance when it comes to bullying. So how do we create environments, programs, and systems that not only respond to bullying when it happens but also are proactive and prevent bullying before it can occur?

Because school systems and networked school districts provide good access to youth, utilizing schools to implement bullying prevention seems to make logical sense, and, over the past two decades, schools have been the primary focus of such prevention/intervention curricula. Research has indicated that bullying can be significantly decreased through comprehensive schoolwide prevention programs developed to work with youth and school/community stakeholders. Vreeman and Carroll (2007) reviewed bullying interventions and found that the most effective interventions used multidisciplinary approaches consisting of school policies, staff training, classroom curricula, conflict resolution training, and individual counseling. Effective programming will be discussed more extensively in the next section.

Systemic Response

Over the past 30 years there has been an extensive development of bullying prevention programs and considerable research on their effectiveness, although many researchers debate the effectiveness and true impact of these programs on bullying incidents. The vast consensus is that these programs typically only have a modest effect (Merrell et al., 2008). A meta-analysis of 44 evaluations of anti-bullying programs was conducted. The studies ranged from 1983 to 2009; about one-third were conducted in the United States and two-thirds were undertaken in other countries (Ttofi & Farrington, 2011). Findings showed that, on average, bullying decreased by 20–23% and victimization decreased by 17–20% following the interventions. However, intensive programs were found to be most effective: these programs typically included parent involvement, trained school staff, and improved child supervision.

Cushman and Clelland (2011) argued that bullying behavior should be conceptualized as a systemic phenomenon often influenced by a wide range of factors that relate to variables such as the individual youth, family system, peers, school environment/culture, community, cultural norms, and social media. Based on their findings, these researchers stated that all bullying interventions should decisively be framed within a systemic solution. The idea of a systemic solution has also been supported by researchers such as Bradshaw et al. (2015) who state that the most effective programs should include a multicomponent prevention approach which addresses different ecological layers and targets multiple risk factors. Studies such as these conclude that anti-bullying programs should take into consideration teacher training, schoolwide approaches and buy-in, parental involvement, community support, and societal factors. All of these elements are key and fundamental to decreasing bullying behaviors.

To put into practice such a systemic approach to bullying prevention, it is necessary to address the challenges involved in bringing about change in how the overall system is currently organized. To begin with, agencies or institutions (schools, public health, mental health, etc.) are siloed and work independently of one another with very little information sharing or collaboration. If we are to prevent bullying, instead of working independently of one another, helping agencies should be operating within a collective system that works to support each other and support the adolescent. For efficacy sake, anti-bullying prevention is not a singular task or focus, but a blended process that is multidimensional in its approaches and needs. This type of shift in focus will take leadership from experts along with community and educational stakeholders.

Case Study: Raleigh

Raleigh is a 14-year-old girl who is a freshman in high school. Raleigh has battled both physical and emotional limitations her entire childhood. She was born with cerebral palsy and experienced neglect from her birth mother prior to being adopted at age 4 by the Henderson family. She has lived with the Henderson's in a small rural community for the past 10 years. While the Henderson family has loved and provided for Raleigh during this time, they have often felt unprepared and unequipped for both her physical and emotional needs. Since the onset of puberty, new issues have emerged, and her adoptive parents seem even more lost in how to support her. At school, Raleigh is withdrawing. Now in high school, she has new teachers, administrators, and school counselors. She loved her teachers at her K-8 school and primarily stayed in two classrooms away from the general student population due to it being an older building with limited accessibility for handicapped students. Raleigh honestly preferred it that way; she felt safe and enjoyed her small bubble of teachers and students.

Now, everything has changed: her new high school is much larger, the new building has greater accessibility, and she now has classes in several different hallways, all with the general student population. This new exposure to other students has been mixed. Raleigh is shy and has always only had one or two friends. Now, other than at lunch, she never sees her friends and all the students seem to stare at her and her wheelchair. Whenever she enters the classroom students stop talking and look at her. She prefers it when they ignore her, but some of the boys make fun of her below their breath. Recently, some of the boys have started sticking notes to the back of her wheelchair or her locker; she even overheard one of them betting $100 if to anyone who would ask her out to the Homecoming game. These changes in school have had a real impact on Raleigh. She's anxious, depressed, and she's getting sick more than usual. Her parents have noticed all these changes over the past few weeks. Whenever they try to talk to Raleigh she states that everything is fine. They have decided to reach out for help. They started by calling her school counselor and asking her to check on Raleigh and see if she'll talk to her. The school counselor was happy to help and did a quick check of her grades; she found they were lower than her 8th-grade averages. She also checked with her teachers, who reported that Raleigh was bright, but unengaged and quiet most days. The school counselor even observed Raleigh in the hallway between classes and found her to be sheepish and avoiding contact with her peers. The school counselor also arranged meetings between Raleigh's teachers, Individualized Education Program (IEP) coordinator, and parents for additional support and collaboration.

After coordination of services and gathering information, her school counselor brought Raleigh into her office for an individual session and asked her if she'd be interested in joining a group of girls that she works with each week. Raleigh reluctantly agreed to join the girl's group. While the Hendersons were pleased to hear that Raleigh was engaging with the school counselor and had agreed to group counseling, they were still concerned about how fatigued Raleigh acted and how often she was having cold symptoms (aches, fatigue, loss of appetite). They decided to reach out to her pediatrician. The pediatrician conducted a full checkup. The pediatrician had been treating Raleigh for 10 years, and they have a good relationship. Raleigh admitted to often feeling sad and even unsure of whether she wanted to live some days. Raleigh had never attempted to hurt herself but had more than once fantasized about taking too many pills before bedtime. Raleigh was diagnosed with depression and prescribed a low dose of anti-anxiety medication. The pediatrician also referred her to a local community mental health (CMH) agency for weekly therapy.

At the local CMH agency Raleigh met Linda, a new therapist who has been practicing about 2 years. Raleigh loved her purple hair and the two began to develop a strong working partnership. Raleigh finally felt like she had people around her who listened. Through her girls' group at school she realized she wasn't the only one who was struggling; Linda helped her have a safe space each week to talk about her feelings; and the medication seemed to be helping her feel less sad and not always on an emotional roller coaster. These combined systemic efforts and continued support from the school, pediatrician, and community health therapist helped guide Raleigh to a path of increased physical and emotional wellness. The local CMH agency even offered a parents group for the Henderson' to help them connect with other parents of teens.

After 6 months of systemic treatment and support, Raleigh and her parents report decreased moodiness, an improvement in grades, and the only medical visits have been for routine follow-ups.

Summary

While the factors that contribute to bullying and school violence discussed in this chapter portray a dismal image, targeted acts of violence are the exception to the rule and not the "norm" for most youth and adolescents. However, universally, schools and communities can do more to ensure the safety of our children and adolescents. Proactively working to identify youth at risk and better understanding warning signs for violent behaviors are both ways in which prevention and interventions can be improved upon. It is time that communities develop collaborative systems to ensure that no youth who is struggling is overlooked or goes unnoticed.

References

Acquah, E. O., Topalli, P. Z., Wilson, M. L., Junttila, N., & Niemi, P. M. (2016). Adolescent loneliness and social anxiety as predictors of bullying victimisation. *International Journal of Adolescence and Youth*, *21*(3), 320–331.

Armstrong, S. B., Dubow, E. F., & Domoff, S. E. (2019). Adolescent coping: In-person and cyber-victimization. *Cyberpsychology: Journal of Psychosocial Research on Cyberspace*, *13*(4).

Barnes, J., Belsky, J., Broomfield, K. A., Melhuish, E., & the National Evaluation of Sure Start (NESS) Research Team. (2006). Neighborhood deprivation, school disorder and academic achievement in primary schools in deprived communities in England. *International Journal of Behavioral Development*, *30*(2), 127–136.

Barnow, S., Lucht, M., & Freyberger, H. J. (2001). Influence of punishment, emotional rejection, child abuse, and broken home on aggression in adolescence: An examination of aggressive adolescents in Germany. *Psychopathology*, *34*(4), 167–173.

Birkett, M., Russell, S. T., & Corliss, H. L. (2014). Sexual-orientation disparities in school: The mediational role of indicators of victimization in achievement and truancy because of feeling unsafe. *American Journal of Public Health*, *104*(6), 1124–1128.

Black, D. W. (2017). Abandoning the federal role in education: The every student succeeds act. *California Law Review*, *105*, 1309.

Boekaerts, M. (2011). Emotions, emotion regulation, and self-regulation of learning: Center for the study of learning and instruction, leiden university, the netherlands, and ku leuven. In *Handbook of self-regulation of learning and performance* (pp. 422–439). Routledge.

Bradshaw, C. P., Sawyer, A. L., & O'Brennan, L. M. (2007). Bullying and peer victimization at school: Perceptual differences between students and school staff. *School Psychology Review*, *36*(3), 361–382.

Bradshaw, C. P., Pas, E. T., Debnam, K. J., & Lindstrom Johnson, S. (2015). A focus on implementation of positive behavioral interventions and supports (PBIS) in high schools: Associations with bullying and other indicators of school disorder. *School Psychology Review*, *44*(4), 480–498.

Bradshaw, C. P., & Waasdorp, T. E. (2009). Measuring and changing a "culture of bullying." *School Psychology Review*, *38*(3), 356–361.

Bullying Statistics. (2013). *Stop bullying, harassment, and anti-bully in school/work*. Retrieved from http://pacer.org

Centers for Disease Control and Prevention (CDC). (2017). Bullying research. Retrieved September 29, 2020, from https://www.cdc.gov/violenceprevention/youthviolence/bullyingresearch/index.html

Chester, K. L., Callaghan, M., Cosma, A., Donnelly, P., Craig, W., Walsh, S., & Molcho, M. (2015). Cross-national time trends in bullying victimization in 33 countries among children aged 11, 13 and 15 from 2002 to 2010. *European Journal of Public Health, 25*(suppl_2), 61–64.

Christie-Mizell, C. A., Keil, J. M., Laske, M. T., & Stewart, J. (2011). Bullying behavior, parents' work hours and early adolescents' perceptions of time spent with parents. *Youth & Society, 43*(4), 1570–1595.

Curtner-Smith, M. E. (2000). Mechanisms by which family processes contribute to school-age boy's bullying. *Child Study Journal, 30*(3), 169–169.

Cushman, P., & Clelland, T. (2011). A health promoting schools' approach to bullying. *SET: Research Information for Teachers, 3*, 17–25.

Dale, J., Russell, R., & Wolke, D. (2014). Intervening in primary care against childhood bullying: An increasingly pressing public health need. *Journal of the Royal Society of Medicine, 107*(6), 219–223.

Dishion, T. J. (1990). The family ecology of boys' peer relations in middle childhood. *Child Development, 61*(3), 874–892.

Dooley, J. J., Gradinger, P., Strohmeier, D., Cross, D., & Spiel, C. (2010). Cybervictimisation: The association between help-seeking behaviours and self reported emotional symptoms in Australia and Austria. *Australian Journal of Guidance and Counselling, 20*, 194–209. doi:10.1375/ajgc.20.2.194

Eaton, D. K., Kann, L., Kinchen, S., Shanklin, S., Flint, K. H., Hawkins, J., . . . Whittle, L. (2012). Youth risk behavior surveillance—United States, 2011. *Morbidity and Mortality Weekly Report: Surveillance Summaries, 61*(4), 1–162.

Eisenberg, M. E., & Aalsma, M. C. (2005). Bullying and peer victimization: Position paper of the Society for Adolescent Medicine. *Journal of Adolescent Health, 36*(1), 88–91.

Espelage, D. L., Bosworth, K., & Simon, T. R. (2000). Examining the social context of bullying behaviors in early adolescence. *Journal of Counseling & Development, 78*(3), 326–333.

Farrell, A. D., Meyer, A. L., & White, K. S. (2001). Evaluation of Responding in Peaceful and Positive Ways (RIPP): A school-based prevention program for reducing violence among urban adolescents. *Journal of Clinical Child Psychology, 30*(4), 451–463.

Farrington, D. P. (2011). Families and crime. In J. Q. Wilson & J. Petersilia (Eds.), *Crime and Public Policy* (pp. 130–157). New York: Oxford University Press.

Fekkes, M., Pijpers, F. I., & Verloove-Vanhorick, S. P. (2004). Bullying behavior and associations with psychosomatic complaints and depression in victims. *Journal of Pediatrics, 144*(1), 17–22.

Finkelhor, D., Turner, H. A., Shattuck, A., & Hamby, S. L. (2015). Prevalence of childhood exposure to violence, crime, and abuse: Results from the National Survey of Children's Exposure to Violence. *JAMA Pediatrics, 169*(8), 746–754.

Fitzpatrick, K. M., Dulin, A., & Piko, B. (2010). Bullying and depressive symptomatology among low-income, African-American youth. *Journal of Youth and Adolescence, 39*(6), 634–645.

Flouri, E., & Buchanan, A. (2003). The role of mother involvement and father involvement in adolescent bullying behavior. *Journal of Interpersonal Violence, 18*(6), 634–644.

Fox, C., & Harding, D. J. (2005). School shootings as organizational deviance. *Sociology of Education, 78*(1), 69–97.

Frydenberg, E. (2008). *Adolescent coping: Advances in theory, research and practice.* Routledge.

Frydenberg, E., & Lewis, R. (1993). Boys play sport and girls turn to others: Age, gender and ethnicity as determinants of coping. *Journal of Adolescence, 16*, 253–266. doi:10.1006/jado.1993.1024

Frydenberg, E., & Lewis, R. (2000). Teaching coping to adolescents: When and to whom? *American Educational Research Journal, 37*, 727–745. doi:10.3102/00028312037003727

Glew, G. M., Fan, M. Y., Katon, W., & Rivara, F. P. (2008). Bullying and school safety. *Journal of Pediatrics, 152*(1), 123–128.

Gladstone, G. L., Parker, G. B., & Malhi, G. S. (2006). Do bullied children become anxious and depressed adults? A cross-sectional investigation of the correlates of bullying and anxious depression. *Journal of Nervous and Mental Disease, 194*(3), 201–208.

Gladden, R. M. (2014). *Bullying surveillance among youths: uniform definitions for public health and recommended data elements.* Version 1.0. Centers for Disease Control and Prevention.

Gómez-Ortiz, O., Romera, E. M., & Ortega-Ruiz, R. (2016). Parenting styles and bullying: The mediating role of parental psychological aggression and physical punishment. *Child Abuse & Neglect, 51*, 132–143.

Greene, M. B. (2006). Bullying in schools: A plea for measure of human rights. *Journal of Social Issues, 62*(1), 63–79.

Hinduja, S., & Patchin, J. W. (2007). Offline consequences of online victimization: School violence and delinquency. *Journal of School Violence, 6*(3), 89–112.

Iyer, R. V., Kochenderfer-Ladd, B., Eisenberg, N., & Thompson, M. (2010). Peer victimization and effortful control: Relations to school engagement and academic achievement. *Merrill-Palmer Quarterly (Wayne State University Press), 56*(3), 361.

Juvonen, J., Wang, Y., & Espinoza, G. (2013). Physical aggression, spreading of rumors, and social prominence in early adolescence: Reciprocal effects supporting gender similarities? *Journal of Youth and Adolescence, 42*(12), 1801–1810.

Kessel Schneider, S., O'Donnell, L., & Smith, E. (2015). Trends in cyberbullying and school bullying victimization in a regional census of high school students, 2006–2012. *Journal of School Health, 85*(9), 611–620.

Kim, M. J., Catalano, R. F., Haggerty, K. P., & Abbott, R. D. (2011). Bullying at elementary school and problem behaviour in young adulthood: A study of bullying, violence and substance use from age 11 to age 21. *Criminal Behaviour and Mental Health, 21*(2), 136–144.

Konishi, C., Hymel, S., Zumbo, B. D., & Li, Z. (2010). Do school bullying and student-teacher relationships matter for academic achievement? A multilevel analysis. *Canadian Journal of School Psychology, 25*(1), 19–39.

Kosciw, J. G., Greytak, E. A., & Giga, N. M. (2015). *The 2015 National School Climate Survey: The experiences of lesbian, gay, bisexual, transgender, and queer youth in our Nation's Schools.* GLSEN.

Lazarus, R. S., & Folkman, S. (1984). *Stress, appraisal, and coping.* Springer

Lester, R., & Maldonado, N. (2014). Perceptions of middle school teachers about an anti-bullying program. Paper presented at the Annual Mid-South Educational Research (MSERA) conference. Knoxville, Tennessee, November 7, 2014.

Leuschner, V., Fiedler, N., Schultze, M., Ahlig, N., Göbel, K., Sommer, F., ... Scheithauer, H. (2017). Prevention of targeted school violence by responding to students' psychosocial crises: The NETWASS program. *Child Development, 88*(1), 68–82.

Li, Q. (2006). Cyberbullying in schools: A research of gender differences. *School Psychology International, 27*, 157–170. doi:10.1177/0143034306064547

Loeber, R., & Dishion, T. (1983). Early predictors of male delinquency: A review. *Psychological Bulletin, 94*(1), 68.

Machmutow, K., Perren, S., Sticca, F., & Alasker, F. D. (2012). Peer victimization and depressive symptoms: Can specific coping strategies buffer the negative impact of cybervictimization? *Emotional & Behavioural Difficulties, 17*, 403–420. doi:10.1080/13632752.2012.704310

Martínez, I., Murgui, S., García, O. F., & García, F. (2019). Parenting in the digital era: Protective and risk parenting styles for traditional bullying and cyberbullying victimization. *Computers in Human Behavior, 90*, 84–92.

Mazzone, A., & Camodeca, M. (2019). Bullying and moral disengagement in early adolescence: Do personality and family functioning matter? *Journal of Child and Family Studies, 28*(8), 2120–2130.

Merrell, K. W., Gueldner, B. A., Ross, S. W., & Isava, D. M. (2008). How effective are school bullying intervention programs? A meta-analysis of intervention research. *School Psychology Quarterly, 23*(1), 26–42

Meyer-Adams, N., & Conner, B. T. (2008). School violence: Bullying behaviors and the psychosocial school environment in middle schools. *Children & Schools, 30*(4), 211–221.

Mulder, S. F., & van Aken, M. A. (2014). Socially anxious children at risk for victimization: The role of personality. *Social Development, 23*(4), 719–733.

Nansel, T. R., Overpeck, M., Pilla, R. S., Ruan, W. J., Simons-Morton, B., & Scheidt, P. (2001). Bullying behaviors among US youth: Prevalence and association with psychosocial adjustment. *Journal of the American Medical Association, 285*(16), 2094–2100.

National Research Council and Institute of Medicine. (2009). *Preventing mental, emotional, and behavioral disorders among young people: Progress and possibilities.* National Academies Press.

Newman, M. L., Holden, G. W., & Delville, Y. (2005). Isolation and the stress of being bullied. *Journal of Adolescence, 28*(3), 343–357.

No Child Left Behind Act of 2001, 20 U.S.C. 70 § 6301 et seq.

Olafsen, R. N., & Viemerö, V. (2000). Bully/victim problems and coping with stress in school among 10- to 12-year-old pupils in Aland, Finland. *Aggressive Behavior, 26*, 57–65.

Olweus, D. (1978). *Aggression in the schools: Bullies and whipping boys.* Hemisphere.

Olweus, D. (1980). Familial and temperamental determinants of aggressive behavior in adolescent boys: A causal analysis. *Developmental Psychology, 16*(6), 644.

Olweus, D. (1993). *Bullying at school: What we know and what we can do.* Blackwell.

Olweus, D. (2013). School bullying: Development and some important challenges. *Annual Review of Clinical Psychology, 9*(1), 751–780.

Pabian, S., & Vandebosch, H. (2016). An investigation of short-term longitudinal associations between social anxiety and victimization and perpetration of traditional bullying and cyberbullying. *Journal of Youth and Adolescence, 45*(2), 328–339.

Patterson, G. R., DeBaryshe, B. D., & Ramsey, E. (1989). A developmental perspective on antisocial behavior (Vol. 44). *Washington, DC: American Psychological Association, 10,* 0146167211405994.

Peckham, S. (2007). Combating bullying. *Education Digest, 73*(1), 73.

Pepler, D., Jiang, D., Craig, W., & Connolly, J. (2008). Developmental trajectories of bullying and associated factors. *Child Development, 79*(2), 325–338.

Perlus, J. G., Brooks-Russell, A., Wang, J., & Iannotti, R. J. (2014). Trends in bullying, physical fighting, and weapon carrying among 6th-through 10th-grade students from 1998 to 2010: Findings from a national study. *American Journal of Public Health, 104*(6), 1100–1106.

Petrosino, A., Guckenburg, S., DeVoe, J., & Hanson, T. (2010). What Characteristics of Bullying, Bullying Victims, and Schools Are Associated with Increased Reporting of Bullying to School Officials? Issues & Answers. REL 2010-No. 092. *Regional Educational Laboratory Northeast & Islands.*

Pettit, G. S., & Bates, J. E. (1989). Family interaction patterns and children's behavior problems from infancy to 4 years. *Developmental Psychology, 25*(3), 413.

Prothrow-Stith, D., & Davis, R. A. (2010). A public health approach to preventing violence. In L. Cohen, V. Chavez, & S. Chehimi (Eds.), *Prevention is primary: Strategies for community well-being* (2nd ed., pp. 323–350). San Francisco, CA: Jossey-Bass.

Rayner, C. (1999). From research to implementation: Finding leverage for prevention. *International Journal of Manpower, 20*, 28–38.

Saluja, G., Iachan, R., Scheidt, P. C., Overpeck, M. D., Sun, W., & Giedd, J. N. (2004). Prevalence of and risk factors for depressive symptoms among young adolescents. *Archives of Pediatrics & Adolescent Medicine, 158*(8), 760–765.

Samara, M., & Smith, P. K. (2008). How schools tackle bullying, and the use of whole school policies: Changes over the last decade. *Educational Psychology, 28*(6), 663–676.

Schreier, A., Wolke, D., Thomas, K., Horwood, J., Hollis, C., Gunnell, D., . . . Salvi, G. (2009). Prospective study of peer victimization in childhood and psychotic symptoms in a nonclinical population at age 12 years. *Archives of General Psychiatry, 66*(5), 527–536.

Schwartz, D., Dodge, K. A., Pettit, G. S., & Bates, J. E. (1997). The early socialization of aggressive victims of bullying. *Child Development, 68*(4), 665–675.

Seals, D., & Young, J. (2003). Bullying and victimization: Prevalence and relationship to gender, grade level, ethnicity, self-esteem, and depression. *Adolescence, 38*(152), 735-747.

Sharp, S., & Smith, P. (2002). *School bullying: Insights and perspectives.* Routledge.

Shetgiri, R., Lin, H., & Flores, G. (2013). Trends in risk and protective factors for child bullying perpetration in the United States. *Child Psychiatry & Human Development, 44*(1), 89–104.

Stanton, L., & Beran, T. (2009). A review of legislation and bylaws relevant to bullying. *McGill Journal of Education/Revue des sciences de l'éducation de McGill, 44*(2), 245–260.

Strassberg, Z., Dodge, K. A., Pettit, G. S., & Bates, J. E. (1994). Spanking in the home and children's subsequent aggression toward kindergarten peers. *Development and Psychopathology, 6*(3), 445–461.

Stuart-Cassel, V., Bell, A., & Springer, J. F. (2011). Analysis of State Bullying Laws and Policies. *Office of Planning, Evaluation and Policy Development, US Department of Education.*

Takizawa, R., Maughan, B., & Arseneault, L. (2014). Adult health outcomes of childhood bullying victimization: evidence from a five-decade longitudinal British birth cohort. *American Journal of Psychiatry, 171*(7), 777–784.

Tenenbaum, L. S., Varjas, K., Meyers, J., & Parris, L. (2011). Coping strategies and perceived effectiveness in fourth through eighth grade victims of bullying. *School Psychology International, 32*(3), 263–287.

Ttofi, M. M., & Farrington, D. P. (2011). Effectiveness of school-based programs to reduce bullying: A systematic and meta-analytic review. *Journal of Experimental Criminology, 7,* 27–56.

Vreeman, R. C., & Carroll, A. E. (2007). A systematic review of school-based interventions to prevent bullying. *Archives of Pediatrics & Adolescent Medicine, 161*(1), 78–88.

Watson, S., & Miller, T. (2012). LGBT oppression. *Multicultural Education, 19*(4), 2–7.

World Health Organization. (2014). *Global status report on violence prevention 2014.* Geneva: World Health Organization.

Ybarra, M. L. (2004). Linkages between depressive symptomatology and Internet harassment among young regular Internet users. *CyberPsychology & Behavior, 7*(2), 247–257.

Ybarra, M. L., & Mitchell, K. J. (2004). Youth engaging in online harassment: Associations with caregiver–child relationships, Internet use, and personal characteristics. *Journal of Adolescence, 27*(3), 319–336.

Ybarra, M. L., Mitchell, K. J., & Korchmaros, J. D. (2011). National trends in exposure to and experiences of violence on the Internet among children. *Pediatrics, 128*(6), e1376–e1386.

9
Antisocial Behavior and Addiction

Overview

This chapter discusses aggression, antisocial behavior, and addiction in youth. These behaviors can include bullying, threatening, intimidation, physical fights, being cruel to people or animals, using weapons, or sexual assault (American Psychological Association, 2010). Antisocial behavior can cause serious and wide-ranging consequences within families, schools, and communities. Major types of aggressive and antisocial behaviors are addressed here, along with their interplay among neurobiological processes, protective factors, and gender variables. In addition, we cover both process addiction and substance abuse in this chapter. Though the grouping of addictions with antisocial behavior may be somewhat controversial, given both the genetic predisposition and behavioral components to addiction we felt that addressing both of these components were pertinent since the biopsychosocial model is a component to understanding and treatment of both. The Centers for Disease Control and Prevention (2019) address both antisocial behaviors and addictions in the Youth Risk Behavior Surveillance System, and addressing these issues in conjunction with generalized risk and contributing factors reflects how these issues often appear together.

Issues of addiction—both process addictions and substance use disorders—encompass an entire field of study within itself, including separate licensures and certifications to practice with individuals struggling with addiction. Hence, a comprehensive overview of addictions in youth is outside the scope of this text, but we felt it was pertinent to address the topic from a systemic perspective. Origin, assessment, interventions, and outcome studies are also reviewed.

Introduction

As a professional you begin to feel your tenure when you work with kids from a young age and watch them grow up and begin to age out of the services you provide. With clients who have been identified as having antisocial behaviors in early childhood, these behaviors can persist and even escalate as they go through adolescence and enter adulthood. These clients can be particularly challenging to work with at times and certainly require a great deal of case management and supportive services; these clients can maintain a presence on your caseload for a long period of time.

> **Case Study: Caleb**
>
> Thirteen years ago, a young child (age 4) walked into my counseling center. He wore denim jeans and a blue dinosaur sweatshirt. At first sight, he was cute and energetic. I could have never predicted what I would learn during the intake session with his grandmother and aunt. Caleb had a tough 4 years of existence. His mother had been in prison for the past 2 years and prior to that her boyfriend (Caleb's father) had been arrested for violence against not only the mother but for neglect and abuse against Caleb. The grandmother and aunt had held primary guardianship since that time. Caleb had never slept well, eaten well, or hit his developmental milestones according to his pediatrician. The grandmother had tried to take a firm hand to Caleb but the more she spanked him the worse he behaved. She and the aunt were desperate, and, thanks to guidance from the Head Start teachers at Caleb's preschool, they had been referred to our center after Caleb's latest incident.
>
> The week prior, Caleb's cousins came for a visit and brought their new puppy along. All the kids were outside running around and playing with it; all seemed fine until the puppy got too excited and bit Caleb. Caleb became enraged; he got so upset that he began to kick the puppy. Caleb got in trouble; his grandmother spanked him and sent him to his room. Later that afternoon, Caleb snuck out of the house, grabbed the puppy, and drowned him in the creek behind their house. The grandmother and aunt were so shocked and appalled by his behavior they didn't even know where to begin. They knew Caleb wasn't well-behaved, but this vengeful and violent behavior shocked them. Caleb also had a 2½-year-old sister named Trisha, and they now were concerned for her safety. They needed to talk to someone quickly, so Monday morning they sought out Caleb's preschool teacher for help.

> That was 13 years ago, and let's just say the case file on Caleb is thick. He has been in and out of individual counseling, group counseling, day treatment, and two 30-day stints of residential treatment. He takes three different types of medication daily (or at least, this is what is prescribed) and is currently under the care of a pediatrician and pediatric psychiatrist. Despite the rural area in which he lives, his grandmother and aunt have been diligent about driving Caleb to specialists for treatment as needed. He's 17 now, and his antisocial behaviors have been consistent throughout childhood, escalating since the onset of puberty. Caleb has been arrested twice for misdemeanor assault charges and is currently in a juvenile justice facility. He turns 18 next month and would like to earn his GED and get a job. Since both of Caleb's parents have been in prison the majority of his life, his services have been provided by the state; however, next month, many of those services will come to an end. Unfortunately for Caleb, despite numerous interventions, his antisocial behaviors only continue to escalate and without continued support there are serious concerns for what adulthood might look like for him. Caleb is not alone in this journey.

There are a lot of other "Caleb's" out there whose behaviors persist and escalate throughout childhood into adolescence and adulthood. Outcomes are often bleak, and resources are minimal at times. However, research does show that there are factors that can positively influence youth like Caleb. In the following sections, those factors, along with origin, assessment, interventions, and outcome studies, are reviewed.

What Is Antisocial Behavior?

When discussing the term "antisocial behavior," you must first acknowledge the breadth of the term. Antisocial behaviors span a wide range and present themselves within a continuum of severity. They are often defined as aggressive, rule-breaking, and troubling behaviors (Connor, 2004). These behaviors can include bullying, threatening, intimidation, physical fights, being cruel to people or animals, using weapons, or sexual assault (American Psychological Association, 2010). Antisocial behavior is most commonly categorized into oppositional-defiant disorder (ODD) and conduct disorder (CD), with ODD focusing on early age-inappropriate or disruptive behaviors and CD focused on aggression and behaviors that involve hurting (e.g., initiating fights), overpowering (e.g., stealing), and status offenses (e.g., truancy) (Hinshaw & Lee, 2003).

Antisocial behavior is a prevalent problem in adolescent development (Nock et al., 2006). Antisocial behavior typically begins to emerge during middle childhood but often experiences a significant increase in frequency in early adolescence (Moffitt, 1993). Antisocial behavior is more commonly exhibited by males, while females are more likely to develop antisocial behavior later in adolescence and in young adulthood (Marmorstein & Iacono, 2005; Silverthorn & Frick, 1999). Youth tend to exhibit antisocial behavior for extended periods of time, and behaviors often fluctuate in severity (Lahey et al., 1995). Antisocial behavior can cause serious and extensive consequences within a school, community or family; therefore, effective interventions for antisocial behavior need to be a priority for researchers, family resource centers, school systems, and community leaders. Despite significant research identifying meaningful and reliable correlations of antisocial behavior, implementing effective interventions on a wide scale has remained challenging in most schools and communities.

Previous studies have indicated that antisocial behavior is associated with a wide number of outcomes across a variety of domains including cognitive development, attachment, personality and temperament, peer relationships, and community (Dodge & Pettit, 2003). Some of these variables persist throughout the adolescent's development into adulthood, while others tend to be more fluid. According to Ward and Beech (2015), additional research is needed to identify causal antecedents, causal consequences, and alternative manifestations of the associated variables.

Research studies have also distinguished those individuals who engage in frequent delinquent behaviors from the general population in ways that extend beyond simply breaking or not breaking the law (Jessor & Jessor, 1977; Na, 2017; Thornberry et al. 1995; Vitaro et al., 2005). Some findings are summarized here.

- In middle childhood, these individuals tend to be overactive, disruptive, oppositional, and have extreme difficulties in forming peer relationships.
- In middle childhood, these individuals tend to be impulsive and seek out risky behaviors/activities.

- In adolescence, these individuals tend to be more inclined to show feelings of depression, have difficulty reading, and use drugs.
- In later adolescents, these individuals tend to struggle with impulse control, which often results in drinking heavily, drug use, unemployment, intimate partner violence, gambling, anger, and violence.

These studies show that the extent to which an adolescent engages in this broader range of behaviors varies greatly. However, it should be noted that any study that examines antisocial behaviors must consider factors involved in driving these behaviors, and, at the root of this broader range of behaviors is an *antisocial lifestyle*, a term often referred to in academic literature.

What Is a Process Addiction?

Process addictions, also known as *behavioral addictions*, are addictions characterized by a strong impulse to partake in a specific behavior. An individual with a process addiction engages in said behavior even when it results in harmful consequences to their emotional, interpersonal, or physical well-being. It is difficult for the person to refrain from partaking in the behavior, which results in the need for treatment or intervention to stop such behavior.

Gaming

As therapists, it is widely known that gambling is one such process addiction. While gambling isn't necessarily such a widespread addiction for teens today, gaming is. Gaming disorder is defined in the 11th Revision of the *International Classification of Diseases* (ICD-11) as a pattern of gaming behavior ("digital-gaming" or "video-gaming") characterized by impaired control over gaming; increasing priority given to gaming over other activities, to the extent that gaming takes precedence over other interests and daily activities; and continuation or escalation of gaming despite the occurrence of negative consequences. For gaming disorder to be diagnosed, the behavior pattern must be of sufficient severity to result in significant impairment in personal, family, social, educational, occupational, or other important areas of functioning, and the pattern is normally evident for at least 12 months (World Health Organization [WHO], 2019). In 2013, the American

Psychiatric Association (APA) determined that internet gaming disorder (IGD) requires further research and data accumulation and included IGD in section III of the *Diagnostic and Statistical Manual of Mental Disorders* (DSM-5; APA, 2013). In the DSM-5, five of the nine diagnosis criteria (preoccupation or obsession, withdrawal, tolerance, loss of control, loss of interest, continued overuse, deceiving, escape of negative feelings, functional impairment) must be met within a year to confirm the diagnosis of IGD. The largest study to date conducted on teenage video game addiction and the effects of video game addiction was published in 2020. Sarah M. Coyne and her team followed 385 adolescents over 6 years. During this time, 10% of gamers exhibited pathological video gaming behavior that got worse over the years (Coyne et al., 2020).

Treatment of IGD may use either cognitive behavior therapy (CBT) or dialectical behavior therapy (DBT). CBT helps teens to identify and modify thought and behavior patterns. CBT supports teens in shifting from negative toward positive behaviors. DBT helps teens acknowledge the unhealthy behaviors they are using to cope with deeper underlying issues. Additionally, DBT helps teens find ways to modify these behaviors. Both CBT and DBT have been found to be helpful interventions for therapists to use with teens addicted to gaming.

Internet and Social Media

Adolescents and teens today have never lived in a world without the internet, Wi-Fi, Bluetooth, and various forms of social media. Adolescents' addictive use of social media and the internet is an increasing concern among parents, teachers, researchers, and others. Excessive use of social networking sites can have negative implications, such as negative mood states, concentration problems, and less interest in spending time with friends and family (Ostovar et al., 2016). Due to the increasingly accelerated development of smartphones and the fact that they are convenient to carry on the person, mobile phones are replacing the internet as a primary addictive source (Barnes et al., 2019). Adolescents have been identified as a group at risk for smartphone addiction, and a recent meta-analysis suggests that one in four adolescents presents problematic smartphone use (Sohn et al., 2021). Whether chasing "likes" on social media platforms, a need to constantly communicate or interact with others, or the desire to share nearly every detail of their lives, adolescents are constantly "plugged in." Symptoms of an internet or social media addiction include identifying with several of the following statements:

1. Finding oneself preoccupied with posting or sharing mundane details of day-to-day life
2. Checking or refreshing apps and social media sites to review an accurate number of likes, comments, or messages
3. Becoming distracted from performing other tasks (including chores, work, or academic assignments) due to being engrossed in social media
4. Having the desire to "log off" or disengage from social media but finding oneself unable to do so
5. Wearing outfits or attending events with the sole purpose of posting on social media
6. Using a device or checking social media as soon as one wakes up
7. Using a device or checking social media up until the moment that one falls asleep
8. The desire or practice of being "plugged in" or having screen time on devices even while in intimate settings or small gatherings (such as during meals, baths, visits with friends or family members)
9. Increased irritability when the use of the internet or a device is unavailable or prohibited
10. Strong changes in mood or affect related to social media interaction (praise, affirmations, number of friend requests or page visits, etc.)

Therapists may provide interventions for adolescents who wish to treat a social media or internet addiction. Often, parents will seek intervention out of concern for their child or in an effort to avoid the negative implications that youth are especially vulnerable to through such addictive behaviors.

Shopping

Though widely accepted as a process addiction, the addiction to shopping, also known as *oniomania*, is not currently recognized in the DSM-5-TR. Because of the financial accessibility required, shopping addiction is not nearly as common among teens as internet or gaming addiction. Due perhaps to lack or inaccessibility of funds, many teens do not have the opportunity to develop a shopping addiction (compulsive or impulsive shopping). In a 2012 study, one of the largest at that time, Grant et al. found that approximately 3.5% of high school students experienced problem shopping, compared to 1.9% of college students and 5.8% of adults, which further supported findings that problem shopping may frequently start in adolescence. In their study, problem shopping was associated with multiple measures of adverse functioning, including occasional and regular smoking, drug use, endorsement of sadness and hopelessness, and other antisocial behaviors such as fighting and carrying weapons (Grant et al., 2011). Students with problem shopping reported symptoms that appear consistent with other addictive behaviors: urges to shop, attempts to cut back, missed opportunities due to behavior, and a calming effect of shopping. Excessive or compulsive shopping may co-occur with other addictive behaviors or substance abuse (e.g., alcohol, drugs, or nicotine).

The highest prevalence of compulsive shopping among adolescents can be seen in females. Furthermore, adolescents who often use toxic substances also experienced a greater frequency of desires to purchase unnecessary products without evaluating the suitability of those products. Additionally, the nonuse of toxic substances was related to a lower score in compulsive buying (Pérez de Albéniz-Garrote et al., 2021). Thus, substance abuse could be considered a risk factor or vulnerability for adolescents to develop co-occurring disorders in the future. This again points to a strong relationship between buying addiction and substance addiction. In increasingly consumerist societies, buying has turned into a leisure activity which creates a short-term feeling of wellness but which can also provoke feelings of guilt. In the United States, it's not uncommon for adolescents to have their own bank accounts, credit cards, or payment apps. For teens, accessibility of funds combined with the prevalence of online stores and shopping apps ensures that shopping can be done at the click of a button. While convenient, this can quickly become an uncontrolled habit or addiction.

Sexting

Sexting includes sexually suggestive texts or images sent digitally, usually via text message or other use of technology. While sexting itself is not a recognized addiction in the DSM-5-TR, we found it important to include in this chapter, mostly due to how closely related sexting is to internet and social media addictions. Adolescents who have behavioral or emotional issues may be especially vulnerable to sexting, which may lead them to engage in other sexual behaviors at an early age (Houck et al., 2014). Several studies have identified a relationship between cyberbullying and sexting behaviors (Darden et al., 2019). In previous years, the body of research regarding sexting behaviors has increased dramatically, especially research focused on adolescent and teenage populations. This subject and related research is of considerable relevance to parents, the education community, and healthcare practitioners working with young people who engage in or are addicted to this behavior.

Many investigations have linked sexting behaviors to impulsivity and substance abuse problems. In addition, sexting is related to bad judgment, sensation seeking, and problematic alcohol and drug use, as well as to suicide (Döring, 2014). The vast majority of studies have found a positive association between depressive symptoms and sexting behaviors (Klettke et al., 2019). Chaudhary et al. (2017) conducted a study with 1,760 teens and found that youth who reported sexting were significantly more likely to report symptomatology of depression and anxiety compared to those who did not report sexting. Specifically, their results showed that between 20% and 27% of youth who sexted had depressive symptoms. The exchange of intimate photos or videos increases the risk of being victimized, not only by the direct sender or recipient of the image-based sexual content but by anyone who might have access to it, as teens might find themselves involuntarily exposed to unwanted sexual content. Teenage boys and girls who engage in sexting behaviors have shown a higher risk of reporting suicidal thoughts even after controlling for cyber victimization and depression (Medrano et al., 2018). Like internet and social media addictions, sexting behavior is extremely common among adolescents and can quickly become a compulsive or addictive behavior for some teens. Because of the negative implications and potential for victimization, it is recommended that therapists and parents alike keep abreast of research related to the correlations and association between mental health and sexting behaviors. Furthermore, knowledge of sexting behavior specifically may aid therapists who assist teens with interventions for other types of addictions that are commonly seen in conjunction with this behavior.

Substance Use and Abuse

Alcohol remains the most widely used substance among America's youth, and drinking by young people poses enormous health and safety risks (National

Institute on Alcohol Abuse and Alcoholism [NIAAA], 2004). The diagnostic criteria for alcohol abuse and dependence are detailed in DSM-5-TR. To meet the diagnosis of abuse, one of four abuse criteria must be met. To meet a diagnosis of dependence, three of seven dependence criteria must be met. In general, *substance abuse* is characterized by a maladaptive pattern of use indicated by continued use despite consequences or recurrent use where such use may be physically hazardous. *Substance dependence* is characterized as a chronic and progressive disorder characterized by loss of control over use, compulsion, and continued use despite consequences (APA, 2022). Family systems exert significant influence on adolescents and on the behaviors in which teens choose to engage. Early identification of children, adolescents, and families with alcohol-related problems is critically important to prevent problem alcohol use among adolescents. Early consumption of larger volumes of alcohol may lead to continuation of this pattern of consumption in adult life with resulting poorer educational achievement, increased welfare benefit receipt, and other substance use disorders. Early symptoms of alcohol use disorder led to increased adult levels of mental health disorders (Boden et al., 2020). According to the 2019 NSDUH, an estimated 414,000 adolescents ages 12–17 had alcohol use disorder. This number includes 163,000 males and 251,000 females. Alcohol remains the most prevalent addiction among adolescents in the United States. Adolescent youth may underestimate the detrimental effects of alcohol abuse simply due to how widespread and common alcohol consumption is, and many parents are fully aware of underage consumption or abuse. Still, therapists should prepare to work diligently with adolescents, educators, and families in an effort to reduce and ultimately eliminate adolescent substance abuse.

The percentage of adolescents reporting substance use decreased significantly in 2021 according to the latest results from the Monitoring the Future survey of substance use behaviors and related attitudes among 8th-, 10th-, and 12th-graders in the United States. These findings represent the largest 1-year decrease in overall illicit drug use reported since the survey began in 1975. According to the National Survey Results on Drug Abuse (Johnston et al., 2021), marijuana use among 8th–12th graders did not increase despite a decrease in adolescents' perceived risk. In fact, the 2021 survey reported significant decreases in use across many substances, including those most commonly used in adolescence: alcohol, marijuana, and vaped nicotine. This year, the study surveyed students on their mental health during the COVID-19 pandemic. Students across all age groups reported moderate increases in feelings of boredom, anxiety, depression, loneliness, worry, difficulty sleeping, and other negative mental health indicators since the beginning of the pandemic. Never before had such dramatic decreases in drug use among teens been observed in just a 1-year period. These data are unprecedented and highlight one unexpected potential consequence of the COVID-19 pandemic, which caused seismic shifts in the day-to-day lives of adolescents.

While exact reasons for the decrease in reported substance abuse by minors could be due to the increase in family cohesiveness or increased parental involvement, further research is needed to explore these theories. Though this downward trend in reported substance abuse by adolescents is favorable, therapists should not be misled: risky, addictive behaviors are still prevalent among teens. In addition to alcohol and marijuana, adolescents also use some of the less common drugs: party drugs such as ecstasy (Molly), cocaine, opioids, and methamphetamines. Behavioral approaches such as CBT, group therapy, and family therapy approaches such as family behavior therapy or multisystemic therapy are effective interventions for use with adolescents trying to overcome substance abuse or addiction issues.

Systemic Factors Related to Antisocial Behavior and Addiction

Genetics

Disentangling the influences of nature and nurture is a fundamental step toward the goal of explaining the origin of antisocial behavior (Dishion & Patterson, 2006; Rhee & Waldman, 2002). Research on the origin of antisocial behavior primarily has focused almost exclusively on the role of dysfunctional family or environmental influences, such as poverty, parental wellness, coercive parenting, abuse, and family conflict. Still, not all youth exposed to social adversity develop antisocial behavior, and some youth become antisocial in spite of having a favorable social or environmental background. Discussions around the development of antisocial behaviors and addiction often focus only on environmental factors and skim over arguments regarding possible genetic influences (Kazdin, 2018). However, within the past decade there is a growing consensus that both individual-specific (genetics) and social (adversity) factors contribute to the development and maintenance of antisocial behavior (Frazier et al., 2019). Specifically, there is increasing evidence that biological factors that are organic to the individual youth intensify the risk of antisocial behaviors for those who live with social adversity. Because previous studies have shown that youth who display disruptive behaviors are more likely to have parents who display antisocial behaviors themselves, it's certainly a logical conclusion to say that antisocial behaviors and addiction are possibly inherited (Brazil et al., 2018). The next extension of course is trying to identify specific genes that demonstrate an increased risk of antisocial behavior. Within this body of research, there is also exploration into early exposure to trauma and the long-lasting impact of abuse and neglect on the brain and overall function (Ryan et al., 2017). At present, there is still a great deal to understand and additional research is needed; however, it is clear that genetic factors are involved and can influence the development of antisocial behavior(s). As therapists, a better understanding of how neurobiology relates to antisocial and aggressive behavior and a predisposition to addiction will be critical for the prevention and treatment of chronic antisocial behavior in youth and adolescents.

Gender

Gender differences between male and female adolescents have been found to exist in the overall frequency of antisocial behaviors (Perkins & Borden, 2003) and in the different types of engagement in antisocial behavior (Underwood, 2004; Rose & Smith, 2018). Typically, adolescent males are more likely to engage in antisocial behavior than females (Vaillancourt & Krems, 2018). Males have also been found to be more blatantly antisocial than females, and females tend to engage in covert behaviors rather than overtly antisocial behaviors (Gorman-Smith & Loeber, 2005; Smaragdi et al., 2017). *Overt antisocial behavior* is described as a direct form of aggression, such as physical or verbal aggression. *Covert antisocial behavior* is described as using modest or unassuming ways of harming others. This type of behavior is designed to damage relationships (especially peer relationships in the adolescent period) or create social isolation; engaging in such acts is an indirect form of antisocial behavior (Loeber et al., 2005).

When examining gender difference in behaviors within a social media realm, males compared to females are more likely to engage in antisocial behaviors when online, such as cyberbullying and misrepresenting positive information about themselves, especially when females were resistant to communication (Guadagno et al., 2012). Males are also much more likely to engage in misogynistic language that demeans females along with engaging in harassing behaviors. Social media is also often a host to overt antisocial behavior such as harassment, which is often centered around outward appearances and weight-based bullying (Thompson et al., 2018).

Family Dynamics

Previous research studies leave little doubt that family dynamics greatly influence a child's likelihood of engaging in antisocial behaviors. Regardless of gender, being born to an unmarried mother almost doubles an individual's risk of participating in risky behaviors, while being born to an unmarried mother under the age of 18 triples the risk (Furstenberg et al., 1987; Maynard, 1997; Crugnola et al., 2019). Of course, it should be noted that there are associations between girls who demonstrate antisocial behaviors and teenage pregnancy, and this can be partnered with risky social connections and lead to poor parenting practices (Moffit & Caspi, 2001; Lange et al., 2019). Decades of research have documented the ties between family dynamics across several dimensions and the development of antisocial behaviors, but less is known about specific subgroups of family functioning and the risks for and protective factors against antisocial behaviors (Braga et al., 2017).

According to the literature, three primary family domains contribute to the development of adolescent antisocial behaviors: family-level functioning, parent–child relationship, and parenting abilities (Fosco & LoBraico, 2019). Family-level functioning (Moos, 1994), is represented by family conflict and positive family climate as two distinct feature domains and is predictive of future development for adolescent behaviors. Family conflict includes anger, aggression, and disregard and predicts adolescent violent behaviors in peer relationships (Benson & Buehler, 2012). The parent–child relationship is also a key indicator in the development of risky behaviors. A strong parent–child relationship, which includes parental involvement and positive adolescent connection with the family, is a protective factor against the development of antisocial behaviors. When the parent–child relationship is weak and includes little time together, poor communication, and little or no joint activities, the adolescent is at more than double the risk of engaging in unwanted behaviors. A strong relationship increases the likelihood that an adolescent is going to be receptive to guidance from the parent, and this ultimately reduces the prospect of poor behaviors. Parenting skills are the core of a positive or negative parent–child relationship. Parent knowledge and supportive discipline are two key factors that make up positive parenting skills. Parent knowledge includes an awareness of what the child/adolescent is engaged in, their whereabouts, and their activities (Kiesner et al., 2009). Parental supervision is pivotal in providing a protective factor for adolescent behaviors. *Supportive discipline* refers to positive reinforcers, reasoning, and exclusion of harsh punishments such as spanking or hitting. The absence of harsh discipline greatly reduces the risk of development antisocial behaviors and, when positive reinforcers are used in a consistent manner, works to support positive prosocial behaviors (Halgunseth et al., 2013).

Family dynamics are also greatly influenced by environmental factors such as poverty, unemployment, and community. Some researchers argue that some environmental factors are only indirectly associated with the development of antisocial behavior and that stronger predictors are linked to the family domains previously mentioned, such as ineffective parenting and poor supervision (Patterson, 2016). Family life certainly is multidimensional, and more than likely it is a combination of numerous variables that contribute to the development of unwanted behaviors in children and adolescents. However, researchers do agree that parenting is a central and critical risk factor for predicting future behaviors (McQuillan & Bates, 2017). Programming to support young parents and delivering resources for providing care and building positive parent–child relationships are key to helping future generations avoid the risk of developing risky and potentially harmful behaviors.

Community and Neighborhoods

Certain elements within the community or neighborhood in which youth live and spend their time may possibly make them more at risk for antisocial behaviors. Early work on risky lifestyles conducted by Sampson and Luritsen (1994) extensively studied community-based risk and found that social disorganization and changes within neighborhoods and communities are two prevalent factors in predicting increased rates of youth violent behaviors and criminal activities. Youth who live in areas of highly concentrated poverty are twice as likely to engage in antisocial behaviors as those in middle-class neighborhoods (Karyda, 2020). An even more alarming finding is that youth living in disorganized neighborhoods with high crime rates, drugs, gangs, and poor-quality housing showed not only a higher propensity for engaging in risky behaviors, but also are more likely to engage in a greater variety of risky and violent acts, especially during late adolescence (Boyle et al., 2019).

According to Fowler et al. (2009), neighborhood and community effects on antisocial behaviors may be particularly impactful during middle childhood. Research has documented that children who are exposed to community violence at early ages are more prone to violent behaviors in adolescence. A similar impact can be seen in children who attend community schools with high delinquency rates; these children are more prone to engage in similar behaviors (Wolf & Baglivio, 2017; Wolf et al., 2017). Understanding the compelling relationship between community and violence risk is important to note when working with youth. Children and youth who dwell in these neighborhoods and communities should be considered at high risk due to their repeated and potentially traumatic exposure to violence.

Schools

If you're a therapist who has ever worked within or in collaboration with a school then you know that the most often received mental health referral is based on rule-breaking behaviors within the classroom. According to Hess et al. (2014), studies have consistently found that behavioral disorders (attention-deficit/hyperactivity disorder, CD, and ODD) are the most frequently diagnosed psychiatric disorders in school-aged children and adolescents. When students who have been diagnosed with a behavioral disorder break classroom norms or rules, they are often removed from the classroom environment, either through in-school suspension or, for more extreme behavior (such as fighting), out-of-school suspension. Bear (2012) explains that the system is established in a way that provides little flexibility to school administrators: strict "zero tolerance" codes of conduct and state legislation often require out-of-school suspension for certain antisocial behaviors. Removal from the classroom often has adverse effects on the student. Eivers et al. (2010) explained that it is essential for children to be present and engaged in the classroom to adjust successfully to the school environment. Ryan and Goodram (2013) stated that dismissing students with disruptive or antisocial behaviors from the classroom has a negative impact on the students' academic, emotional, and social development and that, for the majority of students, removal from the classroom does not influence future behavior. In fact, students often continue to display antisocial behaviors and further perpetuate this cycle of disruptive behaviors and school discipline, which can end with students being placed in an alternative school setting, expulsed, or dropping out.

Intervening with students who are struggling with their behavior is essential. School leaders, therapist, and teachers must all work collaboratively to help students change negative classroom behaviors. When students continually display antisocial behavior they also become increasingly at risk for academic failure, grade level retention, social isolation, and, ultimately, dropping out (Teske, 2011). Excluding students from school does not teach students alternative prosocial behaviors and might reinforce antisocial behavior, which has a negative impact on a student's overall development (Sharkey & Fenning, 2012). Kline (2016) also warned that if preventative measures are not implemented in schools, in addition to interfering with academic success, recurrent antisocial behavior increases the likelihood of students' entering the "school-to-prison pipeline," which results in a burden to both the community and society at large. According to Henggeler and Schoenwald (2011), the juvenile system handles more than 1,000,000 adolescents each year, and yet much still stays the same for these individuals, with only 5% of those adolescents who are high risk receiving mental health services such as family and behavioral therapy.

Finding alternative ways to support and retain students in school while delivering effective evidenced-based interventions to assist students in developing skills to manage behavior must be a priority for every school district. The issue for many school districts is a lack of qualified trained mental health professionals (i.e., school counselors) within the schools (most school counselors carry a caseload that is two to three times higher than recommended by the American School Counseling Association [2019]). School districts also face shortages in regards to programming, which costs money to purchase and supply to students for behavioral modifications and support. However, it should be noted that many children who struggle with behavioral issues do not necessarily qualify for services under the Individuals with Disabilities Education Act (IDEA). Therefore, they may not be receiving modifications within the classroom to help support positive behavioral changes. This is why many school districts across the country have moved to more universal programming, such as Positive Behavioral Interventions and Supports (PBIS), to help address school-wide student outcomes regardless of eligibility (Pas et al. 2019). Egan and Bull (2020) highlight the importance of implementing interventions designed to reduce and prevent high-risk behaviors because, when preventative measures are implemented correctly, research shows positive results in reducing antisocial behavior and school expulsions and increasing academic achievement.

Peer Groups

Consistently throughout professional literature, researchers have found that there is a strong peer connection to antisocial behavior and substance use in youth and adolescence (Cook et al., 2009; Erickson & Jensen, 1977; Shaw & McKay, 1931, 1969; Sijtsema & Lindenberg, 2018; Toro et al., 2004). According to Moffit (1993) teenagers' desire to influence peers is the primary source of most of the delinquency acts that occur during their adolescent developmental period. When compared to behaviors by adults, antisocial behaviors committed by teenagers are much more likely to occur in peer groups (de Jong et al., 2019), and peer pressure has been theorized to be an important instigator of a wide range of troubling behavior in youth, including acts of delinquency, violent offenses, reckless driving, and drug and alcohol use (Waddell et al., 2021).

There are two primary sources of peer influence on risky group behaviors. The first is the consistent exposure to peers during this developmental period. Adolescents spend a large bulk of their time with their peer group, either in school or outside of the school day. This extended period of time provides plenty of opportunities to participate in dangerous or risky behaviors. The secondary source is the importance that adolescents place on peer relationships. During adolescence, peer groups and their opinions, attitudes, and perceptions take on an unprecedented importance, even more so than family or adult perceptions that might have previously had more influence. This is especially true for those adolescents who are particularly vulnerable to outside influences (Mason et al., 2019). Those who care for and work with youth should be aware that individuals tend to gravitate toward others with a similar mindset or interest, which is typically termed *peer similarity* and can encompass involvement with and tolerance of antisocial behaviors (Gardner & Steinberg, 2005). While research has clearly documented how peer influences tend to lessen as individuals move from adolescence to early adulthood, less is known as to exactly why. Additional research is needed to identify why peer dynamics and antisocial behaviors seem to change in early adulthood (Lamblin et al., 2017).

Assessment and Treatments

As the tools for assessing antisocial behaviors have improved, so have treatments and interventions. This is essentially because assessment and treatment go hand in hand. Strong assessments lead to strong interventions and treatments. A robust behavior assessment will not only determine a level of risk, it can also identify factors, contexts, and other variables that can affect behavior for better or worse. From here, the intervention is constructed to formulate an appropriate plan based on the level of treatment required.

Since the 1980s, research related to assessing risky or potentially violent behaviors among youth and adolescents has advanced considerably more slowly than for other populations, such as psychiatric patients or criminal offenders (Hart & Logan, 2011; Heffernan & Ward, 2017). However, some researchers have taken the advances made in adult populations and are applying those to improve behavior assessments for children and adolescents. Further research regarding the accuracy of assessments in predicting the risk of harmful or violent behavior in adolescent populations is lacking, but there have been a few noteworthy findings over the past couple of decades. Research conducted within the past decade or so examines a wider range of risk factors and multiple sources of information (Shoemaker, 2018). This broadened lens has led to stronger predictive validity and promises of more robust future research. Essentially, there is no gold standard for behavior assessments in children and adolescent populations. The more recent consensus among researchers and behavior experts is that the best approach is not a single measure or method, but the use of multiple informants and measures (De Los Reyes et al., 2013; Dirks et al., 2012; Frick et al., 2014; Makol et al., 2020).

Behavior Interventions

Over the past few decades, researchers have made significant progress in developing interventions that exhibit positive effects on youth antisocial behavior (O'Connell et al., 2009). Within the professional literature, there are two primary bodies of work: prevention and therapy. Researchers throughout the literature have identified numerous interventions that prevent or reduce antisocial behavior in adolescent populations for the short term, but evidence of long-term intervention benefits has only recently become available. Given the availability and publication of evidenced-based interventions for antisocial behavior in adolescence, it is concerning that systems that serve youth (e.g., education, mental health, juvenile justice, public health) are still straining to meet the needs of youths at risk for or already demonstrating risky behavior (Henggeler & Schoenwald, 2011). Funding and resources for many of these evidence-based interventions remain low in these systems (Greenwood, 2008), and several interventions (such as wilderness challenge programs) that have been found to have little to no effect or even negative effects on youth continue to be widely used (Lipsey, 2009). Interventions to prevent and treat antisocial behavior in youth attempt to address one or more risk factors. While there is no standard or professional typology to describe these intervention strategies, here we categorize them into four main groups: family and early childhood interventions, youth and adolescent interventions, community-level interventions, and multisystemic interventions.

Family and Early Childhood Interventions
Young parenthood, poverty, inconsistent parenting styles, and erratic supervision by a single parent create a construct of variables that put children at increased risk of future antisocial behavior (Bornstein, 2015). Children born to young and unsupported/unprepared parents are more likely to be neglected and abused and, as a result, are more likely to victimize others later in life (Bland et al., 2018). Inadequate social support of parents is a significant link to a child's antisocial behavior because family factors are key and play an important role in the development of delinquency. Interventions and treatments with families to reduce violent/antisocial behavior can take many forms. Interventions that affect one or more risk factors or support varying strengths in the family are typically most successful. Family and early childhood interventions that have been shown to achieve long-term declines in antisocial behavior and violence prevention include home visitation (which is an essential component) accompanied with early education of all family members (Arango et al., 2018).

Parenting skills are also an important link to children developing antisocial behavior(s). Harsh discipline, lack of supervision, and poor or inconsistent parental monitoring have been shown to be strong predictors in the development of juvenile delinquency (Gard et al., 2017). While parenting skills are not always innate these skills can be taught to young parents. Positive parenting skills are a learned behavior that evolves from observations, engagement, learned experience, and even some trial and error. Numerous programs have been developed by researchers to help support and train parents who are providing inadequate care for their child. Some of the most successful programs have actually helped to develop partnerships between parents, teachers, and community agencies using dual trainings so that the parents are being trained while developing relationships with supportive systems within their network for longitudinal support as the child grows into middle childhood and adolescence (Kazdin, 2017).

Another important predictor is early childhood education. Early school achievement can be an important element in developing self-esteem, achieving academic success, and receiving peer acceptance (Pritchard & Wilson, 2003). Early childhood education can also have an important impact on the later development of behaviors during the adolescent period. Education programs and early interventions can strengthen a student's connection to the school itself and the relationships formed with school stakeholders. By improving school achievement and attachment through social reinforcement of the student role, students are less likely to engage in risky or delinquent behaviors either on school campuses or within their community (Reynolds et al., 2004). When we consider the cost of delinquency and antisocial behaviors compared to the costs of programming such as parenting skills interventions and early childhood education, the programming seems like a bargain. Investing in our young parents and early childhood education could make a significant difference in our next generation.

Youth and Adolescent Interventions

As previously discussed, numerous factors contribute to youth developing antisocial behaviors. Peer groups, poverty, poor parenting, genetics, community, and academic achievement are all potential contributors to a child developing risky or delinquent behaviors as they transition into adolescence. These behaviors can also be triggered by abusive or violent treatment from either a caretaker or peer. Interventions that target these behaviors are typically geared toward youth, but more recently interventions are being developed and utilized with younger populations as a source of prevention. Prevention programming is typically constructed to improve students' social, problem-solving, and anger management skills and promote nonviolent beliefs and thought patterns while educating and increasing student knowledge about conflict and violent behavior (Edwards et al. 2005). Research evaluating such programming is limited, additional research including control studies are needed, and most of the research available shows mixed or modest results (Park-Higgerson et al., 2008). More recent research states that prevention should be focused on elementary-age children, while youth and adolescents benefit from interventions such as mentoring, life skills training, peer counseling, vocational training, and employment services (Fagan & Catalano, 2013). Many of these skills can be delivered through school-based programming. School-based programming has been shown to have a modest impact on preventing or reducing violence when used as a part of a school-wide curriculum and implemented over multiple points throughout the academic calendar (Garrard & Lipsey, 2007). These types of school-based interventions typically use instruction methods based in cognitive behavioral techniques that include role-play and didactic instruction. This type of intervention provides students the opportunity to practice skills with their peers to avoid aggressive and possibly violent behaviors. Schools can also seek to supplement this training by using peer influences for those students who need more targeted intervention for their behavior. Older peers can be utilized to serve as behavioral support role models or peer mediators. Role models work to develop a positive peer relationship with the student and model socially acceptable behaviors within the school and community, while peer mediation focuses on conflict resolution and managing issues by finding a nonviolent resolution (Cutrin et al., 2015). Most programming of this type is primarily teacher-led, is universal in its application, and is meant for the general student population. More intensive programming is needed for those students who have already shown a propensity for violent acts or are considered at high risk for developing antisocial behaviors.

Community-Based Interventions
Rates of crime and violence involving youth are directly related to neighborhood rates of poverty, unemployment, and social disorganization (Fagan et al., 2018). Neighborhoods with high crime rates are usually characterized by high housing density, resident mobility, underresourced public schools, limited participation in community organizations, and youth with little or no supervision. Unfortunately, these types of neighborhood and communities are overwhelmed by different types of challenges. One contributing but

often overlooked and undervalued challenge is the lack of community interventions shown to be effective in evidenced-based studies. Research has shown that many community-based interventions are not centered on evidence-based studies regarding what works to prevent violence or reduce problem behaviors (Muratori et al., 2019). Durlak et al. (2010) states there is evidence that well-implemented, community-based programs can lead to positive behavioral outcomes for young people, including those who are disadvantaged and socially excluded. In addition, a meta-analysis by Durlak et al. (2010) of 68 after-school programs for US children and adolescents aged 5–18 years living in high-crime neighborhoods indicated that, compared to controls, participants demonstrated a significant decrease in problem behaviors and improvements in their self-perceptions, bonding to school, positive social behaviors, school grades, and levels of academic achievement. Community-based interventions and prevention programs vary greatly in their approach and in their potential to impact children's and adolescent's life outcomes, and additional rigorous evaluation studies are needed. Along with additional research, additional resources and funding are needed in at-risk communities to not only help fund evidenced-based programming but also to ensure that participants are trained and supervised to ensure the efficacy of the interventions.

Multisystemic Interventions

Multisystemic interventions are typically intensive, networked, home- and community-based interventions that are known within the professional literature to reduce the number of out-of-home placements and recidivism among youth with antisocial or risky behavior (Henggeler et al., 2009). These types of interventions typically target 12- to 18-year-old adolescents at risk of out-of-home placement due to their severe problem behavior. In some cases, multisystemic interventions can be used as an alternative to inpatient treatment. These interventions focus on supportive services that encourage socially acceptable behaviors in adolescents while strengthening support systems for the family (Henggeler & Schaeffer, 2016). These interventions work specifically on the contributing factors of antisocial behavior in the natural environment. This working perspective understands a young person's behavior within multiple systems including the family, peer, school, and community (Markham, 2018). Primary treatment goals of multisystem interventions include keeping the child at home, staying in school, and avoiding incidents with the police or criminal justice system. Secondary treatment goals include but are not limited to improved parenting skills, improved family relationships, improved social support, academic/school success, and an increase in socially accepted behaviors (Tan and Fajardo, 2017). Recently, the target population has been expanded to serve youth with a history of sex offending, substance abuse, chronic illness, and severe emotional disorders (Henggeler & Schaeffer, 2016).

Summary

This chapter has highlighted how antisocial behavior in youth can take on many attitudes and forms. These aggressive behaviors often escalate with age and development, regularly leaving parents, schools, and communities uncertain about how to best address these issues. The most promising interventions for youth with aggressive behaviors use a variety of approaches and include parents, schools, and community services (Kimonis et al., 2014). Most experts agree that a two-pronged approach that includes early prevention and ongoing interventions best serve youth, parents, schools, and the community at large. In the situations highlighted throughout this chapter, many researchers emphasize working with parents, counselors, and community partners if we are to be effective and efficient in providing best practices to youth and adolescents who continuously exhibit these types of troubling behaviors. As discussed in this chapter, youth continue to struggle with process addictions, drug or alcohol addiction, or both. While it is important to get the truth in session, especially when an inventory or assessment is taking place, it is also paramount that the therapist and client achieve open communication, with a maintained level of respect and acceptance for the minor. It should also be noted that a therapist can accept a client without condoning her behavior.

Case Study: Reed

Reed is a 13-year-old girl from Ethiopia. She was adopted by an American couple at the age of 6 and moved to the United States. The transition to a new culture, new language, new parents, and a new home was difficult during those first few years. During middle childhood, Reed often acted out with burst of anger and tantrums when she was overwhelmed with emotions. While her parents tried to support her and love her through these difficult episodes, they were often left overwhelmed themselves. Soon they sought out behavior and emotional support. They first moved Reed to a private school with smaller classrooms and more individualized attention. Second, following the recommendation of a friend, they sought out an adoption support group. The support group was a wonderful resource, and they quickly made friends (both parents and Reed) and found an outlet for their fears, frustrations, and hope. Their new family seemed to settle in, routines were established, and, for the most part, Reed and her adoptive parents seemed to reconcile some sense of normalcy and deepen their relationship. However, as Reed transitioned from middle childhood into adolescence new behaviors began to emerge. Mood swings, refusal to do her homework, withdrawing from friends, and even self-injury were discovered. Reed began bullying other girls, fighting, and experimenting with alcohol. Reed was spiraling, and her parents felt blindsided by these behaviors. One night, Reed was caught sneaking out of the house. When her parents tried to stop her from leaving the home, Reed began violently hitting her mother repeatedly: the mother's jaw was broken in three places and she was hospitalized for her injuries. Reed was arrested and sent to a 7-day mental health in-patient treatment center. Through the juvenile justice system, Reed received 12 months of probation and required mental health counseling. When Reed returned home, she entered into intensive counseling (twice a week), and the parents began seeing a counselor as well.

The relationship they had worked so hard to build seemingly crumbled overnight. The parents knew they needed help, and lots of it. They had committed years ago to Reed, and they did not intend to give up on their family. Following the counselor's advice, they began to read about trauma and the impact of trauma on adolescent brain development. Soon things began to make more sense. The emergence of antisocial behaviors, withdraw, and poor performance in school had all been triggered by something, but what? Through counseling, Reed finally disclosed that a boy at school had tried to kiss her, grabbed her breasts, and kept giving her unwanted attention on a daily basis. The harassment didn't stop at school; in the evenings he would send her texts and messages on various social media platforms. At first she tried to avoid him, delete his messages, and block his accounts but when that didn't work she decided to fight back. She became hostile: she tried to be so aggressive that no one, including her parents would want to be around her. She wanted to withdraw from everyone so that she could feel safe again. The more affection her parents tried to show her, the angrier she got. These recent incidents had brought up long-suppressed memories of physical and sexual abuse experienced long before her adoption.

While counseling had helped in several ways, the parents began to realize that they needed support from varying perspectives. They needed additional services that could support their entire family. Reed's family decided to switch to a therapist who operated within a multisystemic perspective. The parents entered parent training to help better communicate, listen, and support Reed. Reed began group therapy in addition to her individual counseling. The family began to receive home visits, and Reed's parents worked on sensitivity training and received parenting supervision from their therapist. The supervision provided new behavioral strategies to provide boundaries for Reed's behavior and support for her positive behaviors. The intensive sessions lasted for 5 months, during which Reed and her parents experienced significant positive changes. Reed reported feeling a greater sense of being understood and support, and she was beginning to interact and engage with friends and school. Reed's parents reported better communication, reduced parental stress, increased parental confidence, and an enhanced relationship with Reed.

After the completion of the intensive systemic intervention, Reed and her parents returned to traditional weekly therapy for continued support and emotional maintenance.

References

American Psychological Association. (2010). *Publication manual of the American Psychological Association* (6th ed.). Author.

American Psychiatric Association. (2022). Diagnostic and statistical manual of mental disorders (5th ed., text rev.). https://doi.org/10.1176/appi.books.9780890425787

American School Counselor Association. (2019). ASCA National Model: A framework for school counseling programs (4th ed., Executive Summary). Retrieved from https://www.schoolcounselor.org/asca/media/asca/ASCA%20National%20Model%20Templates/Fourth-Edition/ANMExecutiveSummary-4.pdf

Arango, C., Díaz-Caneja, C. M., McGorry, P. D., Rapoport, J., Sommer, I. E., Vorstman, J. A., . . . Carpenter, W. (2018). Preventive strategies for mental health. *The Lancet Psychiatry*, 5(7), 591–604.

Barnes, S. J., Pressey, A. D., & Scornavacca, E. (2019). Mobile ubiquity: Understanding the relationship between cognitive absorption, smartphone addiction and social network services. *Computers in Human Behavior, 90*, 246–258. https://doi.org/10.1016/j.chb.2018.09.013

Bear, G. G. (2012). Both suspension and alternatives work, depending on one's aim. *Journal of School Violence, 11*(2), 174–186.

Benson, M. J., & Buehler, C. (2012). Family process and peer deviance influences on adolescent aggression: Longitudinal effects across early and middle adolescence. *Child Development, 83*(4), 1213–1228.

Bland, V. J., Lambie, I., & Best, C. (2018). Does childhood neglect contribute to violent behavior in adulthood? A review of possible links. *Clinical Psychology Review, 60*, 126–135.

Boden, J., Blair, S., & Newton-Howes, G. (2020). Alcohol use in adolescents and adult psychopathology and social outcomes: Findings from a 35-year cohort study. *Australian & New Zealand Journal of Psychiatry, 54*(9), 909–918. https://doi.org/10.1177/0004867420924091

Bornstein, M. H. (2015). Children's Parents. Handbook of Child Psychology and Developmental Science. Vol.4: Ecological settings and processes in developmental systems (7th ed., pp. 55–132). Hoboken, NJ: Wiley.

Boyle, M. H., Georgiades, K., Duncan, L., Wang, L., Comeau, J., & 2014 Ontario Child Health Study Team. (2019). Poverty, neighbourhood antisocial behaviour, and children's mental health problems: Findings from the 2014 Ontario Child Health Study. *Canadian Journal of Psychiatry, 64*(4), 285–293.

Braga, T., Gonçalves, L. C., Basto-Pereira, M., & Maia, A. (2017). Unraveling the link between maltreatment and juvenile antisocial behavior: A meta-analysis of prospective longitudinal studies. *Aggression and Violent Behavior, 33*, 37–50.

Brazil, I. A., van Dongen, J. D., Maes, J. H., Mars, R. B., & Baskin-Sommers, A. R. (2018). Classification and treatment of antisocial individuals: From behavior to biocognition. *Neuroscience and Biobehavioral Reviews, 91*, 259–277.

Centers for Disease Control and Prevention. (2019). *Youth risk behavior survey data*. Retrieved from www.cdc.gov/yrbs.

Chaudhary, P., Peskin, M., Temple, J. R., Addy, R. C., Baumler, E., & Ross, S. (2017). Sexting and mental health: A school-based longitudinal study among youth in Texas. *Journal of Applied Research on Children, 8*(1), 1–27.

Connor, D. F. (2004). *Aggression and antisocial behavior in children and adolescents: Research and treatment*. Guilford.

Cook, E. C., Buehler, C., & Henson, R. (2009). Parents and peers as social influences to deter antisocial behavior. *Journal of Youth and Adolescence, 38*(9), 1240–1252.

Coyne, S. M., Stockdale, L. A., Warburton, W., Gentile, D. A., Yang, C., & Merrill, B. M. (2020). Pathological video game symptoms from adolescence to emerging adulthood: A 6-year longitudinal study of trajectories, predictors, and outcomes. *Developmental Psychology, 56*(7), 1385–1396. https://doi.org/10.1037/dev0000939

Crugnola, C. R., Ierardi, E., Bottini, M., Verganti, C., & Albizzati, A. (2019). Childhood experiences of maltreatment, reflective functioning and attachment in adolescent and young adult mothers: Effects on mother-infant interaction and emotion regulation. *Child Abuse & Neglect, 93*, 277–290.

Cutrín, O., Gómez-Fraguela, J. A., & Luengo, M. Á. (2015). Peer-group mediation in the relationship between family and juvenile antisocial behavior. *European Journal of Psychology Applied to Legal Context, 7*(2), 59–65.

Darden, M. C., Ehman, A. C., Lair, E. C., & Gross, A. M. (2019). Sexual compliance: Examining the relationships among sexual want, sexual consent, and sexual assertiveness. *Sexuality & Culture, 23*(1), 220–235. https://doi.org/10.1007/s12 119-018-9551-1

de Jong, E., Bernasco, W., & Lammers, M. (2019). Situational correlates of adolescent substance use: An improved test of the routine activity theory of deviant behavior. *Journal of Quantitative Criminology, 36*(4), 823–850.

De Los Reyes, A., Bunnell, B. E., & Beidel, D. C. (2013). Informant discrepancies in adult social anxiety disorder assessments: Links with contextual variations in observed behavior. *Journal of Abnormal Psychology, 122*(2), 376.

Dirks, M. A., De Los Reyes, A., Briggs-Gowan, M., Cella, D., & Wakschlag, L. S. (2012). Annual Research Review: Embracing not erasing contextual variability in children's behavior–theory and utility in the selection and use of methods and informants in developmental psychopathology. *Journal of Child Psychology and Psychiatry, 53*(5), 558–574.

Dishion, T. J., & Patterson, G. R. (2006). *The development and ecology of antisocial behavior in children and adolescents*. Wiley.

Dodge, K. A., & Pettit, G. S. (2003). A biopsychosocial model of the development of chronic conduct problems in adolescence. *Developmental Psychology, 39*(2), 349.

Döring, N. (2014). Consensual sexting among adolescents: Risk prevention through abstinence education or safer sexting? *Cyberpsychology, 8*(1), 1–9. https://doi.org/10.5817/CP2014-1-9

Durlak, J. A., Weissberg, R. P., & Pachan, M. (2010). A meta-analysis of after-school programs that seek to promote personal and social skills in children and adolescents. *American Journal of Community Psychology, 45*(3), 294–309.

Edwards, D., Hunt, M. H., Meyers, J., Grogg, K. R., & Jarrett, O. (2005). Acceptability and student outcomes of a violence prevention curriculum. *Journal of Primary Prevention, 26*(5), 401–418.

Egan, V., & Bull, S. (2020). Social support does not moderate the relationship between personality and risk-taking/antisocial behaviour. *Personality and Individual Differences, 163*, 110053.

Eivers, A. R., Brendgen, M., & Borge, A. I. (2010). Stability and change in prosocial and antisocial behavior across the transition to school: Teacher and peer perspectives. *Early Education and Development, 21*(6), 843–864.

Erickson, M. L., & Jensen, G. F. (1977). "Delinquency is still group behavior!": Toward revitalizing the group premise in the sociology of deviance. *Journal of Criminal Law and Criminology, 68*, 262–273. doi:10.2307/1142849

Fagan, A. A., & Catalano, R. F. (2013). What works in youth violence prevention: A review of the literature. *Research on Social Work Practice, 23*(2), 141–156.

Fagan, A. A., Hawkins, J. D., & Catalano, R. F. (2018). *Communities that care: Building community engagement and capacity to prevent youth behavior problems*. Oxford University Press.

Fosco, G. M., & LoBraico, E. J. (2019). Elaborating on premature adolescent autonomy: Linking variation in daily family processes to developmental risk. *Development and Psychopathology, 31*(5), 1741–1755.

Fowler, P. J., Tompsett, C. J., Braciszewski, J. M., Jacques-Tiura, A. J., & Baltes, B. B. (2009). Community violence: A meta-analysis on the effect of exposure and mental health outcomes of children and adolescents. *Development and Psychopathology, 21*(1), 227–259.

Frazier, A., Ferreira, P. A., & Gonzales, J. E. (2019). Born this way? A review of neurobiological and environmental evidence for the etiology of psychopathy. *Personality and Neuroscience, 2*, e8.

Frick, P. J., Ray, J. V., Thornton, L. C., & Kahn, R. E. (2014). Can callous-unemotional traits enhance the understanding, diagnosis, and treatment of serious conduct problems in children and adolescents? A comprehensive review. *Psychological Bulletin, 140*(1), 1.

Furstenberg Jr, F. F., Brooks-Gunn, J., & Morgan, S. P. (1987). *Adolescent mothers in later life.* Cambridge University Press.

Gard, A. M., Waller, R., Shaw, D. S., Forbes, E. E., Hariri, A. R., & Hyde, L. W. (2017). The long reach of early adversity: Parenting, stress, and neural pathways to antisocial behavior in adulthood. *Biological Psychiatry: Cognitive Neuroscience and Neuroimaging, 2*(7), 582–590.

Gardner, M., & Steinberg, L. (2005). Peer influence on risk taking, risk preference, and risky decision making in adolescence and adulthood: An experimental study. *Developmental Psychology, 41*(4), 625.

Garrard, W. M., & Lipsey, M. W. (2007). Conflict resolution education and antisocial behavior in US schools: A meta-analysis. *Conflict Resolution Quarterly, 25*(1), 9–38.

Gorman-Smith, D., & Loeber, R. (2005). Are developmental pathways in disruptive behaviors the same for girls and boys? *Journal of Child and Family Studies, 14*(1), 15–27.

Grant, J. E., Potenza, M. N., Krishnan-Sarin, S., Cavallo, D. A., & Desai, R. A. (2011). Shopping problems among high school students. *Comprehensive Psychiatry, 52*(3), 247–252. https://doi.org/10.1016/j.comppsych.2010.06.006

Greenwood, P. (2008). Prevention and intervention programs for juvenile offenders. *The Future of Children*, 185–210.

Guadagno, R. E., Okdie, B. M., & Kruse, S. A. (2012). Dating deception: Gender, online dating, and exaggerated self-presentation. *Computers in Human Behavior, 28*(2), 642–647.

Hagan, M. P., & King, S. L. (1997). Accuracy of psychologists' short-term predictions of future criminal behavior among juveniles. *Journal of Offender Rehabilitation, 25*, 129–141.

Halgunseth, L. C., Perkins, D. F., Lippold, M. A., & Nix, R. L. (2013). Delinquent-oriented attitudes mediate the relation between parental inconsistent discipline and early adolescent behavior. *Journal of Family Psychology, 27*(2), 293.

Hart, S. D., & Logan, C. (2011). Formulation of violent risk using evidence-based assessments: The structured professional judgement approach. In P. Sturmey & M. McMurran (Eds.), *Forensic case formulation* (pp. 3–32). Wiley.

Heffernan, R., & Ward, T. (2017). A comprehensive theory of dynamic risk and protective factors. *Aggression and Violent Behavior, 37*, 129–141.

Henggeler, S. W., & Schaeffer, C. M. (2016). Multisystemic therapy: Clinical overview, outcomes, and implementation research. *Family Process, 55*, 514–528. https://doi.org/10.1111/famp.12232.

Henggeler, S. W., Schoenwald, S. K., Borduin, C. M., Rowland, M. D., & Cunningham, P. B. (2009). *Multisystemic therapy for antisocial behavior in children and adolescents*, 2nd ed. Guilford.

Henggeler, S. W., & Schoenwald, S. K. (2011). Evidence-based interventions for juvenile offenders and juvenile justice policies that support them and commentaries. *Social Policy Report, 25*(1), 1–28.

Hess, R. S., Pejic, V., & Castejon, K. S. (2014). Best practices in delivering culturally responsive, tiered-level supports from youth with behavioral challenges. In P. Harrison & A. Thomas (Eds.), *Best practices in school psychology* (pp. 157–168). Bethesda, MD: National Association of School Psychologists.

Hinshaw, S. P., & Lee, S. S. (2003). Conduct and oppositional defiant disorders. In E. J. Mash, & R. A. Barkeley (Eds.), *Child psychopathology* (pp. 144–198). New York: The Guilford Press.

Houck, C. D., Barker, D., Rizzo, C., Hancock, E., Norton, A., & Brown, L. K. (2014). Sexting and sexual behavior in at-risk adolescents. *Pediatrics, 133*(2), e276–e282.

Jessor, R., & Jessor, S. (1977). *Problem behavior and psychosocial development*. Academic Press.

Johnston, L. D., Miech, R. A., O'Malley, P. M., Bachman, J. G., Schulenberg, J. E., Patrick, M. E., & University of Michigan, Institute for Social Research. (2021). *Monitoring the future national survey results on drug use, 1975-2020: Overview, key findings on adolescent drug use*. Institute for Social Research.

Karyda, M. (2020). The influence of neighbourhood crime on young people becoming not in education, employment or training. *British Journal of Sociology of Education, 41*(3), 393–409.

Kazdin, A. E. (2017). Parent management training and problem-solving skills training for child and adolescent conduct problems. In J. Weisz and A. Kazdin (Eds.), *Evidence-based psychotherapies for children and adolescents* (3rd ed.) (pp. 142–158). New York: Guilford Press.

Kazdin, A. E. (2018). Developing treatments for antisocial behavior among children: Controlled trials and uncontrolled tribulations. *Perspectives on Psychological Science, 13*(5), 634–650.

Kiesner, J., Dishion, T. J., Poulin, F., & Pastore, M. (2009). Temporal dynamics linking aspects of parent monitoring with early adolescent antisocial behavior. *Social Development, 18*(4), 765–784.

Kimonis, E. R., Frick, P. J., & McMahon, R. J. (2014). Conduct and oppositional defiant disorders. In: E. J. Mash & R. A. Barkley (Eds.), *Child Psychopathology*, Third Edition (pp. 145–179). New York: Guilford Press.

Klettke, B., Hallford, D. J., Clancy, E., Mellor, D. J., & Toumbourou, J. W. (2019). Sexting and psychological distress: The role of unwanted and coerced sexts. *Cyberpsychology, Behavior and Social Networking, 22*(4), 237–242. https://doi.org/10.1089/cyber.2018.0291

Kline, D. M. S. (2016). Can restorative practices help to reduce disparities in school discipline data? A review of the literature. *Multicultural Perspectives, 18*(2), 97–102.

Lahey, B. B., Loeber, R., Hart, E. L., Frick, P. J., Applegate, B., Zhang, Q., . . . Russo, M. F. (1995). Four-year longitudinal study of conduct disorder in boys: Patterns and predictors of persistence. *Journal of Abnormal Psychology, 104*(1), 83.

Lamblin, M., Murawski, C., Whittle, S., & Fornito, A. (2017). Social connectedness, mental health and the adolescent brain. *Neuroscience & Biobehavioral Reviews, 80*, 57–68.

Lange, B. C., Callinan, L. S., & Smith, M. V. (2019). Adverse childhood experiences and their relation to parenting stress and parenting practices. *Community Mental Health Journal, 55*(4), 651–662.

Lipsey, M. W. (2009). The primary factors that characterize effective interventions with juvenile offenders: A meta-analytic overview. *Victims and Offenders, 4*(2), 124–147.

Loeber, R., Lacourse, É., & Homish, D. L. (2005). *Homicide, violence, and developmental trajectories*. Guilford.

Makol, B. A., Youngstrom, E. A., Racz, S. J., Qasmieh, N., Glenn, L. E., & De Los Reyes, A. (2020). Integrating multiple informants' reports: How conceptual and measurement models may address long-standing problems in clinical decision-making. *Clinical Psychological Science, 8*(6), 953–970.

Markham, A. (2018). A review following systematic principles of multisystemic therapy for antisocial behavior in adolescents aged 10–17 years. *Adolescent Research Review, 3*(1), 67–93.

Marmorstein, N. R., & Iacono, W. G. (2005). Longitudinal follow-up of adolescents with late-onset antisocial behavior: A pathological yet overlooked group. *Journal of the American Academy of Child & Adolescent Psychiatry, 44*(12), 1284–1291.

Mason, M., Mennis, J., Russell, M., Moore, M., & Brown, A. (2019). Adolescent depression and substance use: The protective role of prosocial peer behavior. *Journal of Abnormal Child Psychology, 47*(6), 1065–1074.

Maynard, R. (Ed.). (1997), *Kids having kids: Economic costs and social consequences of teen pregnancy.* Urban Institute Press

McQuillan, M. E., & Bates, J. E. (2017). Parental stress and child temperament. In *Parental Stress and Early Child Development* (pp. 75–106). Springer, Cham. doi:10.1007/978-3-319-55376-4_4.

Medrano, J. L. J., Lopez Rosales, F., & Gámez-Guadix, M. (2018). Assessing the links of sexting, cybervictimization, depression, and suicidal ideation among university students. *Archives of Suicide Research, 22*(1), 153–164. https://doi.org/10.1080/13811 118.2017.1304304

Moffitt, T. E. (1993). Adolescence-limited and life-course-persistent antisocial behavior: A developmental taxonomy. *Psychological Review, 100*(4), 674.

Moffitt, T. E., & Caspi, A. (2001). Childhood predictors differentiate life-course persistent and adolescence-limited antisocial pathways among males and females. *Development and Psychopathology, 13*(2), 355–375.

Moos, R. H. (1994). *Family environment scale manual: Development, applications, research.* Consulting Psychologists Press.

Muratori, P., Bertacchi, I., Masi, G., Milone, A., Nocentini, A., Powell, N. P., . . . Romero, D. (2019). Effects of a universal prevention program on externalizing behaviors: Exploring the generalizability of findings across school and home settings. *Journal of School Psychology, 77*, 13–23.

Na, C. (2017). The consequences of school dropout among serious adolescent offenders: More offending? More arrest? Both? *Journal of Research in Crime and Delinquency, 54*(1), 78–110.

National Institute on Alcohol Abuse and Alcoholism (NIAAA). NIAAA council approves definition of binge drinking. *NIAAA Newsletter 3*, Winter 2004. Retrieved March 5, 2018, from https://pubs.niaaa.nih.gov/publications/Newsletter/winter2004/Newsletter_Number3.pdf.

National Institute on Alcohol Abuse and Alcoholism (NIAAA). Underage drinking. 2020. Retrieved December 8, 2020, from https://pubs.niaaa.nih.gov/publications/UnderageDrinking/UnderageFact.h . . . .

Nock, M. K., Kazdin, A. E., Hiripi, E. V. A., & Kessler, R. C. (2006). Prevalence, subtypes, and correlates of DSM-IV conduct disorder in the National Comorbidity Survey Replication. *Psychological Medicine, 36*(5), 699.

O'Connell, M. E., Boat, T., & Warner, K. E. (2009). Committee on the prevention of mental disorders and substance abuse among children, youth, and young adults: Research advances and promising interventions. *Preventing Mental, Emotional, and Behavioral Disorders Among Young People: Progress and Possibilities.*

Ostovar, S., Allahyar, N., Aminpoor, H., Moafian, F., Nor, M. B. M., & Griffiths, M. D. (2016). Internet addiction and its psychosocial risks (depression, anxiety, stress and loneliness) among Iranian adolescents and young adults: A structural equation model in a cross-sectional study. *International Journal of Mental Health and Addiction, 14*(3), 257–267. https://doi.org/10.1007/s11469-015-9628-0

Park-Higgerson, H. K., Perumean-Chaney, S. E., Bartolucci, A. A., Grimley, D. M., & Singh, K. P. (2008). The evaluation of school-based violence prevention programs: A meta-analysis. *Journal of School Health, 78*(9), 465–479.

Pas, E. T., Ryoo, J. H., Musci, R. J., & Bradshaw, C. P. (2019). A state-wide quasi-experimental effectiveness study of the scale-up of school-wide positive behavioral interventions and supports. *Journal of School Psychology, 73*, 41–55.

Patterson, G. R. (2016). Coercion theory: The study of change. In T. J. Dishion & J. J. Snyder (Eds.), *The oxford handbook of coercive relationship dynamics* (pp. 7–22). Oxford University Press.

Pérez de Albéniz-Garrote, G., Medina-Gómez, M. B., & Buedo-Guirado, C. (2021). Compulsive buying in adolescents: The impact of gender and alcohol and cannabis use. *Sustainability (Basel, Switzerland), 13*(7), 3982. https://doi.org/10.3390/su13073982

Perkins, D. F., & Borden, L. M. (2003). Positive behaviors, problem behaviors, and resiliency in adolescence. In R. M. Lerner, M. A. Easterbrooks, & J. Mistry (Eds.), *Handbook of psychology*. Vol. 6: Developmental psychology (pp. 373–394). New York: Wiley.

Pritchard, M. E., & Wilson, G. S. (2003). Using emotional and social factors to predict student success. *Journal of College Student Development, 44*(1), 18–28.

Reynolds, A. J., Ou, S. R., & Topitzes, J. W. (2004). Paths of effects of early childhood intervention on educational attainment and delinquency: A confirmatory analysis of the Chicago Child-Parent Centers. *Child Development, 75*(5), 1299–1328.

Rhee, S. H., & Waldman, I. D. (2002). Genetic and environmental influences on antisocial behavior: A meta-analysis of twin and adoption studies. *Psychological Bulletin, 128*(3), 490.

Rose, A. J., & Smith, R. L. (2018). Gender and peer relationships. In W. M. Bukowski, B. Laursen, & K. H. Rubin (Eds.), *Handbook of peer interactions, relationships, and groups* (2nd ed., pp. 571–589). Guilford Press.

Ryan, K., Lane, S. J., & Powers, D. (2017). A multidisciplinary model for treating complex trauma in early childhood. *International Journal of Play Therapy, 26*(2), 111.

Ryan, T. G., & Goodram, B. (2013). The impact of exclusionary discipline on students. *International Journal of Progressive Education, 9*(3), 169–177. Retrieved from http://inased.org/ijpe.htm

Sampson, R. J., & Lauritsen, J. L. (1994). Violent victimization and offending: Individual-, situational-, and community-level risk factors. *Understanding and Preventing Violence, 3*, 1–114.

Sharkey, J. D., & Fenning, P. A. (2012). Rationale for designing school contexts in support of proactive discipline. *Journal of School Violence, 11*(2), 95–104.

Shaw, C. R., & McKay, H. D. (1931). *Report on the causes of crime, vol. II*. Government Printing Office.

Shaw, C. R., & McKay, H. D. (1969). *Juvenile delinquency in urban areas* (revised ed.). University of Chicago Press.

Shoemaker, D. J. (2018). *Theories of delinquency: An examination of explanations of delinquent behavior*. Oxford University Press.

Sijtsema, J. J., & Lindenberg, S. M. (2018). Peer influence in the development of adolescent antisocial behavior: Advances from dynamic social network studies. *Developmental Review, 50,* 140–154.

Silverthorn, P., & Frick, P. J. (1999). Developmental pathways to antisocial behavior: The delayed-onset pathway in girls. *Development and Psychopathology, 11*(1), 101–126.

Smaragdi, A., Cornwell, H., Toschi, N., Riccelli, R., Gonzalez-Madruga, K., Wells, A., . . . Fairchild, G. (2017). Sex differences in the relationship between conduct disorder and cortical structure in adolescents. *Journal of the American Academy of Child & Adolescent Psychiatry, 56*(8), 703–712.

Sohn, S. Y., Rees, P., Wildridge, B., Kalk, N. J., & Carter, B. (2021). Correction to: Prevalence of problematic smartphone usage and associated mental health outcomes among children and young people: A systematic review, meta-analysis and GRADE of the evidence. *BMC Psychiatry, 21*(1), 52–52. Retrieved from https://doi.org/10.1186/s12 888-020-02986-2

Tan, J. X., & Fajardo, M. L. R. (2017). Efficacy of multisystemic therapy in youths aged 10–17 with severe antisocial behaviour and emotional disorders: Systematic review. *London Journal of Primary Care, 9*(6), 95–103.

Teske, S. C. (2011). A study of zero tolerance policies in schools: A multi-integrated systems approach to improve outcomes for adolescents. *Journal of Child and Adolescent Psychiatric Nursing, 24*(2), 88–97.

Thompson, F., Smith, P. K., Blaya, C., Shubhdip, K., & Sundaram, S. (2018). Exchanging ideas. Anti-bullying intervention including peer and parent support strategies. In P. K. Smith, S. Sundaram, B. Spears, C. Blaya, M. Schäfer, & D. Sandhu (Eds.), *Bullying, cyberbullying and pupil well-being in schools: Comparing European, Australian and Indian Perspectives* (pp. 255–284). Cambridge: Cambridge University Press.

Thornberry, T. P., Huizinga, D., & Loeber, R. (1995). Prevention of serious delinquency and violence: Implications from the program of research on the causes and correlates of delinquency. In J. C. Howell, B. Krisberg, et al. (Eds.), *Sourcebook on serious, violent, and chronic juvenile offenders* (pp. 213–237). Thousand Oaks, CA: Sage.

Toro, P. A., Urberg, K. A., & Heinze, H. J. (2004). Antisocial behavior and affiliation with deviant peers. *Journal of Clinical Child and Adolescent Psychology, 33*(2), 336–346.

Underwood, M. K. (2004). Gender and peer relations: Are the two gender cultures really all that different? In J. B. Kupersmidt & K. A. Dodge (Eds.), *Children's peer relations: From developmental science to intervention to policy* (pp. 21–36). Washington, DC: American Psychological Association.

Vaillancourt, T., & Krems, J. A. (2018). An evolutionary psychological perspective of indirect aggression in girls and women. In S. M. Coyne & J. M. Ostrov (Eds.), *The development of relational aggression* (pp. 111–126). Oxford, England: Oxford University Press.

Vitaro, F., Brendgen, M., Larose, S., & Trembaly, R. E. (2005). Kindergarten disruptive behaviors, protective factors, and educational achievement by early adulthood. *Journal of Educational Psychology, 97*(4), 617.

Waddell, J. T., Sternberg, A., Bui, L., Ruof, A. R., Blake, A. J., Grimm, K. J., & Chassin, L. (2021). Relations between child temperament and adolescent negative urgency in a high-risk sample. *Journal of Research in Personality, 90,* 104056.

Ward, T., & Beech, A. R. (2015). Dynamic risk factors: A theoretical dead-end? *Psychology, Crime & Law, 21*(2), 100–113.

Wolff, K. T., & Baglivio, M. T. (2017). Adverse childhood experiences, negative emotionality, and pathways to juvenile recidivism. *Crime & Delinquency, 63*(12), 1495–1521.

Wolf, S., Magnuson, K. A., & Kimbro, R. T. (2017). Family poverty and neighborhood poverty: Links with children's school readiness before and after the Great Recession. *Children and Youth Services Review, 79*, 368–384.

World Health Organization (WHO). (2019). International Statistical Classification of Diseases and Related Health Problems (11th ed.). Retrieved from https://icd.who.int/

10
Abuse and Trauma

Overview

Many clinicians will work with trauma and abuse in their career. More specifically, childhood trauma and abuse should be seen as a public health issue because approximately two-thirds of children in the United States have reported a traumatic incident occurring by the age of 16 (Substance Abuse and Mental Health Services Administration [SAMHSA], 2015). Due to this, clinicians should be well-equipped to identify childhood abuse and/or trauma and provide effective and efficient treatment. Additionally, clinicians working with adults would benefit from knowing this information given the long-term effects of abuse and trauma. In this chapter, we explore the short- and long-term impacts of abuse and trauma on children and adolescents within a cultural context. We provide guidelines for trauma-informed care with youth.

Introduction

Childhood abuse is widespread in the United States. The latest statistics show that 1 in 7 children were victims of child abuse and neglect (CDC, 2022). Furthermore, of those, approximately 1,840 died as a result in 2019 (Child Welfare Information Gateway, 2021). Childhood abuse often leads to trauma and is the leading cause of trauma in adulthood. In this chapter, we discuss types of abuse and its effects on children and adolescents.

> **Case Study: Mario**
>
> Mario is an 8th-grade, middle school student in a rural community approximately 250 miles outside of a major city. Mario and his family

moved to this rural community when his mother married Mario's new stepfather 1 year ago. Mario has had some issues transitioning to his new school and town. He had many friends at his old school and participated in after-school theater. Mario constantly felt like he just did not fit in with this new place and had trouble making new friends. One day, Mario's PE coach Patricia noticed that Mario did not wear his PE uniform and instead wore pants outside during a very hot April afternoon. Because this was out of the ordinary and because Mario was usually a rule-follower, Patricia did not think much of it and passed it off as Mario having a bad day. Mario was allowed to participate in PE activities that day. The next day, Patricia noticed that again Mario did not wear his PE uniform. This time the coach asked Mario about this and he stated, "My mom forgot to wash it again." Patricia again let this pass and Mario was allowed to participate in PE activities.

When this happened 3 days in a row, the coach contacted Mario's mother. When asked about the real reason for his avoiding the PE uniform, Mario said he was clumsy and fell down outside and didn't want to be teased by the other kids at school. After this same incident happened 2 weeks in a row, Patricia referred Mario to the school counselor and suggested that their mother be brought in for a meeting. This experience left Mario embarrassed and fearful of what was to happen next.

Abuse in Childhood

Childhood abuse happens when a guardian, parent, or caregiver causes harm, injury, or in some cases death to a minor (i.e., younger than 18 years). According to the Centers for Disease Control (CDC), 1 in 7 children experience abuse within any one year. Abuse is usually done by someone the child is familiar with (i.e., parent or family member), which is possibly why they are less likely to disclose the abuser to authorities, and this leads to an underreported statistic. In addition to this, the COVID-19 pandemic that began in 2020 and remains ongoing has led to an increase in child mental health issues (Panchal et al., 2021) and an increase in family violence (Boserup et al., 2020; Evans et al., 2021), leaving mental health clinicians in a severe state of burnout and crisis (Aafjes-van Doorn et al., 2020; Litam et al., 2021).

Types of Abuse

The four common types of childhood abuse are physical, sexual, emotional, and neglect. Other types of abuse that may be less common include medical abuse and human trafficking. Any type of childhood abuse is extremely detrimental to that individual's physical and mental health and needs to be addressed. Definitions of each type of abuse will vary depending on state; here we discuss general descriptions of each. The National Child Traumatic Stress Network (NCTSN; https://www.nctsn.org) is a good resource for clinicians: it reports on childhood trauma, treatment, resources, and trauma-informed care. Generally speaking, childhood abuse in all forms occur despite age, race, economic background, and community, thus confirming the argument that childhood abuse is largely a public health issue.

Childhood physical abuse is likely the most common type that clinicians find in their practice with minor children and adolescents. As such, it is crucial for those working with clients to recognize physical injury characteristics such as bruising or broken bones. Childhood physical abuse includes an act of physical injury by the parent and/or guardian and may involve accidental harm. The effects of physical abuse are well known and include both medical (i.e., high blood pressure, physical symptoms) and mental health (i.e., anger, anxiety, depression; Banker et al., 2019; Springer et al., 2007) as well as potential relational issues.

Childhood sexual abuse happens when an adult or another child sexually stimulates a minor for the purpose of the perpetrator. This includes touch and non-touch (e.g., child pornography) interactions. Sexual abuse in childhood has long-term effects well into adulthood including the potential to be revictimized, posttraumatic stress disorder (PTSD), and mental health issues (James & Gilliland, 2017).

Childhood emotional abuse, sometimes called *psychological abuse*, occurs when an adult attempts to control the minor through emotional means. Examples of emotional abuse include yelling, mean jokes, and withholding affection. This type of abuse usually results in shaming or embarrassing the child. While this type of abuse is likely the most difficult to recognize, children experiencing emotional abuse in the home will show signs of low self-worth and perhaps delayed emotional development. Childhood emotional abuse is associated with anxiety and depression (Al-Modallal et al., 2020) and with substance use disorders (Watts et al., 2020).

Childhood neglect occurs when a parent or guardian fails to provide care for the minor. Examples of childhood neglect include leaving a child alone for an extended time or not providing a child with a safe living environment. Children who experience neglect may be seen hoarding food at school or stealing food or money, or they may have poor hygiene due to lack of parental resources. It is important to note here that instances of neglect do not include those families with a lack of resources; rather, this concept is defined by those with the financial means but who are providing inadequate care.

All of these abuse types have the likelihood to develop into trauma responses. The Adverse Childhood Experiences (ACE) Study (Felitti et al., 1998) is a large-scale study that identified the long-term effects of abuse experienced in childhood. Childhood abuse is linked to issues of mental health (e.g., depression, substance use, suicide), physical health issues (e.g., cancer, psychosis, obesity), neurological development (e.g., memory, emotion regulation; Navalta et al., 2018), and life satisfaction (e.g., negative relationship satisfaction; Wheeler et al., 2021). With knowledge of the ACEs study in mind, clinicians are attempting to figure out a way to integrate trauma-informed care into their daily practice with clients.

Signs and Symptoms of Childhood Abuse

While there are several signs and symptoms of childhood abuse, we discuss here some common themes. Please note that just because you see one of these in a client, it does not necessarily mean that they are being abused; rather, it is something to be aware of and perhaps explore further with the child.

One important sign includes changes in routine and/or behavior in the minor. These include behaviors such as aggression toward others, fighting at school, changes in friendships, or running away. These also include any type of withdrawal, such as no longer participating in activities that normally they would enjoy (i.e., sports, dance, etc.) and no longer engaging with peers and/or friends.

Other common signs of which clinicians should be aware include

- Consistent absences from school
- Mental health concerns, such as depression or anxiety
- Any markings found on the body

When thinking about working with childhood abuse from a systemic perspective rather than just on an individual level, the clinician may consider factors such as (a) parent/guardian mental health, (b) supportive networks, (c) access to services, and (d) other community factors.

Naturally, clinicians working with children will also need to engage with parents on some level. Because of this, it is crucial for clinicians to be knowledgeable about parental and/or guardian mental health and how this may impact the child or family. An unstable family environment and poor parental mental health are predictors to childhood abuse (CDC, 2022; Child Welfare Information Gateway, n.d.). Unstable family environments include factors like financial stress and poverty and persistent family conflict. Common parental mental health issues include depression and substance abuse. If parental mental health goes unresolved or untreated, the cycle of abuse in families may continue, and recurring intergenerational trauma may be likely. Families having supportive networks such as strong family and peer relationships and involvement in their communities are more likely to feel connected, and the risk for childhood abuse decreases.

Access to services, treatment, or care may prevent problems or improve the mental well-being of children and their families. Families that live in rural areas for instance may find a shortage of mental health providers. Rural clinicians frequently encounter treatment shortages and resource limitations (Wilson et al., 2018; Witt & McNichols, 2014). In addition, those living in poverty and who may lack resources face added barriers. For example, those parents who come from a lower-income family and have experienced ACEs themselves are more likely to have negative relationships and life satisfaction and a higher level of psychological distress (Wheeler et al., 2021).

In addition to limited access, those who have experienced childhood sexual abuse specifically are more likely to mistrust medical providers and are less likely to seek medical care for physical illness (Regal et al., 2020). This is crucial to note because children experiencing abuse are more likely to have medical conditions such as high blood pressure (Banker et al., 2019) and substance use disorder (Watts et al., 2020) in adulthood (among other illnesses).

Other community factors discussed here include risk factors such as community violence and social isolation, and protective factors such as community involvement and community resources (Centers for Disease Control [CDC], 2022). Community violence includes gang violence, frequent rioting, drive-by shootings, and the like. Social isolation may be more likely to happen with families living in rural areas. These two risk factors may increase the likelihood of continued childhood abuse. Community involvement, such as belonging to a religious organization, and community resources, such as education, housing, and health services, may decrease the likelihood of continued childhood abuse. Providing families with established housing and quality access to education and healthcare help to create a stable community and thereby contribute to overall well-being. It is important for clinicians to understand these risk and protective factors in order to recognize signs and symptoms of abuse and be able to report incidents when necessary.

Reporting Child Abuse

At this point in the chapter, you may be asking yourself, "When do I report this and to whom?" Congratulations: you are using your clinical judgment and your knowledge, experience, expertise, and thought processes to make the best clinical decision for your client. The best answer to the question of when to report is: If you have suspicions, report it. Report even when in doubt. However, there are several factors to consider here, the two main ones being legislation in your state and ethical codes.

Clinicians working with minors have a responsibility to know the laws in the state in which they practice. Considerations here include laws protecting minors against abuse, mandated reporting, and legal definitions. For example, in Texas, you can find the legal definitions of child abuse and neglect on the Texas Department of Family Protective Services website (see https://www.dfps.state.tx.us). Mandatory reporting laws are implemented in many states.

Currently, in the United States, 18 states have laws requiring that anyone suspecting child abuse report the incident. Furthermore, and of most importance to those in the mental health field, all states have laws related to mandated reporting by those professions who are in constant contact with children. These professions certainly include counselors, social workers, and child psychologists but also include other professions such as teachers, child care workers, and clergy, among many others.

The two main entities to consider when reporting are child protective services (CPS) and emergency services (i.e., police, 911). If your client is in immediate danger, your first point of contact will be 911. Aside from this, it is important for anyone working with minors to become familiar with CPS reporting guidelines. CPS offices have 24/7 hotlines as well as online reporting systems in some states.

Now that we have answered the when and who, the next questions you may be asking yourself are "How do I report abuse? What do I report? And what happens if I fail to report?" The following is a general step-by-step process for reporting. Always remember to consult the laws in your state, the ethical codes of your profession, and colleagues in your field when in doubt.

The "how" to reporting involves the choice between CPS or 911. When abuse is witnessed or suspected, the clinician should call and/or report the abuse utilizing the CPS reporting number or website in their state. Due to a slower response time (i.e., usually at least 48 hours), in more urgent situations (i.e., the child is currently in danger in their living situation or needs medical treatment), always call the hotline provided for investigation within 24 hours. Of course, in emergency situations (i.e., life-threatening), call 911 immediately.

Generally speaking, report information might include

- Names of those involved: the minor, parent/guardian, anyone else involved
- Location of the minor: home address, daycare or school address
- Any other information about the minor: date of birth, descriptive information, health information, other people living inside the home
- Description of the abuse incident (be as specific as possible): who, what, where, when, how

The CPS office receives this report and identifies whether an investigation is necessary. Failure to report child abuse is against the law, and punishment may include paying a fine, going to jail, and/or losing one's license to practice. In addition to reporting, if a clinician suspects abuse, utilizing your clinical skills such as relationship-building and asking open-ended questions will help the child disclose and clarify information.

Societal Impact of Abuse

Peterson et al. (2018) reported on childhood maltreatment from 2015 and found astonishing results. The impact to the economy of childhood maltreatment included $830,829 per non-fatal victim and $16.6 million per fatal victim. As you can see, financially, abuse has quite an impact on our economic system. In addition, those who have experienced abuse in childhood may experience other effects such as homelessness (de Vries et al., 2018), educational failure, absenteeism from school and work, unemployment, teen pregnancy, and incarceration (CDC, 2016; Felitti et al.,1998; Liu et al., 2013), all of which impact society through added costs to public housing and public health resources.

Trauma in Youth

Trauma as a concept was unknown until approximately 50 years ago. Since then, the Substance Abuse and Mental Health Services Administration (SAMHSA) has been at the forefront of research and treatment related to trauma. In an interview, Bessel van der Kolk, a well-known psychiatrist in the field of trauma work, defines trauma as "an event that overwhelms the nervous system." He goes on to describe the environmental impact of trauma and the lack of healthy response from a support system as affecting whether abuse becomes worse and leads to a trauma reaction and further into a PTSD diagnosis.

There are a few important key themes to remember when thinking about identifying trauma in clients. First, trauma is about a person's subjective experience. Thus, the most important factor here is how the child experiences the event and not only the event itself. Exposure to the traumatic event (or multiple events) can include direct experience (e.g., child victim of physical abuse), witnessing the experience (e.g., child witnessing parent being physically abused), or hearing about the experience (e.g., physical abuse happens to a cousin and the child learns about it either directly from the cousin or from others; American Psychiatric Association [APA], 2022). Other examples of more common traumatic events in childhood other than abuse include school violence, natural disasters, family deaths, and vehicular accidents.

Trauma in and of itself does not necessarily cause a diagnosis of PTSD; rather, there is a correlation between experiencing trauma and developing PTSD. It is important to distinguish that the trauma event itself is an occurrence (singular or plural), while PTSD is a continuation of symptomatology and distress.

The *Diagnostic and Statistical Manual of Mental Disorders* (DSM-5-TR) provides clinicians with the criteria for diagnosing PTSD in individuals (see APA, 2022). Most important are those factors that are specific to PTSD in children, especially those 6 years and younger. Clinicians should be knowledgeable about two important factors related to PTSD in children: (a) they may express and depict the traumatic event through repeated play and (b) children may have recurring nightmares. For children younger than 6, the APA (2022) includes a special section to aid clinicians in diagnosis.

Childhood trauma has been known to have long-term effects later in adulthood. Effects such as anxiety, depression, and addiction (Copeland et al., 2018) are all common mental health issues seen in adults with trauma in childhood.

Societal Impacts of Childhood Trauma

You may be thinking, "What does trauma have to do with a society as a whole?" It's not uncommon for those working within mental health to focus more on individual-level issues. For example, a child comes into your office with their parent. Parent begins to describe that the child has started to have accidents at night. In addition, the child hasn't been able to focus at school and is being bullied by some peers. As a clinician, our efforts will likely be on building a relationship with the parent and child, treatment planning, diagnosing, etc. These are all important aspects of working with clients. But however important working with those on an individual level is, it is equally imperative to recognize how childhood abuse and trauma may impact society as a whole.

Because of the increased awareness of how trauma interacts with physical and mental health, a number of efforts have been made at the local, state, and federal levels. For example, SAMHSA has funded several projects related to trauma-informed approaches. Furthermore, the Department of Defense has focused on trauma prevention in the military. Taking this systemic approach to treating trauma is a crucial public health matter.

Trauma-Informed Care with Youth

The SAMHSA and Justice Strategic Initiative (2014) as well as the US Department of Health and Human Services prepared a document with the purpose of developing a consensus on trauma-informed services. This framework was built to encourage differing systems in client care (i.e., justice, mental health, education, etc.) to understand the link between trauma and behavioral health. The initiative amalgamated information from research, practice, and trauma survivor's perspectives in order to do this. One of the first missions of this initiative was to develop a robust definition that clinicians and communities could use to aid in their efforts to combat trauma. Their definition reads as follows:

> Individual trauma results from an event, series of events, or set of circumstances that is experienced by an individual as physically or emotionally harmful or life threatening and that has lasting adverse effects on the individual's functioning and mental, physical, social, emotional, or spiritual well-being. (p. 7)

The initiative then focuses on the three E's in this definition.

The three Es	Questions to ask yourself
Events	What occurred?
	Was it a single event or recurring?
Experience	What is the child's perception of the event?
	How do they internally and externally experience this event?
	What does the event mean to the child?
	Does the child understand the event?
	What feelings are associated with the event (e.g., shame, fear, humiliation)?
Effects	Are there long-lasting effects?
	When did these effects begin occurring?
	What are the effects (e.g., avoidance, hypervigilance)?

Because trauma affects youth in all populations, communities, and settings, your response to this experience will be crucial when working with children, adolescents, and families. Thus, clinicians are recommended to follow a trauma-informed approach to treatment or trauma-informed care. Essentially, this means that, as treatment providers, we approach client care from a holistic and informed focus where we take into consideration contextual factors. SAMHSA (2014) provides clinicians with four assumptions of trauma-informed care:

- Realization
- Recognize
- Responds
- Resists re-traumatization

In a trauma-informed approach, all parties involved hold a basic notion that trauma affects not only the individual but also the larger community and systems. Next, they are able to identify the signs of childhood trauma. Then, they respond with a trauma-informed approach. Last, they prevent any re-traumatization. SAMHSA (2014) also identifies six principles of trauma-informed care:

1. Safety
2. Trustworthiness and transparency
3. Peer support
4. Collaboration and mutuality
5. Empowerment, voice, and choice
6. Cultural, historical, and gender issues (p. 10)

These six principles can easily be incorporated in any field or setting. Additionally, clinicians should focus their energy on developing a solid therapeutic alliance, building knowledge on abuse and trauma signs and symptoms, and providing effective evidence-based treatment. The therapeutic alliance, also known as the therapeutic or counseling relationship (or simply the professional relationship with clients) is a known effective factor in outcomes. Many of the above SAMHSA principles require a strong relationship with clients in order to provide safety. It is also important for clinicians to not only be aware of the signs and symptoms of abuse and trauma (as described earlier in this chapter), but to also know when and how to intervene, which is where evidence-based practice comes in. Last, clinicians should ensure that any treatment is age- and developmentally appropriate. For example, interventions for an adolescent will likely look different from those for a younger child. In many instances, play therapy has some promise as being effective with children 6 years and younger (Wheeler & Jones, 2015).

From an evidenced-based perspective, several treatments are applicable to youth and families including

- Trauma-focused cognitive behavioral therapy (TF-CBT)
- Eye-movement desensitization and reprocessing (EMDR)
- Cognitive behavioral therapy (CBT)
- Cognitive processing therapy (CPT)

An empirical review by Blankenship (2017) found that EMDR and TF-CBT are highly effective when working with children, and we discuss these two therapies here. Other considerations or strategies include:

- Psychoeducation
- Meditation
- Yoga
- Play therapy
- Neurofeedback
- Family therapy

Trauma-Focused Cognitive Behavioral Therapy
TF-CBT, developed by Cohen, Mannarino, and Deblinger (2006) has the most evidence-based backing for treatment of trauma in children and adolescents. This therapy incorporates trauma interventions with CBT philosophies. Additional factors include family and attachment, humanism, and neurobiology. For those interested in training in TF-CBT, you can find a certificate program for mental health providers at https://tfcbt.org/.

Eye-Movement Desensitization and Reprocessing
EMDR, developed by Shapiro (2012), is becoming more prevalent in mental health fields. This seven-phase treatment incorporates bilateral stimulation, desensitization, and reprocessing of the trauma. For those interested in training in EMDR, you can find information for mental health providers at https://www.emdr.com/what-is-emdr/ and at https://www.emdria.org/about-emdr-therapy/.

Overall issues with both TF-CBT and EMDR are well known. First, both treatments can be quite costly to mental health providers. Second, studies comparing TF-CBT and EMDR have found that both treatments are equally effective in treating trauma in youth. Specific to EMDR, there has not been extensive evidence on which pieces of EMDR are most effective and how EMDR is effective, making some skeptical of the bilateral stimulation portion specifically.

Summary

While childhood abuse and trauma are certainly related, it is important for clinicians to be able to recognize each of these in order to provide best practices in client and family care. In addition to care at the individual level, clinicians may also consider advocacy efforts in all areas in order to provide a systemic perspective on the prevention and treatment of abuse and trauma. Collaborating with other health professions as well as with communities from a public health perspective will help decrease abuse and trauma statistics. This chapter has highlighted the importance of trauma-informed care in the overall healthcare of children and adolescents.

Case Study: Victoria

Victoria is a 16-year-old junior in high school. She is a cheerleader and active on school leadership projects. Victoria is hopeful to become Valedictorian and attend an Ivy League school majoring in pre-law. She is known by her teachers and peers to be a rule-follower, good student, and kind individual. One day after cheerleading practice, Victoria is in a head-on collision with another vehicle. Both parties survive but not without physical and emotional injury. A month since the accident, Victoria has been forced to take a break from cheerleading and her grades have slipped. At school, she is withdrawn and when confronted about it, she becomes aggressive in speech. Teachers, peers, and family have growing concern for Victoria. The high school counselor has started to see Victoria. Because Victoria already had a good working relationship with the school counselor through a peer mentorship program she was involved in, she felt safe opening up to her. Victoria began by explaining to the school counselor that she hasn't felt like herself lately. She is no longer interested in her normal activities, does not study for tests, and does not even understand the point of college. In addition to this, she has not been sleeping at night because every night since the accident she wakes up feeling panicky and unsafe. When she does fall asleep, she frequently has nightmares of the few seconds prior to the collision. Last, Victoria's doctor has cleared her for driving again, yet she refuses to get behind the wheel and even feels extremely anxious entering a vehicle.

After the school counselor listens empathetically to Victoria's experience and symptomatology, he has a hunch that she may be experiencing some PTSD symptoms. The school counselor tells Victoria about his hunch and recommends they set a meeting with her parents. Victoria agrees, and they set a meeting for the next day.

During the session, Victoria described her experiences and the school counselor discussed with her parents the likelihood of PTSD symptoms. The school counselor, wanting to be as collaborative as possible, asked the family for their input on next steps. Victoria and her family were open to counseling. The school counselor also mentioned that perhaps a psychiatrist or medical doctor may be worth seeing as well due to Victoria's lack of sleep at night and how that may impact her mental health and well-being. Victoria agreed and stated that she would like to visit her regular medical doctor first as she was more comfortable with her. Together, they set up goals for contacting these different entities to provide appropriate care for Victoria while she healed. Victoria received short-term medication for sleep and has been seeing a licensed professional counselor who utilizes TF-CBT with adolescents.

References

Aafjes-van Doorn, K., Békés, V., Prout, T. A., & Hoffman, L. (2020). Psychotherapists' vicarious traumatization during the COVID-19 pandemic. *Psychological Trauma: Theory, Research, Practice, and Policy*, *12*(S1), S148–S150. https://doi.org/10.1037/tra0000868

Al-Modallal, H., Al-Omari, H., Hamaideh, S., & Shehab, T. (2020). Childhood domestic violence as an ancestor for adulthood mental health problems: Experiences of Jordanian Women. *The Family Journal*, *28*(4), 390–395. https://doi.org/10.1177/1066480720909845

American Psychiatric Association. (2022). Diagnostic and statistical manual of mental disorders (5th ed., text rev.). https://doi.org/10.1176/appi.books.9780890425787

Banker, J., Witting, A. B., & Jensen, J. (2019). Hormones and childhood trauma: Links between the physical and psychological. *The Family Journal*, *27*(3), 300–308. https://doi.org/10.1177/1066480719844026

Blankenship, D. M. (2017). Five efficacious treatments for posttraumatic stress disorder: An empirical review. *Journal of Mental Health Counseling*, *39*(4), 275–288. doi:10.17744/mehc.39.4.01

Boserup, B., McKenney, M., & Elkbuli, A. (2020). Alarming trends in US domestic violence during the COVID-19 pandemic. *American Journal of Emergency Medicine, 38*, 2753–2755. https://doi.org/10.1016/j.ajem.2020.04.077

Centers for Disease Control and Prevention. (2022). Child abuse and neglect prevention. Retrieved from https://www.cdc.gov/violenceprevention/childabuseandneglect/index.html\

Centers for Disease Control and Prevention National Center for Injury Prevention and Control, Division of Violence Prevention. (2016). Association between ACEs and negative outcomes. Retrieved from https://www.cdc.gov/violenceprevention/childabuseandneglect/acestudy/ace-graphics.html

Centers for Disease Control and Prevention National Center for Injury Prevention and Control. (2022). Fast facts: Preventing child abuse and neglect. Retrieved from https://www.cdc.gov/violenceprevention/childabuseandneglect/fastfact.html

Child Welfare Information Gateway. (2021). Child abuse and neglect fatalities 2019: Statistics and interventions. U.S. Department of Health and Human Services, Administration for Children and Families, Children's Bureau. Retrived from https://www.childwelfare.gov/pubpdfs/fatality.pdf

Child Welfare Information Gateway (n.d.). Mental health of parents and caregivers. Retrieved from https://www.childwelfare.gov/topics/can/factors/parentcaregiver/mentalhealth/

Cohen, J. A., Mannarino, A. P., & Deblinger, E. (2006). *Treating trauma and traumatic grief in children and adolescents.* Guilford.

Copeland, W. E., Shanahan, L., Hinesley, J., Chan, R. F., Aberg, K. A., Fairbank, J. A., . . . Costello, E. J. (2018). Association of childhood trauma exposure with adult psychiatric disorders and functional outcomes. *JAMA Network Open, 1*(7), e184493–e184493. doi:10.1001/jamanetworkopen.2018.4493

de Vries, S. R., Juhnke, G. A., & Trahan Keene, C. (2018). PTSD, complex PTSD, and childhood abuse: Gender differences among a homeless sample. *Journal for Social Action in Counseling & Psychology, 10*(2), 1–15.

Evans, D. P., Hawk, S. R., & Ripkey, C. E. (2021). Domestic violence in Atlanta, Georgia before and during COVID-19. *Violence and Gender, 8*(3), 140–148. https://doi.org/10.1089/vio.2020.0061

Felitti, V. J., Anda, R. F., Nordenberg, D., Williamson, D. F., Spitz, A. M., Edwards, V., & Marks, J. S. (1998). Relationship of childhood abuse and household dysfunction to many of the leading causes of death in adults: The Adverse Childhood Experiences (ACE) Study. *American Journal of Preventive Medicine, 14*(4), 245–258. doi:10.1016/s0749-3797(98)00017-8

James, R. K., & Gilliland, B. E. (2017). *Crisis intervention strategies* (8th ed.). Cengage Learning.

Litam, S. D., Ausloos, C., & Harrichand, J. J. (2021). Stress and resilience among professional counselors during the COVID-19 pandemic. *Journal of Counseling & Development, 99*, 384–395. https://doi.org/ 0.1002/jcad.12391

Liu, Y., Croft, J. B., Chapman, D. P., Perry, G. S., Greenlund, K. J., Zhao, G., & Edwards, V. J. (2013). Relationship between adverse childhood experiences and unemployment among adults from five US states. *Social Psychiatry and Psychiatric Epidemiology, 48*(3), 357–369. doi:10.1007/s00127-012-0554-1

Navalta, C. P., McGee, L., & Underwood, J. (2018). Adverse childhood experiences, brain development, and mental health: A call for neurocounseling. *Journal of Mental Health Counseling, 40*(3), 266-278. https://doi.org/10.17744/mehc.40.3.07

Panchal. U., Salazar de Pablo, G., Franco, M., Moreno, C., Parellada, M., Arango, C., & Fusar-Pol, P. (2021). The impact of COVID-19 lockdown on child and adolescent mental health: Systematic review. *European Child & Adolescent Psychiatry*, 1-27. https://doi.org/10.1007/s00787-021-01856-w

Peterson, C., Florence, C., & Klevens, J. (2018). The economic burden of child maltreatment in the United States, 2015. *Child Abuse & Neglect, 86*, 178-183. https://doi.org/10.1016/j.chiabu.2018.09.018

Regal, R. A., Wheeler, N. J., Daire, A. P., & Spears, N. (2020). Childhood sexual abuse survivors undergoing cancer treatment: A case for trauma-informed integrated care. *Journal of Mental Health Counseling, 42*(1), 15-31. https://doi.org/10.17744/mehc.42.1.02

Shapiro, F. (2012). EMDR therapy: An overview of current and future research. *European Review of Applied Psychology, 62*, 193-195. doi:10.1016/j.erap. 2012.09.005

Springer, K. W., Sheridan, J., Kuo, D., & Carnes, M. (2007). Long-term physical and mental health consequences of childhood physical abuse: Results from a large population-based sample of men and women. *Child Abuse & Neglect, 31*(5), 517-530. https://doi.org/10.1016/j.chiabu.2007.01.003

Substance Abuse and Mental Health Services Administration (SAMHSA). (2015). Understanding child trauma. Retrieved from https://www.samhsa.gov/child-trauma/understanding-child-trauma

Substance Abuse and Mental Health Services Administration (SAMHSA) and Justice Strategic Initiative (2014). SAMHSA's concept of trauma and guidance for a trauma-informed approach. Retrieved from https://ncsacw.samhsa.gov/userfiles/files/SAMHSA_Trauma.pdf

Watts, J. R., O'Sullivan, D., Panlilio, C., & Daniels, A. D. (2020). Childhood emotional abuse and maladaptive coping in adults seeking treatment for substance use disorder. *Journal of Addictions & Offender Counseling, 41*(1), 18-34. doi:10.1002/jaoc.12073

Wheeler, N., & Jones, K. D. (2015). DSM-5 PTSD in children six and younger: Implications for assessment and treatment. *Journal of Child and Adolescent Counseling, 1*(2), 119-134. doi:10.1080/23727810.2015.1090289

Wheeler, N. J., Regal, R. A., Griffith, S. A. M., & Barden, S. M. (2021). Dyadic influence of adverse childhood experiences: Counseling implications for mental and relational health. *Journal of Counseling & Development, 99*(1), 24-36. doi:10.1002/jcad.12351

Wilson, T. A., Knezevic, B., Kibugi, B., Peterson, P., & Polacek, E. (2018). Experiences and retention among rural mental health counselors. *Journal of Mental Health Counseling, 40*(3). 240-248. https://doi.org/10.17744/mehc.40.3.05

Witt, K. J., & McNichols, C. (2014). Assessing the needs of rural counselor supervisors in Texas. *Journal of Professional Counseling, 41*(2), 15-29.

PART III
AFFECTING CHANGE

11
Engaging Communities in Need

Overview

Communities can have a significant impact on youth and adolescent development. In this chapter, we provide an overview of issues, challenges, and services to those communities in need but lacking access to care. We highlight differences in urban and rural poverty and methods to increase resources for and services to affected areas.

Introduction

Case Study: Michelle

Michelle grew up in a single-parent household. Her mother never really worked a steady job, mostly bounced around and never lasted anywhere more than a few weeks. Their monthly income consisted of Temporary Assistance for Needy Families (TANF) checks and food stamps. Government and community services were a staple in their household. Government commodities such as women, infants, and children (WIC) vouchers, community food pantries, local church organizations, and the county health departments were routinely utilized for sustainability. Michelle's mother depended on community resources to survive. They lived in a small rural community. There was no public transportation, so walking was routine (to church, grocery store, doctor, etc.). They lived in public housing, so for Michelle this lifestyle was normal and most of her peers operated in the same day-to-day mode: survival. For Michelle, school was a safe haven in certain ways. Her school offered food, shelter, and consistent utilities (something that often came and went at home). However, Michelle consistently struggled with her school work.

> Her mother could not read, so help at home was minimal and often undervalued. So, while school offered her survival, it was also her first lesson at how life was different for her than for many others.
>
> Michelle's mother suffered from chronic anxiety and depression. While her mother was loving and attentive, she was unpredictable. She often made erratic decisions based on emotions instead of logic. She was fearful and paranoid of most strangers. She was nomadic and consistently moved herself and Michelle from housing project to housing project. This inconsistency made schooling difficult for Michelle and made accessing routine services difficult for Michelle's mother. In all, Michelle moved seven times before she exited elementary school. She had been held back twice, once in first grade and again in third grade. As she got older her school transitions made it easy for her to fall under the radar, and none of the schools dug too far into her history.
>
> Michelle and her mother's relationship with community and school-wide systems was complicated and complex. While they needed them to survive, they also needed to escape them from time to time, otherwise things could get even tougher for them. Since Michelle's mom couldn't read she couldn't always fill out the paperwork needed to get resources like child support from Michelle's father. When things got overly complex, they left again, moved on to the next apartment complex, the next school, and the next small town. This movement wasn't always easy but it was perceived as necessary.

Community resources are often limited, no matter where you are, but especially in rural areas. Trust is low, need is high, and life is fluid. Michelle and her mother are just one example of families who depend of the support of others within their community to get by and often bounce from place to place, school to school, agency to agency, looking to survive another day.

Communities

Communities can have a significant impact on youth and adolescents. The environment in which one lives can provide both positive and negative influences. Research has documented these influential factors through relationships, collective efficacy, and community resources (Riina et al., 2013). These three factors will guide an outline of our discussion on communities.

Relationships

The importance and value that a community places on relationships can be seen throughout its system. The framework and mechanisms for these relationships are primarily driven by parenting, parenting skills, and familial attachment. Living in neighborhoods with high crime rates is often associated with poor parental involvement (Farrington, 2011). Weak family systems plagued with insecure attachments (Bowlby, 1979) are much more likely to into systems with deeper divides, ambivalence, and avoidance. Systems defined in such ways are cancer to neighborhoods and communities. Strong communities begin in strong households. Children who develop with secure attachments are much more likely to develop healthy relationships with their peers. Children with healthy parental attachments are also much more likely to relate positively to other adults in their lives. These family factors can mediate the relationship between community violence and community engagement.

Collective Efficacy

Collective efficacy is defined as "the group's shared belief in its conjoint capabilities to organize and execute courses of action required to produce given levels of attainments" (Bandura, 1997, p. 477). According to Bandura (1997), an individual's beliefs in collective efficacy influence the futures they seek to achieve through collective action, how well they use their resources, how much effort they put into their group activities, their persistence when collective efforts fail to produce results or confront powerful opposition, and their vulnerability to the discouragement that can affect people taking on difficult social issues (p. 76). The cornerstones of social cohesion and collective efficacy are relationships (previously discussed) and trust. When a community has well-established relationships and a sense of trust among neighbors, the adults take on a role of monitoring or watching out for each other's children. For example, neighbors would be more likely to observe if a child is skipping school or engaged in activities that could be risky (i.e., drug or substance use, selling narcotics, fighting). Communities such as these are also more likely to pool resources to provide positive activities for children and adolescents, such as playgrounds, aquatic centers, or ball fields. Researchers have also documented that communities with strong collective efficacy are more likely to have reduced community violence, violent victimization, and homicide rates (Hipp & Wo, 2015). Additionally, researchers found a negative relationship between collective efficacy and adolescent antisocial behaviors (Fagan et al., 2014). These types of studies outline the importance of communities, neighbors, and collective trust. Neighborhoods pulling together and merging resources certainly can have a positive impact on the lives of children and adolescents within them. This construct is better known as *neighborhood sense of community* (SOC).

Neighborhood SOC is founded in ideas of collective efficacy and neighboring (Perkins & Long, 2002) and has been historically categorized as a perceived sense of belongingness and a shared belief that community members' needs will be met through established relationships (McMillan & Chavis, 1986). Researchers agree that neighborhood SOC positively influences individuals and neighborhoods and also drives how community members engage in activism for social change (Elfassi et al., 2016). According to McMillan and Chavis (1986), there are four dimensions to neighborhood SOC:

- *Membership*: A sense of belongingness or connectedness to the community
- *Influence*: A sense of contribution or making a difference in the community
- *Needs fulfillment*: The belief that community members will meet one another's needs through established relationships
- *Emotional connection*: A shared social and emotional connection or attachment, through experiences or common places

Several instruments have resulted from McMillan and Chavis's (1986) model and been modified to assess SOC. The Sense of Community Index (SCI), by Chavis et al. (1986), has most often been utilized within empirical studies. Recent studies have demonstrated a relationship between SOC and protecting against the negative impacts of neighborhood violence, disorganization, and drug and alcohol abuse (Lardier et al., 2017); predicting academic achievement (Garcia-Reid et al., 2013); and the relationship between community participation, neighborhood SOC, and ethnic identity (Lardier, 2018). Studies illuminate the role of neighborhood SOC in youth development and health promotion, but continued research is needed to further validate these paradigms within younger populations such as children and adolescents.

Community Resources

System resources typically refer to the availability, accessibility, quality, and affordability of services within a community. These services might include but are not limited to social, recreational, educational, medical, mental, childcare, or employment resources. High-poverty communities and neighborhoods are plagued by low resources which complicate their members' ability to provide support and meet the needs of their children and adolescents. However, poverty is not the only risk factor for communities that suffer from low levels of services or stripped-downed services. Instability, high unemployment rates, low community participation, and high crime rates are all contributing factors that put communities at risk for inadequate resources. On the flip side, there are also protective factors that can be found within a community to help moderate risk and help to support communities in providing resources to youth and adolescents. Communities have the ability to provide opportunities for youth to overcome barriers and protect them from certain risks. The more connectedness an adolescent has to their community the more likely they are to experience positive outcomes (academic, social, or career development) (Kim et al., 2016). Evidence also suggests that youth who participate in or belong to community organizations are also less likely to involve themselves in antisocial behaviors or engage in substance abuse (Bond et al., 2007). These studies build the case for all communities (especially those that suffer from risk factors) to establish community resources to ensure high quality and available programming for youth.

Underserved Communities

The Department of Health and Human Services defines underserved communities as those that have shortages within their public health system (which includes mental health services) and are marked by high poverty, high unemployment, low academic attainment, high infant mortality, and/or a high elderly population (US Department of Health and Human Services, Health Resources and Services Administration, 2012). More than 10 million children, nearly 1 in 7 (14.4%) live in poverty (Trisi & Saenz, 2019). The child poverty rate is 1.5 times higher than that for adults ages 18–64 (9.4%) and adults 65 and older (8.9%). According to Aber and Chaudry (2010), these discrepancies between adult and child poverty rates highlight the need for investing in services specifically designed for children and adolescents. Based on these figures, it is imperative that those children living near or below the poverty line remain a focus of research and future state and federal funding to support both prevention and intervention within underserved communities.

A major contributor to these disparities is a lack of resources. These resources include funding, infrastructure, research, available workforce, and engagement. Even when services are available, numerous systemic factors impact whether community members access or receive care, including barriers such as lack of transportation, low mental health literacy, stigma, and negative perceptions of care providers (Crumb et al., 2019).

Adolescents in underserved communities consistently lack the resources and skills needed to develop cognitively and emotionally (Hooper et al., 2021). Social competence, problem-solving, self-awareness, and resilience help youth envision and have hope for the future.

Rural Communities

Families living in rural communities often have fewer resources and poorer access to services that meet their needs. These families often suffer from severe stress due to financial and social restraints that influence their everyday lives. These family systems are more likely to experience food shortages, divorce, poor physical/mental health, job loss, and violence (Felner & DeVries, 2013). Rural community members often experience isolation while lacking needed resources to make personal and professional gains. Marginalization and stigmatization plague these communities, and while basic resources are scarce, larger-scale services such as hospitals, rehabilitation services, and physicians with specializations are almost nonexistent (Douthit, et al., 2015). Rural communities are excessively impacted by health issues such as cancer (Moy et al., 2017) and heart disease (Kulshreshtha et al., 2014), which drives this population to experience a higher morbidity rate. These same communities on average have a higher percentage of members who experience substance abuse and have a mental health diagnosis (Smalley et al., 2010). Moving beyond diagnosis, due to several unfortunate factors (i.e., lack of resources, treatment options, and mental health stigma), the suicide rate was nearly 1.5 times higher in rural than in urban counties between 2001 and 2015 (Ivey-Stephenson et al., 2017). These shortages place children and adolescents in these rural communities at a significant disadvantage and at greater risk for engaging in risky behaviors. These children and adolescents are also much more likely to experience poor mental, emotional, and overall wellness. A study of teens in a rural county in Mississippi found that youth who experience depression or anxiety report fewer visits to pediatric offices but more visits to hospital emergency rooms, county health department clinics, and school-based clinics (Rickert et al., 1996). These patterns suggest that rural communities need to better support agencies that can link services among healthcare providers.

According to Yoshikawa et al. (2012), research has established a clear and significant relationship between rural poverty-stricken communities and an adolescent's risk of developing issues related to wellness (emotional, mental, physical, or behavioral). Research has demonstrated that "poverty is a critical risk factor for many of the mental, emotional, and behavioral disorders of youth and adolescents" (Yoshikawa et al., 2012, p. 272). Accounting for the numerous risk factors that children and adolescents living in poverty face, they are almost destined to experience some type of negative outcome later in life. However, protective factors, if present in a youth's life, can mediate those risks. For example, a positive school environment can be influential in helping to develop life-long skills like grit and resilience for adulthood.

Urban Communities

Around 85% of the US population resides in urban counties, even though 63% percent of US counties are classified as rural (Rothwell et al., 2014). Regardless of location, however, studies have shown that the pervasiveness of health concerns are similar between urban and rural communities (Crumb et al., 2018). Specifically, when examining mental health, researchers estimate that mental disorders affect about 20% of the rural population, which is similar to urban populations (Gamm et al., 2010). Despite the prevalence of mental health issues, access to healthcare and other wellness resources varies greatly between rural and urban or metropolitan areas. Rural and urban communities unfortunately experience similar barriers that prevent access to public health and community resources; these common barriers include lack of insurance, low mental health literacy, stigma, and shortage of affordable resources.

Youth in urban communities, specifically Black youth or people of color, face challenges that are distinct from those faced by rural youth. These challenges put them at a high risk of experiencing lower levels of overall wellness, including environmental stressors related to a lack of affordable housing (Gallagher et al., 2018), lack of quality public health resources (Patel et al., 2019), and repeated exposure to violence (Warner, 2019). Research also indicates that students in urban schools are more likely to experience racism when attending school systems that use curricula that do not cater to all students' needs and cultural or ethnic experiences (Aguayo, 2019). Further studies show that repeated exposure to discrimination is significantly linked with elevated levels of stress and anxiety; this can ultimately lead to decreased mental wellness (Hughes et al., 2015).

Challenges and Oppression

Intersectionality

Academic and youth advocates often use the term "intersectionality" to discuss the impact of multiple factors that can influence an adolescent's wellness or development. Essentially, this term seeks to better understand what happens when an adolescent simultaneously experiences several oppressions at the same time or during the same period of development. This term was originally introduced by Crenshaw (1991), who stated that gender, race, social class, and sexuality are inseparable dimensions of oppression that are not always recognized by current legal constructs or systems. Initially, these studies explored the intersection of identities that Black women experience. Intersectionality is now utilized throughout disciplines to highlight how these intertwining systems of oppression influence each other.

Psychology and counseling literature has shown an increased interest in intersectionality frameworks and theories (Galliher et al., 2017). For instance, Shin (2015) has encouraged counselors to attend to a combination of factors and internal social identities when working with clients. However, this work is showing up outside of publications and academic journals, as youth activists and their allies within the United States and across the world are working in a variety of fields that include police reform, education, and immigration. These concepts, research studies, and daily activism are helping the field to better understand how youth function within their own unique selves and configure their social identities (Harris & Patton, 2019). Here, we discuss several of the marginalizing forces that youth can experience within their communities during adolescent development.

Racism

Jones (1972) defined racism as "the exercise of power against a racial group defined as inferior by individuals and institutions with the intentional or unintentional support of the entire culture" (p. 117). According to Jones, racism manifests itself in three forms: individual, institutional, and cultural. Later, Bonilla-Silva (1997) challenged individuals to reinterpret racism and highlight the role of organized systems in which public policies, organizational practices, and cultural representations work together to reinforce and perpetuate racial inequities. Almost 25 years later, racism scholars continue to explore the complexities and constructs of prejudice behaviors. According to Sue et al. (2007), youth of color experience direct, indirect, second-hand, and subtle forms of racism every day. These indignities communicate negativity to these emerging adults and reflect a systemic, multi-level construct that has evolved and influenced generations for hundreds of years.

While a large emphasis of previous literature has focused on racism and the individual, a new focus within counseling and psychology is to examine institutional, structural, and cultural racism and their impacts on adolescent health (Jones & Neblett, 2017). One example, is Critical Race Theory (CRT), which focuses on the intersection of numerous oppressions and social identities as determinants of the social context that influences physical, emotional, and mental health development among adolescents (Ford & Airhihenbuwa, 2010). However, current research within this new focus is limited in scope, and those limitations are influencing the field's ability to develop new multisystemic programming and policies to address the impact of racism on youth's overall wellness and development.

Residential Segregation

One of the most extensively studied arenas for institutional racism is residential segregation. Residential segregation illuminates the differences in neighborhood and community quality of life, living conditions, and access to opportunity (White et al., 2012). Neighborhoods with limited mobility, access, and resources such as early childhood education and employment opportunities are susceptible to high levels of poverty, crime, and poor health outcomes. Long-standing racism and institutional neglect in poor, segregated communities contribute to weakened communities and impact neighborhood relationships and trust among community members. Simply put, residential segregation by race (especially Hispanic and Black communities) has created environments for children and adolescents that inflict more adversity and poor physical and mental health outcomes as compared to those experienced by Whites living in more affluent neighborhoods. A national study of individuals in early adulthood found that the removal of residential segregation would eliminate Black–White differences in earnings, high school graduation rates, and unemployment and reduce racial differences in single-motherhood by two-thirds (Cutler & Glaeser, 1997). Families and communities play a crucial role in protecting children and youth from the external stressors and influences of racism; therefore, the stronger the neighborhood/community and the more resilient the family an individual has, the less likely they are to be negatively influenced by toxic stress imposed by prejudice and discrimination (Brody et al., 2017). The challenge facing the mental health community is to focus more research and advocacy efforts on confronting and illuminating the influence of structural, organizational, and cultural racism on child and adolescent development.

Barriers to Sexual Minority Youth

TIME magazine, in 2005, had a White male teen on its cover with the title "The Battle Over Gay Teens." Almost two decades later, LGBTQ bullying in schools and youth suicide have received increased national media attention and youth supportive community resources. Within this climate, the average age of coming out as LGBTQ has dropped to around 13 years. Twenty-five percent of transgender people also come out about their gender identity in young adulthood (younger than 25) (Riggs & Patterson, 2009). As youth come out earlier in adolescence, they also confront peer, adult, and community attitudes and reactions for longer periods of time and at a more vulnerable stage of development that may make it difficult to manage prejudice and homophobia. Families, schools, neighborhoods, churches, and the child welfare system assist in the development of children and adolescence; however, these same institutions can also be spaces of homophobia and transphobia for LGBTQ youth. These issues are potentially amplified for LGBTQ youth of color who, in addition to dealing with attitudes of homophobia, also have to contend with racism (Rosenberg, 2017).

Community resources, policies, and interventions are vital to the health and success of LGBTQ youth as they move into early adulthood. According to Choi et al. (2019), LGBTQ individuals in the United States experience poverty at higher rates compared to heterosexual people. Their research also showed that transgender individuals experience the highest rates of economic insecurity. However, there is limited research into why LGBTQ individuals experience poverty at greater levels. While economic insecurity is a complex issue, studies have shown that childhood poverty is linked to adult poverty (Carpenter et al., 2020). Therefore, communities with high rates of children in poverty should be aware of these links and use them to predict and prevent poor future economic outcomes for their community members. Barriers such as low educational opportunities, unemployment, low wages, high cost of living, housing instability, and transportation are all factors that might influence these outcomes.

Homelessness and Poverty

Morton et al. (2017) estimate that 700,000 US youth experience some form of homelessness each year. Many of these youth also experience the detrimental effects of being homeless, such as substance abuse, violence, or incarceration. Prior to leaving home, many experienced childhood sexual or physical abuse (Bender et al., 2015), and many also report that they have a parent with substance abuse or mental health issues. This exposure to trauma so early in life has the potential to impact youth long after they leave home (Tyler et al., 2018). Combining early trauma and homelessness creates vulnerability for revictimization while living on the street. These risk factors lead youth to cope and manage their circumstances in different ways. Managing the stress of being homeless often leads to drug and alcohol abuse (Tyler & Melander, 2015). Moreover, youth who experience additional trauma while homeless are even more likely to abuse substances and experience even more severe mental health issues such as anxiety, depression, and suicidal ideation (Narendorf et al., 2017). These studies highlight a call for action among community leaders and child advocates.

Drug and Alcohol Abuse

Substance abuse has been identified as one of the main causes of death among youth (Kann et al., 2018). It is also interrelated with issues such as poor mental health (anxiety, depression), criminal behavior (aggression), and negative social relationships. According to Berge et al. (2016), once these behaviors are adopted in adolescence, the negative consequences can extend well into adulthood. Therefore, these behaviors are a major public health concern for youth.

For decades, federal reports based on Neighborhood Disorganization Theory have documented the significant relationship between criminal activity and substance abuse (Substance Abuse and Mental Health Administration, 2009) for both adult and youth populations (Jang, 2018). According to this theory, neighborhoods that have high levels of criminal activity and violence more often have a higher number of members who also struggle with alcohol and drug addiction. However, research utilizing multilevel modeling suggests there is a lack of consensus about neighborhood-level influences (Algren et al., 2015). In 2014, a meta-analysis of 23 studies of neighborhood effects on youth substance abuse reported no evidence for a role of residential mobility, crime, employment, neighborhood attitudes toward drinking, social capital, and collective efficacy (Jackson et al., 2014).

More recent literature calls for further research and believes previous studies may be missing part of the story due to a lack of controls in moderating and influential factors. In sum, researchers and youth advocates must continue to evaluate multilevel factors and intersectionality when it comes to the complex influences that contribute to youth substance abuse. Unfortunately, with resources waning in both urban and rural communities, the cycle of violence and abuse is only being fueled by the COVID-19 pandemic and economic slump currently being faced in the United States.

Protective and Moderating Factors

Neighborhood Partnerships

Neighborhood partnerships include adults in the community who can use their talents and resources to create stability and support. Promotion of wellness at the local level, integral approaches, local partnerships, and community engagement have all been well supported and encouraged in the literature (Weiss et al., 2016). However, despite the evidence, access to quality programs for children and youth are still lacking in many areas across the United States. These collaborations are key to addressing complex needs, which in turn can support community recovery and provide protective factors for the vulnerable. Examples of collaborative community programs include promotion of health and overall well-being in child and adolescent populations. Local governments are key in addressing inequalities due to their ability to create and enforce policies concerning social and health services.

A key limitation to neighborhood partnerships occurs before youth are ever actually involved: this limitation is the disconnect between evidence-based programming and practice-based participation. Many researchers publish studies and develop programs without meaningful participation and feedback from those who will actually be implementing the programs. Partnerships require mutually agreed upon principles; shared vision; clear, consistent communication; cultural awareness; and a working knowledge of community needs. This type of collaboration is key to creating valuable and sustainable partnerships that deliver community-specific approaches that target the needs of adolescents across systems.

Community-Based Interventions

Adolescence is a crucial time period in which to learn healthy behaviors and create patterns that improve and sustain physical and mental wellness. While some youth have family support and live in communities that are rich in resources, others are not as fortunate and may be at particular risk for developing poor behaviors and lack of access to quality care/support. Mental health issues in adolescents that are left untreated can easily extend into adulthood, which can lead to both physical and mental health impairments (Nelson et al., 2020). Thus, it is essential that youth advocates (pediatricians, psychiatrists, counselors, community leaders, schools) find evidence-based interventions to enhance those protective mental factors that might discourage the development of risky behaviors within this population.

Programs guided by communities are greatly needed to raise awareness and develop strategies to address risk factors for mental wellness among youth. *Community-based participatory research* (CBPR) offers a model by which to engage communities in research and intervention that involves all partners and recognizes strengths in collaboration. According to Stacciarini et al. (2011), CBPR is an especially effective instrument to engage underserved minority communities when focusing on mental health risk factors and outcomes. CBRP has also been recognized for its utility in health promotion and in highlighting health disparities within communities (Stadnick et al., 2016).

When it comes to community-based services, there are long-standing problems especially when discussing mental health services. These problems include but are not limited to access, discontinuation of support, funding, lack of integrated care, and system fragmentation. Some experts argue the need for *integrated community-based youth service hubs* (ICYSHs) to provide more comprehensive youth-focused services. This type of model could be considered a "one stop shop" that offers youth and families access to social services, medical care, and mental health services. Previously conducted research on behavioral health integration in primary care settings has suggested overall benefits to clients (Njoroge et al., 2016). As policymakers and key stakeholders continue to debate the transformation of youth mental health services, collaborative community-based partnerships should be key in their development of new approaches. Many of the issues previously mentioned in this chapter can potentially be addressed by integrating existing services and upholding existing partnerships through additional funding, support, and community outreach.

Youth Empowerment

Self-efficacy can influence the motivation to engage in specific behaviors (Bandura, 1977). *Positive youth development* focuses on the potential of youth in their development of constructive behaviors. This perspective is drawn from experiences with youth overcoming hardships, showing grit, being resilient, and serving as local change agents (Floyd & McKenna, 2003). While there are many working definitions of positive youth development, Hamilton (1999) offer a foundational description: "youth development has traditionally been and is still most widely used to mean a natural process: the growing capacity of a young person to understand and act on the environment" (Hamilton, 1999, p. 3). Later, Damon (2004) wrote that positive youth development takes a strength-based approach to defining and understanding the developmental process. Specifically, it "emphasizes the manifest potentialities rather than the supposed incapacities of young people" (2004, p. 15). This perspective represents a shift in the community's mindset. The growing acknowledgment that youth are influential in community development has led, in part, to a growing emphasis on youth participation in decision-making and leadership (Adams & Oshima, 2014). Research has shown for decades that this type of engagement for adolescents can empower individuals and further self-efficacy beliefs by encouraging youth to think and act independently, create meaning in their lives, and understand how their single contributions can benefit the community at large (Conger & Kanungo, 1988).

The focus of these types of models organizes systems to foster and develop the strengths of youth and adolescents. These initiatives move beyond prevention or responsive services and key in on the process of developing positive behaviors and beliefs. Communities and organizations utilizing these models can work with youth to instill hope, build relationships, and teach youth how to make independent choices while assuming community responsibilities. Youth are an asset and a resource to any community. This population has tremendous energy and talents, and they offer communities a new perspective, one that differs from previous generations. While youth certainly have needs and should be supported and cared for by their communities, they also have a great capacity to contribute and be engaged.

Summary

The demand for care and services for youth and adolescents only seems to be increasing, especially for long-term counseling and therapy. Adolescents have disproportionally experienced worse mental health outcomes since the start of the COVID-19 pandemic, with around 74% reporting that their mental health worsened during this time period (Czeisler et al., 2021). In most communities, especially those with the greatest demand, the delivery of services must be re-evaluated to ensure that effective, accessible, and equitable services are available to youth who are in need and most at risk for developing risky behaviors. As noted throughout this chapter, research has clearly documented limitations within the delivery of services. However, communities have the ability to provide opportunities and services for youth to assist them with overcoming barriers and protect them from certain risks. Moving forward, partnerships that promote wellness should be considered integral to support and encourage the development of wellness in our communities, especially when addressing the needs of youth and adolescents.

Case Study: Trinity

Trinity is a 13-year-old African American girl. Trinity's family lives in a city located in the midwestern part of the United States, with a population of around 600,000 people. Trinity lives in a two-bedroom downtown apartment that she shares with her mother, grandmother, and three siblings. She is the oldest of four children and has several responsibilities around the apartment. After she comes home from school each day, she is responsible for helping watch her siblings, feed them, and give them a bath each evening. Her mother and grandmother both work the second shift at the hospital downtown. These responsibilities leave her little time to hang out with her friends, watch television, or do her homework. She is typically an average student, but lately she has trouble concentrating and completing her homework.

Two weeks ago, on her way home from school, she witnessed a violent crime. Just as she got off the bus in the afternoon, she witnessed two men outside a bar fighting. One man grabbed a knife from his pocket and stabbed the other man. The assailant ran away and left the other man to die on the streets. In all the chaos, Trinity was shoved to the side of the street, with a front row seat to watch the crime play out. Since then, she's had nightmares, been afraid to go to school, and no longer wants to walk around her neighborhood without her mom or grandmother. On top of all of this, the police now want her to try to identify the man with the knife.

Trinity's mother and grandmother have become increasingly worried about her. Once a confident and secure teenage girl, Trinity now seemed anxious, distant, and preoccupied. Her mother tried repeatedly to ease her worries, but the nightmares are becoming more and more frequent and seemed more intense. The biggest red flag occurred when her mother and grandmother came home from work and found Trinity in her closet, crying, seemingly frozen in fear. Trinity stated she heard a loud noise outside the window, panicked, grabbed her siblings, and hid with them in the closet for hours. Her mother realized that Trinity needed support and couldn't be left alone in charge of her siblings. The next day, she reached out to a local community organization for children and youth where Trinity and her siblings could go after school.

Villages Children and Youth Program was new to the community and eager to reach and serve as many children and adolescents as possible. The Villages center planned to operate under a different approach from that of most youth programs, with a goal to serve the whole child. The center not only provided a safe space after school, but they also offered tutoring, nutrition, games, college prep, and physical and mental services for those in need. This multifaceted approach is supported by the local school district, child welfare center, and local pediatric group. Every week, these groups send volunteers, which include teachers, counselors, and nurse practitioners, to the center and provide programming and direct services.

Trinity and her siblings began attending the center routinely. There they received help with homework and evening meals, and Trinity began seeing a counselor every other week. On, the weeks she did not see her counselor, she attended a girl's group where she learned more about the challenges that girls her age were also experiencing in her neighborhood. Through these experiences she learned that she wasn't so alone in her feelings; she wasn't the only one who felt afraid sometimes. After several sessions with her counselor, she began to feel less anxious and more comfortable functioning in her routine activities. The center also helped to relieve some of the other stressors on Trinity: for example, she no longer was solely responsible for helping her siblings with their homework or preparing the evening meal.

Her mother and grandmother noticed the changes in Trinity and her siblings. Trinity's grades were rebounding, and she is talking about taking the SAT next year. The community center has reached out to Trinity's parents to meet with their team. There Trinity's mom learns about Trinity's progress at the center and is pleased with how her daughter has grown

> in her short time there. She wonders where these types of resources have been: if only this center had been available years ago, her family would have been much better off.

For many children and youth, the support of a community partnership operating under a team approach can help to identify and address the many challenges that kids face each day. Trinity's situation offers just one example of the barriers that can impact wellness and prevent a successful transition into adulthood. Partnerships between collaborators, parents, and community members are a critical component in helping students live healthy lives. Certainly, the functionality of such a model and its results will vary because of individual needs, available resources, and unique challenges within each community. However, the fundamental contributor to these types of successful partnerships is the development and maintenance of strong relationships between collaborators. Unfortunately, far too often these types of partnerships start with resources, energy, and passion for change but over time resources run short, volunteers decline, and partnerships deteriorate, leaving kids and families searching once again for the support needed to face the multitude of challenges that impact their daily lives.

References

Aber, L., & Chaudry, A. (2010). *Low-income children, their families and the Great Recession: What next in policy?* Urban Institute.

Adams, S., & Oshima, K. (2014). *Engaging youth through community-driven development operations: Experiences, findings, and opportunities*. Social Development Department, World Bank.

Algren, M. H., Bak, C. K., Berg-Beckhoff, G., & Andersen, P. T. (2015). Health-risk behaviour in deprived neighbourhoods compared with non-deprived neighbourhoods: A systematic literature review of quantitative observational studies. *PloS One, 10*(10), e0139297.

Aguayo, D. (2019). Dismantling racism in public schools using critical race theory and Whiteness studies. Urban Education. Advance online publication. doi:10.1177/0042085918783822.

Bandura, A. (1977). Self-efficacy: Toward a unifying theory of behavioural change. *Psychological Review, 84*(2), 191–215.

Bandura, A. (1997). *Self-Efficacy: The Exercise of Control*. New York: W H Freeman/Times Books/Henry Holt & Co.

Bender, K., Brown, S. M., Thompson, S. J., Ferguson, K. M., & Langenderfer, L. (2015). Multiple victimizations before and after leaving home associated with PTSD, depression, and substance use disorder among homeless youth. *Child Maltreatment, 20*, 115–124.

Berge, J., Sundell, K., Ojehagen, A., & Håkansson, A. E. (2016). Role of parenting styles in adolescent substance use: Results from a Swedish longitudinal cohort study. *BMJ Open, 6*(1), 1–9.

Bond, L., Butler, H., Thomas, L., Carlin, J., Glover, S., Bowes, G., & Patton, G. (2007). Social and school connectedness in early secondary school as predictors of late teenage substance use, mental health, and academic outcomes. *Journal of Adolescent Health, 40*(4), 357–366.

Bonilla-Silva, E. (1997). Rethinking racism: Toward a structural interpretation. *American Sociological Review, 62*, 465–480. http://dx.doi.org/10.2307/2657316

Bowlby, J. (1979). The Bowlby-Ainsworth attachment theory. *Behavioral and Brain Sciences, 2*(4), 637–638.

Brody, G., Yu, T., Chen, E., & Miller, G. (2017). Family-centered prevention ameliorates the association between adverse childhood experiences and prediabetes status in young black adults. *Preventive Medicine, 100*, 117–122.

Carpenter, C. S., Eppink, S. T., & Gonzales, G. (2020). Transgender status, gender identity, and socioeconomic outcomes in the United States. *ILR Review, 73*(3), 573–599.

Chavis, D. M., Hogge, J. H., McMillan, D. W., & Wandersman, A. (1986). Sense of community through Brunswik's lens: A first look. *Journal of Community Psychology, 14*(1), 24–40.

Choi, S. K., Badgett, M. V. L., & Wilson, B. D. M. (2019). *State profiles of LGBT poverty in the United States*. The Williams Institute.

Conger, J. A., & Kanungo, R. N. (1988). The empowerment process: Integrating theory and practice. *Academy of Management Review, 13*(3), 471–482.

Crenshaw, K. (1991). Mapping the margins: Intersectionality, identity politics, and violence against women of color. *Stanford Law Review, 43*, 1241–1299.

Crum, L., Mingo, T. M., & Crowe, A. (2018). "Get over it and move on": The impact of mental illness stigma in rural, low-income United States populations. *Mental Health & Prevention, 13*, 143–148.

Crumb, L., Haskins, N., & Brown, S. (2019). Integrating social justice advocacy into mental health counseling in rural, impoverished American communities. *Professional Counselor, 9*(1), 20–34.

Cutler, D. M., & Glaeser, E. L. (1997). Are ghettos good or bad? *Quarterly Journal of Economics, 112*, 827–872.

Czeisler, M. É., Lane, R. I., Petrosky, E., Wiley, J. F., Christensen, A., Njai, R., ... Rajaratnam, S. M. (2021). Mental health, substance use, and suicidal ideation during the COVID-19 pandemic: United States. *Morbidity and Mortality Weekly Report, 69*(32), 1049.

Damon, W. (2004). What is positive youth development? *Annals of the American Academy of Political and Social Science, 591*(1), 13–24.

Douthit, N., Kiv, S., Dwolatzky, T., & Biswas, S. (2015). Exposing some important barriers to health care access in the rural USA. *Public Health, 129*(6), 611–620.

Elfassi, Y., Braun-Lewensohn, O., Krumer-Nevo, M., & Sagy, S. (2016). Community sense of coherence among adolescents as related to their involvement in risk behaviors. *Journal of Community Psychology, 44*(1), 22–37.

Fagan, A. A., Wright, E. M., & Pinchevsky, G. M. (2014). The protective effects of neighborhood collective efficacy on adolescent substance use and violence following exposure to violence. *Journal of Youth and Adolescence, 43*(9), 1498–1512.

Farrington, D. P. (2011). Families and crime. In J. Wilson & J. Petersilla (Eds.), *Crime and public policy* (pp. 130–157). New York: Oxford University Press.

Felner, R. D., & DeVries, M. L. (2013). Poverty in childhood and adolescence: A transactional–ecological approach to understanding and enhancing resilience in contexts of disadvantage and developmental risk. In S. Goldstein & R. B. Brooks (Eds.), *Handbook of resilience in children* (pp. 105–126). New York: Springer.

Floyd, D. T., & McKenna, L. (2003). National youth serving organizations in the United States: Contributions to civil society. *Handbook of Applied Developmental Science: Promoting Positive Child, Adolescent, and Family Development Through Research, Policies, and Programs, 3*, 11–26.

Ford, C. L., & Airhihenbuwa, C. O. (2010). The public health critical race methodology: Praxis for antiracism research. *Social Science & Medicine, 71*, 1390–1398. http://dx.doi.org/10.1016/j.socscimed.2010.07.030

Gallagher, M., Burnstein, E. T., & Oliver, W. (2018). *How affordable housing providers can boost residents' economic mobility.* Urban Institute.

Galliher, R., McLean, K., & Syed, M. (2017). An integrated developmental model for studying identity in context. *Developmental Psychology, 53*, 2011–2022. doi:10.1037/dev0000299

Gamm, L., Stone, S., & Pittman, S. (2010). Mental health and mental disorders: A rural challenge: A literature review. *Rural Healthy People, 1*(1), 97–114.

Garcia-Reid, P., Peterson, C. H., Reid, R. J., & Peterson, N. A. (2013). The protective effects of sense of community, multigroup ethnic identity, and self-esteem against internalizing problems among Dominican youth: Implications for social workers. *Social Work in Mental Health, 11*(3), 199–222.

Hamilton, S. F. (1999). *A three-part definition of youth development.* Unpublished manuscript, Cornell University College of Human Ecology, Ithaca NY.

Harris, J., & Patton, L. (2019). Un/doing intersectionality through higher education research. *Journal of Higher Education, 90*, 347–372. doi:10.1080/00221546.2018.1536936

Hipp, J. R., & Wo, J. C. (2015). Collective efficacy and crime. *International encyclopedia of social and behavioral sciences, 4*, 169–173.

Hooper, L., Puhl, R., Eisenberg, M. E., Crow, S., & Neumark-Sztainer, D. (2021). Weight teasing experienced during adolescence and young adulthood: Cross-sectional and longitudinal associations with disordered eating behaviors in an ethnically/racially and socioeconomically diverse sample. *International Journal of Eating Disorders, 54*(8), 1449–1462.

Hughes, M., Kiecolt, K. J., Keith, V. M., & Demo, D. H. (2015). Racial identity and well-being among African Americans. *Social Psychology Quarterly, 78*(1), 25–48.

Ivey-Stephenson, A. Z., Crosby, A. E., Jack, S. P., Haileyesus, T., & Kresnow-Sedacca, M. J. (2017). Suicide trends among and within urbanization levels by sex, race/ethnicity, age group, and mechanism of death—United States, 2001–2015. *MMWR Surveillance Summaries, 66*(18), 1.

Jackson, N., Denny, S., & Ameratunga, S. (2014). Social and sociodemographic neighborhood effects on adolescent alcohol use: A systematic review of multi-level studies. *Social Science and Medicine, 115*, 10–20.

Jang, S. J. (2018). Religiosity, crime, and drug use among juvenile offenders: A test of reciprocal relationships over time. *International Journal of Offender Therapy and Comparative Criminology, 62*(14), 4445–4464.

Jones, J. (1972). *Prejudice and racism*. Addison Wesley.

Jones, S. C. T., & Neblett, E. W. (2017). Future directions in research on racism-related stress and racial-ethnic protective factors for Black youth. *Journal of Clinical Child and Adolescent Psychology, 46*, 754–766.

Kann, L., McManus, T., Harris, W. A., Shanklin, S. L., Flint, K. H., Queen, B., ... Ethier, K. A. (2018). Youth risk behavior surveillance—United States, 2017. *MMWR Surveillance Summaries, 67*(8), 1.

Kulshreshtha, A., Goyal, A., Dabhadkar, K., Veledar, E., & Vaccarino, V. (2014). Urban-rural differences in coronary heart disease mortality in the United States: 1999–2009. *Public Health Reports, 129*, 19–29.

Kim, B. E., Gilman, A. B., Hill, K. G., & Hawkins, J. D. (2016). Examining protective factors against violence among high-risk youth: Findings from the Seattle Social Development Project. *Journal of Criminal Justice, 45*, 19–25.

Lardier Jr, D. T. (2018). An examination of ethnic identity as a mediator of the effects of community participation and neighborhood sense of community on psychological empowerment among urban youth of color. *Journal of Community Psychology, 46*(5), 551–566.

Lardier Jr, D. T., Bermea, A. M., Pinto, S. A., Garcia-Reid, P., & Reid, R. J. (2017). The relationship between sexual minority status and suicidal ideations among urban Hispanic adolescents. *Journal of LGBT Issues in Counseling, 11*(3), 174–189.

McMillan, D. W., & Chavis, D. M. (1986). Sense of community: A definition and theory. *Journal of Community Psychology, 14*(1), 6–23.

Morton, M. H., Dworsky, A., & Samuels, G. M. (2017). *Missed opportunities: Youth homelessness in America National estimates*. Chapin Hall at the University of Chicago.

Moy, E., Garcia, M. C., Bastian, B., Rossen, L. M., Ingram, D. D., Faul, M., & Iademarco, M. F. (2017). Leading causes of death in non-metropolitan and metropolitan areas: United States, 1999–2014. *Morbidity and Mortality Weekly Report: Surveillance Summaries, 66*, 1–8.

Narendorf, S., Cross, M. B., Santa Maria, D., Swank, P. R., & Bordnick, P. S. (2017). Relations between mental health diagnoses, mental health treatment, and substance use in homeless youth. *Drug and Alcohol Dependence, 175*, 1–8.

Nelson, C. A., Scott, R. D., Bhutta, Z. A., Harris, N. B., Danese, A., & Samara, M. (2020). Adversity in childhood is linked to mental and physical health throughout life. *BMJ. (Clinical Research Ed), 371*, m3048. https://doi.org/10.1136/bmj.m3048

Njoroge, W. F., Hostutler, C. A., Schwartz, B. S., & Mautone, J. A. (2016). Integrated behavioral health in pediatric primary care. *Current Psychiatry Reports, 18*(12), 1–8.

Patel, M. R., Israel, B. A., Song, P. X., Hao, W., TerHaar, L., Tariq, M., & Lichtenstein, R. (2019). Insuring good health: Outcomes and acceptability of a participatory health insurance literacy intervention in diverse urban communities. *Health Education & Behavior, 46*(3), 494–505. doi:10.1177/1090198119831060

Perkins, D. D., & Long, D. A. (2002). Neighborhood sense of community and social capital: A multi-level analysis. In A. Fisher, C. Sonn, & B. Bishop (Eds.), *Psychological sense of community: Research, applications, and implications* (pp. 291–318). New York: Plenum.

Rickert, V. I., Hassed, S. J., Hendon, A. E., & Cunniff, C. (1996). The effects of peer ridicule on depression and selfimage among adolescent females with Turner syndrome. *Journal of Adolescent Health, 19*(1), 34–38.

Riggs, Damien W., & Amy Patterson. (2009). The smiling faces of contemporary homophobia and transphobia. *Gay and Lesbian Issues and Psychology Review, 5*(3), 185–190.

Riina, E. M., Martin, A., Gardner, M., & Brooks-Gunn, J. (2013). Context matters: Links between neighborhood discrimination, neighborhood cohesion and African American adolescents' adjustment. *Journal of Youth and Adolescence, 42*(1), 136–146.

Rosenberg, R. (2017). The whiteness of gay urban belonging: Criminalizing LGBTQ youth of color in queer spaces of care. *Urban Geography, 38*(1), 137–148.

Rothwell, C., Madans, J., & Arispe, I. (2014).2013 NCHS urban-rural classification scheme for counties. Retrieved fromhttps://www.cdc.gov/nchs/data_access/urban_rural.htm

Shin, R. Q. (2015). The application of critical consciousness and intersectionality as tools for decolonizing racial/ethnic identity development models in the fields of counseling and psychology. In A. J. Marsella (Ed.), *Decolonizing "multicultural" counseling through social justice* (pp. 11–22). Springer.

Smalley, K. B., Yancey, C. T., Warren, J. C., Naufel, K., Ryan, R., & Pugh, J. L. (2010). Rural mental health and psychological treatment: A review for practitioners. *Journal of Clinical Psychology, 66*(5), 479–489.

Substance Abuse and Mental Health Services Administration, Office of Applied Studies. (2009). National Survey of Substance Abuse Treatment Services (N-SSATS), 2009. Data on Substance Abuse Treatment Facilities, DASIS Series: S-49, HHS Publication No. (SMA) 09-4451

Sue, D. W., Capodilupo, C. M., Torino, G. C., Bucceri, J. M., Holder, A., Nadal, K. L., & Esquilin, M. (2007). Racial microaggressions in everyday life: implications for clinical practice. *American Psychologist, 62*(4), 271.

Stadnick, N., Haine-Schlagel, R., & Martinez, J. (2016). Using observational assessment to help identify factors associated with parent participation engagement in community-based child mental health services. *Child & Youth Care Forum, 45*(5), 745–758.

Stacciarini, J. R., Shattell, M. M., Coady, M., & Wiens, B. (2011). Review: Community based participatory research approach to address mental health in minority populations. *Community Mental Health Journal, 47*, 489–497. doi:10.1007/s10597-010-9319-z

Tyler, K. A., & Melander, L. A. (2015). Child abuse, street victimization, and substance use among homeless young adults. *Youth & Society, 47*, 502–519.

Tyler, K. A., & Schmitz, R. M. (2018). A comparison of risk factors for various forms of trauma in the lives of lesbian, gay, bisexual and heterosexual homeless youth. *Journal of Trauma & Dissociation, 19*(4), 431–443.

Trisi, D., & Saenz, M. (2019). Economic Security Programs Cut Poverty Nearly in Half Over Last 50 Years. *Center on Budget and Policy Priorities, updated November, 26.*

US Department of Health and Human Services (HHS), Health Resources and Services Administration. (HRSA). The Office of Rural Health Policy Rural Guide to Health Professions.(Rockville, Md: HRSA, 2012). https://www.ruralhealthinfo.org/assets/4946-22086/ruralhealthprofessionsguidance.pdf

Warner, T. D. (2019). Book review: Communities and crime: An enduring American challenge. *International Criminal Justice Review, 29*(2), 209–211.

Weiss, D., Lillefjell, M., & Magnus, E. (2016). Facilitators for the development and implementation of health promoting policy and programs–a scoping review at the local community level. *BMC Public Health, 16*(1), 1–15.

White, K., Haas, J., & Williams, D. (2012). Elucidating the role of place in health care disparities: The example of racial/ethnic residential segregation. *Health Services Research, 47*, 1278–1299.

Yoshikawa, H., Aber, J. L., & Beardslee, W. R. (2012). The effects of poverty on the mental, emotional, and behavioral health of children and youth: Implications for prevention. *American Psychologist, 67*(4), 272.

12
Putting It All Together
Systemic Change for Positive Mental Health in Youth

Overview

In this chapter we focus on mental health promotion, prevention, and intervention when working with youth in school and community settings. We emphasize the importance of developing positive mental health through expanding services, promoting prevention activities, and the addition of interventions for mental health disorders. We address advocating for change and identifying and implementing successful programs with youth from a systemic perspective.

Developing a Response to the Multifaceted Nature of Youth Mental Health

Throughout this text we have highlighted the multifaceted nature of mental health problems from a biopsychosocial model including genetic predispositions to addiction, antisocial behavior, and depression; system influences, such as family and peer groups; educational settings; social service settings and services to unaccompanied immigrant minors (UIMs); and the relationship between various systems, such as mental health programs and facilities, schools, juvenile justice programs, and UIM services. So how do we develop an effective response to these pertinent issues?

Prevention and *early intervention* programs may be touted as solutions to addressing the challenges of youth mental health. Prevention programs are difficult to implement, given the need to demonstrate evidence of the need for a program designed to address a problem that may not be firmly established. In other words, the nature of prevention requires proof that, without intervention, a problem will become worse. Instead, establishing the need for early intervention programs may be easier once a problem or issue has taken root and needs to be addressed before worsening. One way to establish need is to focus on risk factors that are prevalent within a system or community. O'Connell et al. (2009) detailed risk and protective factors for youth, taking into account individual, family, and community systems across various developmental stages (see Table 12.1). Though the list of risk and protective factors is quite comprehensive, the ability to intervene with these issues is quite limited.

When accounting for risk factors, many individual issues (e.g., temperament, anxiety, hyperactivity) are not easily addressed quickly or can be resolved through education or a didactic program. Within the family or social context (e.g., family, school, peer group, community), issues of permissive parenting, parental attachment, and family substance use and violence, along with bullying, poor peer interactions, or substance use among peers require a broader intervention because these represent systemic problems. Often agencies and organizations that initiate programs to address risk factors can only operate from a singular perspective. For example, schools may address issues concerned with the student but lack the opportunity to engage with the family. Counseling agencies can engage in individual and family interventions but may lack perspective on what happens in the schools. Finally, a sole focus on risk factors may be challenging due to the nature of addressing change from a problem-focused approach. Successful interventions may be more likely from a strength-based rather than a problem-focused approach (Kottler & Balkin, 2017; Oddli & Ronnestad, 2012). Thus, incorporating protective factors is pertinent to promoting healthy well-being in youth.

A focus on protective factors often occurs within the context of social emotional learning in the schools; programs focused on family engagement, such as multisystemic therapy; and through community partnerships such as the Big Brothers Big Sisters Community-Based Mentoring Program. When accounting for protective factors, O'Connell et al. (2009) identified elements such as self-regulation, self-esteem, and achievement motivation on the individual level; protection, consistent discipline, adequate economic resources, and supportive relationships at the family level; and healthy peer groups, school/family engagement, positive school policies, and psychological safety at the community level. When addressing protective factors, interventions that incorporate a strength-based approach may be more empowering than those that focus on problems in which limited control or ability to influence is an impediment to growth and change (Kotter & Balkin, 2017).

Table 12.1 Risk and Protective Factors for Youth

Stage	Persons	Risk factors	Protective factors
Infancy/ Early childhood	Individual	Difficult temperament	Self-regulation Secure attachment Mastery of communication and language skills Ability to make friends and get along with others
	Family	Cold and unresponsive mother behavior Parental modeling of drug/alcohol use	Reliable support and discipline from caregivers Responsiveness Protection from harm and fear Opportunities to resolve conflict Adequate socioeconomic resources for the family
	School, peers, community		Support for early learning Access to supplemental services such as feeding, and screening for vision and hearing Stable, secure attachment to childcare provider Low ratio of caregivers to children Regulatory systems that support high quality of care
Middle school	Individual	Poor impulse control Low harm avoidance Sensation seeking Lack of behavioral self-control/regulation Aggressiveness Anxiety Depression Hyperactivity/ADHD Antisocial behavior Early persistent problem behaviors Early substance use	Mastery of academic skills (math, reading, writing) Following rules for behaviors at home, at school, and in public places Ability to make friends Good peer relationships

(continued)

Table 12.1 Continued

Stage	Persons	Risk factors	Protective factors
	Family	Permissive parenting Parent-child conflict Inadequate supervision and monitoring Low parental warmth Lack of or inconsistent discipline Harsh discipline Low parental aspirations for child Child abuse/maltreatment Substance use among parents or siblings Parental favorable attitudes toward alcohol and/or drugs	Consistent discipline Language-based, rather than physical, discipline Extended family support
	School, peers, community	School failure Low commitment to school Accessibility/availability Peer rejection Laws and norms favorable toward use Deviant peer group Peer attitudes toward drugs Interpersonal alienation Extreme poverty for those children antisocial in childhood	Healthy peer groups School engagement Positive teacher expectations Effective classroom management Positive partnering between school and family School policies and practices to reduce bullying High academic standards
Adolescence	Individual	Behavioral disengagement coping Negative emotionality Conduct disorder Favorable attitudes toward drugs Rebelliousness Early substance use Antisocial behavior	Positive physical development Emotional self-regulation High self-esteem Good coping skills and problem-solving skills Engagement and connections in two or more of the following contexts: at school, with peers, in athletics, employment, religion, culture
	Family	Substance use among parents or siblings Lack of adult supervision Poor attachment with parents	Family provides structure, limits, rules, monitoring, and predictability Supportive relationships with family members Clear expectations for behavior and values

Table 12.1 Continued

Stage	Persons	Risk factors	Protective factors
	School, peers, community	School failure Low commitment to school Associating with drug-using peers Not college bound Aggression toward peers Norms (e.g., advertising) favorable toward alcohol use Accessibility/availability	Presence of mentors and support for development of skills and interests Opportunities for engagement within school and community Positive norms Clear expectations for behavior Physical and psychological safely
Young adulthood	Individual	Lack of commitment to conventional adult roles Antisocial behavior	Identity exploration in love, work, and world view Subjective sense of self-sufficiency, making independent decisions, becoming financially independent Future orientation Achievement motivation
	Family	Leaving home	Balance of autonomy and relatedness to family Behavioral and emotional autonomy
	School, peers, community	Not attending college Substance-using peers	Opportunities for exploration in work and school Connectedness to adults outside of family

Numerous prevention and intervention programs have been developed with varying rates of efficacy. The Interagency Working Group on Youth Programs (IWGYP, 2016) is a collaboration among 22 federal agencies to address programs and services focusing on youth. The IWGYP has developed a program directory to identify effective interventions and programs. Programs are evaluated based on extant research and identified as *no effects, promising,* or *effective*. A program that is promising or effective contains at least one randomized controlled trial (RCT) or a multisite study indicating a positive effect for the treatment condition.

RCTs are a cornerstone in determining the effectiveness of a program. RCTs include random assignment into a treatment or control group to determine if the program or intervention was effective. When statistically significant differences are found in favor of participants placed in the treatment group, researchers tend to place a higher level of confidence in the effectiveness of the program. However, RCTs can be very difficult to implement, especially in school and community settings. Random assignment may seem like a simple procedure, but identifying youth who receive or do not receive an intervention can be a controversial issue fraught with ethical concerns. In addition, when such studies are undertaken, a multitude of safety and consent procedures must take place. For examples, administrators of a school or agency have to agree with implementation of the study. Stakeholders, such as teachers, youth advocates, or mental health professionals, may be hesitant to engage in the study. Consent of parents or guardians is necessary, along with youth assent. All of these contingencies rest on approval from an Institutional Review Board (IRB). In other words, collecting data with youth is extremely difficult, and the additional constraints of a RCT can make implementation of the study more challenging.

So far, implementing effective interventions that create lasting change seems rather daunting. However, there are some common elements that effective interventions demonstrate.

Principles of Effective Programs

The National Institute on Drug Abuse (NIDA, 2020) published principles for developing and implementing efficacious prevention and intervention programs. Effective programs have the following characteristics:

- Protective factors strengthened or risk factors reduced
- Community engagement
- Culturally responsiveness
- Family involvement
- Designed to address holistic needs of youth, developmentally, psychologically, and socially
- Improved educational outcomes, including enhanced academic achievement, reduction in behavior problems, reduction in school dropouts, and improved socialization
- Include teacher or parent training
- Include repeated interventions

Programs that include at least two of the primary systems (individual, family, school/community) tend to have stronger effects. This is especially true for school- and family-based programs (NIDA, 2020; Robertson et al., 2003). The multisystemic approach—utilizing more than one system in an intervention—reinforces a relational approach. Programs that are successful in reducing risk factors and strengthening protective factors utilize an approach that conveys information, promotes skill development, provides strategies, and utilizes a relational approach. Examples of relational approaches include individual, family, and group counseling or mentoring by peers or adults.

For example, the Big Brothers Big Sisters Community-based mentoring program matches youth (between the ages of 6 and 18) with an adult mentor (usually between the ages of 22 and 49). The mentor–mentee pairs go on outings in the community, usually twice monthly at a minimum. Compared to a control group, youth in the program exhibited reduced absenteeism in school, a significantly reduced rate of initial drug use and antisocial behavior, and improved grades. The program uses mentoring and community experiences to encourage a reduction in risk factors and to strengthen protective factors (National Institute of Justice, 2011a).

In terms of effective interventions, an important consideration is the relevance of indirect effects. *Indirect effects* occur when supplemental benefits of an intervention are identified in addition to or in the absence of the primary outcomes identified in the program/intervention. We often see indirect effects in school-based initiatives. For example, *Cognitive Behavioral Intervention for Trauma in Schools* was developed as a group therapy intervention program to be delivered in urban schools attended by youth from high-crime neighborhoods. A desired outcome for school-based interventions is improved academic achievement. The belief is that improved mental health will promote a more positive learning environment, which will impact academic outcomes. Despite the decrease in depression and trauma symptoms for youth between ages 10 and 14, no discernible improvement was made in classroom behavioral problems (National Institute on Justice, 2011b).

Now, you might be wondering, if the focus is on trauma, wouldn't the reduction in depression and posttraumatic stress disorder (PTSD) symptoms constitute a primary effect? Maybe, and that is a sound argument. But remember that this was a school-based intervention, and the goal of services delivered in the schools is to improve educational outcomes. Recall that, back in Chapter 1, the systemic services delivered by public schools often go beyond academics to encompass health screenings (e.g., vision, hearing, scoliosis, vaccination records), nutrition (e.g., breakfast and lunch), social emotional learning, and childcare. The idea is that if a school can address the holistic needs of the child, then the opportunity gap in educational achievement can be alleviated. The logic of this point is sound. After all, if kids are not healthy, experience food insecurity, or are traumatized, how likely are they to engage in the learning environment and succeed academically? Unfortunately, the limitations of programs like Cognitive Behavioral Intervention for Trauma in Schools in impacting academic achievement are all too common. Programs can demonstrate headway in reducing absenteeism, behavioral referrals, or classroom misbehavior, but their influence on student achievement remains elusive despite the corollaries between social emotional constructs and academic achievement. Despite this challenge, schools remain an important setting in which to implement youth interventions and programs due to their access to youth and the role of schools in public health.

Programs and interventions may fall short in school settings due to the higher influence of family and community settings. Particularly when a number of risk factors are present and the family and community environments are chaotic and possibly even unsafe, opportunities to meaningfully address concerns, remediate ill effects, and strengthen protective factors in a limited amount of time may face obstacles that may at times be insurmountable. Because meaningful change is often difficult (Kottler & Balkin, 2020), paying attention to indirect effects and meaningful evaluation of effects that go beyond the stated goals of a program is pertinent. To reinforce this latter point, consider the Drug Abuse Resistance Education (DARE) program.

The DARE program was started in 1983, as a collaborative partnership between the Los Angeles Police Department and the Los Angeles School District (Ingraham, 2017; Newton, 1993). Police officers delivered a drug education prevention program to elementary school children with the goal of teaching children skills to resist peer pressure and deter initial drug use. By 1993, DARE was in use in all 50 states, and, by 2002, the program was funded by the US government with an annual budget exceeding $10 million.

One of the advantages of DARE is that communities were able to hire more police officers given this support and funding from the federal government. Not only were more police officers hired, but the success of the DARE program led to more officers interacting with children in schools. But, by the early 1990s, studies began to emerge that were critical of DARE, particularly with regards to its effectiveness in preventing drug use. A decade later, funding was reduced due to the program's ineffectiveness in preventing substance use (Ingraham, 2017).

As you can see, the primary focus for DARE was to reduce drug use in youth. In addition, the program provided a substantial amount of money to communities to increase their police presence. Because of this funding, police officers were present in schools to deliver the DARE program. If a program is not effective in its primary goal of reducing substance use, should the program be defunded? This is what occurred with DARE, but the unfortunate part of the defunding was the lack of any attention paid to indirect effects. Consider the following:

- How was an increased police presence in the school perceived by students, teachers, and the community?
- How was the relationship between youth in the community and police officers impacted?
- How did the delivery of skills designed to strengthen protective factors impact the perception of duties performed by police officers?
- How do positive interactions with youth influence their own perceptions of work in the community?

The answer to each of these questions is, "We don't know" because these questions were never investigated. We know that DARE did not impact drug use in youth. What we do not know is whether or not the relational qualities of police officers positively interacting with youth in communities had a positive impact on the perception of police officers. In addition, we do not know if the opportunity for police officers to engage in youth-oriented program changed their own perceptions of the community.

For example, after delivery of DARE in an elementary school classroom, could some youth have left school that day thinking, "The police officer was nice. I liked the police officer. I want to be a police officer." Could the police officer have left the school thinking, "I enjoyed talking to the youth." Or perhaps the police officer left with more empathy toward the community she serves.

Of course we do not know if any of these effects were apparent because the research question was never asked. Once it was determined that, after more than a decade of implementation, the DARE program did not reduce substance use among youth, the program was cut. But perhaps there were benefits—indirect effects—that made the program worthwhile.

The point of this heuristic example is to note that behavioral change is difficult. The problems faced by youth are complicated and are not likely to be resolved by a single program or intervention. But that does not mean any one single intervention is ineffective. Rather, evaluations should examine the both primary and secondary effects of an intervention.

In terms of the complex nature of youth problems and the ability to address issues through programs and interventions, consider the following exercise.

Case Study: Bad Habits

Think of a bad habit you have and have engaged in for a long time. For example maybe you do one of these:

- Not exercise enough
- Eat too much fast food
- Use tobacco or nicotine
- Bite your fingernails
- Get too little sleep
- Spent too much time on the internet or social media
- Procrastinate
- Use profanity

You get the idea. It might be one of these or something else. But whatever it is, you have probably been doing it a long time. Furthermore, if you are reading this book, it is likely that you are in a graduate-level class, which will place you at around the top 5% of educated people when you earn your graduate degree.

So far, we have established that you have a bad habit that you indulge over a long period of time, and you are among the most educated of people. No doubt you are aware of your bad habit. Maybe you have even engaged in some interventions from time to time to change your bad habit or have gone through a lot of material to understand your bad habit, only to find yourself going back to it. So, why haven't you changed?

> It's a tough question. But the point is that, despite being educated and knowledgeable, change is difficult and even arming yourself with knowledge about a bad habit may be insufficient to produce a meaningful change. If such change is difficult for the most educated adults, you can imagine the challenge of addressing issues with youth and why programs and interventions may only have modest impact.

Advocating for Change

The premise of this text is that we must address the challenges faced by youth through a multidimensional lens and systemic perspective. There are numerous foundations across the country with varying interests and emphases that compete for funds to promote change in youth. Unfortunately, sometimes the communities in most need have the fewest resources. For example, the Mississippi Delta, which includes portions of Mississippi, Arkansas, and Louisiana suffers from inequities related to income, child nutrition, resources for education, and health disparities. The Mississippi Delta is among the most impoverished regions of the United States (Gray et al., 2016). Despite investments from major foundations, both challenges and a dearth of resources remain.

To change systemic disparities, a collaborative system is necessary. Funding agencies, foundations, universities, and the like should develop strategies to identify communities that need help and the programs, interventions, and services that can address those communities' needs. Communities and schools often struggle to obtain resources due to isolation, lack of expertise to pursue funding, unfamiliarity with available services and resources that can address needs, and an inability to compete for existing resources when faced with larger or more populous regions with similar needs. For example, obtaining federal money to implement a drug court in a rural community may be challenging if the community must compete with major urban centers for the same funding. In addressing health disparities in youth, collaborations with universities that have resources to pursue grant money and establish relationships with federal agencies and foundations can be pertinent to extending resources to communities in need.

Universities are in an ideal position to assume leadership responsibilities to advocate for change. Consider the following characteristics that make universities ideal institutions to lead the charge for systemic change in youth mental health.

Expertise in research and evaluation. Faculty at universities are trained in research and evaluation. The ability to obtain external funds to engage communities is within the scope of training of doctoral-level professionals.

System of recognition. Teaching, research, and service represent the traditional scope of work for university faculty. Hence, universities provide a system through which to encourage community engagement and university partnerships.

Dedicated human capital. Most universities have offices dedicated to research and sponsored programs. Within these offices, universities focus on grant support, budgets, federal compliance, memorandums of understanding, and legal counsel, which are necessary mechanisms to promote human subjects research and collaborative activities with external agencies.

Training in research ethics and compliance. The United States has a long, troubled history related to research ethics dating back to the early 20th century, when the federal government engaged in a study of syphilis using Black Americans as research subjects; these men were subsequently denied penicillin in order for medical professionals to observe the course of the disease. As a result, research ethics is the only type of ethical code that the federal government mandates and oversees (Balkin & Kleist, 2022). Hence, agencies and organizations that engage in research using human subjects are required to comply with federal codes and have this compliance overseen by an IRB. The IRB consists of individuals within the agency or organization—typically universities and hospitals—who have training in research ethics as it pertains to human subjects and who oversee all human subjects research conducted at the institution.

Grant writing. Although private foundations can set their own standards, the numerous government agencies that oversee grant funding have complex procedures that require training, expertise, and experience to navigate. Familiarity with complex budgeting, logic models, scholarly review, and research and evaluation represent some of the skills required to obtain external funding. Once again, universities offer training and expertise in these areas.

The reality is that schools and communities that are in most need often lack the resources and expertise to obtain assistance. This is when universities typically can employ their expertise and structure to build collaborative partnerships to provide pertinent research information and help to make meaningful systemic changes to communities that serve youth. Collaborative partnerships have the capacity to be inclusive and to promote involvement with communities, schools, medical facilities, offices of juvenile justice, and social service agencies. Without a comprehensive system in place to promote cooperation, each organization can get stuck in its own silo, attempting to impact youth in only a limited capacity.

Summary

Throughout this chapter, we provided an overview of risk and protective factors as well as the characteristics of successful programs and interventions. Despite knowing what successful programs do, the multifaceted nature of youth problems requires complex solutions. Hence, change occurs slowly and in small increments. A key to creating lasting change for youth lies in collaborations across systems. Universities are uniquely suited to provide leadership in this area due to their resources and personnel who have the skills to develop creative and scholarly programs and pursue collaborative partnerships and external funding opportunities.

References

Balkin, R. S., & Kleist, D. M. (2022). *Counseling research: A practitioner-scholar approach* (2nd ed.). American Counseling Association.

Gray, V. B., Byrd, S. H., Fountain, B. J., Rader, N. E., & Frugé, A. D. (2016). Childhood nutrition in the Mississippi Delta: Challenges and opportunities. *Health Promotion International, 31*(4), 857–868. https://doi.org/10.1093/heapro/dav072

Ingraham, C. (2017, July 12). A brief history of DARE, the anti-drug program Jeff Sessions wants to revive. *The Washington Post*. Retrieved June 11, 2022, from https://www.washingtonpost.com/news/wonk/wp/2017/07/12/a-brief-history-of-d-a-r-e-the-anti-drug-program-jeff-sessions-wants-to-revive/

Interagency Working Group on Youth Programs. (2016). Retrieved June 9, 2022, from https://youth.gov/pathways-youth-strategic-plan-federal-collaboration

Kottler, J. A., & Balkin, R. S. (2017). *Relationships in counseling and the counselor's life*. American Counseling Association.

Kottler, J. A., & Balkin, R. S. (2020). *Myths, misconceptions, and invalid assumptions about counseling and psychotherapy*. Oxford University Press.

National Institute on Drug Abuse. (2020, June 10). Prevention principles. Retrieved June 9, 2022, from https://nida.nih.gov/publications/preventing-drug-use-among-children-adolescents/prevention-principles

National Institute on Justice. (2011a). Program profile: Big Brothers Big Sisters (BBBS) Community-Based Mentoring (CBM) Program. Retrieved June 10, 2022, from https://crimesolutions.ojp.gov/ratedprograms/112#ar

National Institute on Justice. (2011b). Program profile: Big Brothers Big Sisters (BBBS) Community-Based Mentoring (CBM) Program. Retrieved June 10, 2022, from https://crimesolutions.ojp.gov/ratedprograms/139

Newton, J. (1993, September 9). DARE marks a decade of growth and controversy: Youth: Despite critics, anti-drug program expands nationally. But some see declining support in LAPD. *Los Angeles Times*. Retrieved June 11, 2022, from https://www.latimes.com/archives/la-xpm-1993-09-09-mn-33226-story.html

O'Connell, M. E., Boat, T., & Warner, K. E. (2009). *Preventing mental, emotional, and behavioral disorders among young people: Progress and possibilities*. National Academies Press and US Department of Health and Human Services.

Oddli, H. W., & Rønnestad, M. H. (2012). How experienced therapists introduce the technical aspects in the initial alliance formation: Powerful decision makers supporting clients' agency. *Psychotherapy Research, 22*(2), 176–193. https://doi.org/10.1080/10503307.2011.633280

Robertson, E., David, S., & Rao, S. (2003). Preventing drug use among children and adolescents: A research-based guide for parents, educators, and community leaders (2nd ed.). Retrieved from http://www.drugabuse.gov/sites/default/files/preventingdruguse.pdf

Index

For the benefit of digital users, indexed terms that span two pages (e.g., 52–53) may, on occasion, appear on only one of those pages.

Tables, figures, and boxes are indicated by *t*, *f*, and *b* following the page number

AAFP (American Academy of Family Physicians), 42
Aber, L., 219–20
abuse. *See* childhood abuse
accommodation, 27
ACEs. *See* adverse childhood experiences
ACE Study. *See* Adverse Childhood Experiences Study
ACF Office of Refugee Resettlement, 12–13
achievement, identity, 26
Acquah, E. O., 147
acquired capability, 109
active consent, 70–71
active suicidal ideation, 109
acute care, 115–16
    defined, 10
    indications and goals for, 43–44
ADA (American Disability Act), 60
addiction, 163. *See also* process addictions; substance use and abuse
    antisocial behavior and, 163
    systemic factors related to, 173–80
ADHD. *See* attention deficit hyperactivity disorder
Adler, Alfred, 8
adolescence developmental stage, 239*t*
adolescence developmental tasks, 29, 30*b*
adolescent identity development theory, 26
adverse childhood experiences (ACEs), 200
    school services and, 62–63
    suicidal attempts and, 101
Adverse Childhood Experiences (ACE) Study, 62–63, 199

advocacy, 247–49
    examples of, 49
    in suicide aftermath, 117
AFSP (American Foundation for Suicide Prevention), 114
alcohol use and abuse, 171–73
    community influences and, 226–27
    school services for, 60
    sexual activity and, 122
Ali, M. M., 40
ally, defined, 125*t*
American Academy of Family Physicians (AAFP), 42
American Disability Act (ADA), 60
American Foundation for Suicide Prevention (AFSP), 114
American Medical Association's Guidelines for Adolescent Preventative Services, 66
American Psychiatric Association (APA), 23, 124–28, 167–68, 203–4
American Psychiatric Association (APA) Division 12, 47
American School Counseling Association (ASCA), 178–79
American School Counseling Association (ASCA) 2012 Ethical Code, 135
Angelou, Maya, 48
animals, cruelty to, 163, 164, 165–66
anorexia nervosa, 48
antisocial behavior, 163–67
    assessment and treatment, 180–85
    case studies, 164–65, 185–87
    collective efficacy and, 217–18
    covert, 174
    defined, 165–66

antisocial behavior (*cont.*)
   emergence of, 166
   explained, 165–67
   interventions for, 180–85
   outcomes associated with, 166
   overt, 174
   research findings, 166–67
   systemic factors related to, 173–80
anxiety, 40
   bullying and, 144–45, 147
   childhood abuse and, 198
   in children of color, 48–49
   cognitive behavioral therapy for, 48
   generalized anxiety disorder, 129
   homelessness and, 225–26
   percentage of children diagnosed with, 40
   percentage of students with, 60
   sexting behaviors and, 171
   social, 147
APA. *See* American Psychiatric Association
Applied Suicide Intervention Skills Training (ASIST), 115
Arizona, 69–70
ASCA. *See* American School Counseling Association
asexual, defined, 125*t*
Asian/Pacific Islander LGBTQ youth, 128
ASIST (Applied Suicide Intervention Skills Training), 115
asylum seekers, 80, 93*t*
attention deficit hyperactivity disorder (ADHD), 58–59, 63, 177–78
autism spectrum disorder (ASD), 63
autonomy *vs.* shame and doubt (psychosocial identity development theory), 25
avoidance-focused coping strategies, 152

Bandura, A., 217–18
Beech, A. R., 166
behavioral addictions. *See* process addictions
behavior disorders, 40, 48–49, 58–59, 60
Berge, J., 226
Big Brothers Big Sisters Community-Based Mentoring Program, 238, 243
Binet, Alfred, 27

biopsychosocial model, 163
biphobia, defined, 125*t*
bipolar disorder, 73–74
bisexual, defined, 125*t*
Black youth
   homicide in, 60
   LGBTQ+, 128
   residential segregation and, 224
   suicidal attempts in, 5
   teen pregnancy and parenthood in, 137
   in urban communities, 222
Blankenship, D. M., 207
Blodgett, C., 62–63
Blueprints, 47
Bonilla-Silva, E., 223
Border Patrol, 85–86
Boston, 84–85
boundaries, lack of, 123*t*
Boyd, R. C., 107–8
Bradbury, S. L., 152
Bradshaw, C. P., 154
Bronfenbrenner, U., 89–90
Bull, S., 178–79
bullying, 141–57
   case studies, 141–42, 155–56
   common behaviors, 144
   coping skills and, 152–53
   covert, 144
   cyber- (*see* cyberbullying)
   defined, 142–43
   face-to-face relational, 143
   implications of, 144–45
   legislation on, 148
   mental health and, 146–47
   overt, 144, 153
   physical, 143
   of pregnant teens and teen parents, 135–36
   prevalence of, 142–43
   protective factors and, 151–53
   public health and, 146
   responding to, 153
   in schools, 156–57
   social development and, 145
   systemic response to, 154–56
   unreported, 153
   verbal, 143
   violence and, 149–51

INDEX 253

Camodeca, M., 151
capacity (school mental health services), 69
cartel violence, 81–82
case studies
   antisocial behavior, 164–65, 185–87
   bad habits, 246–47
   bullying, 141–42, 155–56
   childhood abuse, 196–97
   community issues, 215–16, 230–32
   depression, 110–11
   immigrants and refugees, 82, 83, 85
   school interventions, 56–57, 73–74
   systemic failure, 7–8, 9–12, 13–14
   system of care, 50–52
   trauma, 208–9
CBPR (community-based participatory research), 228
CBT. *See* cognitive behavioral therapy
CCPT (child-centered play therapy), 34
CD. *See* conduct disorder
CDC. *See* Centers for Disease Control and Prevention
cellular phones, 122, 168–69
Centers for Disease Control and Prevention (CDC), 62–63, 104, 121, 143, 163, 197
Central American immigrants, 81–82
Chachamovich, E., 107–8
character education programs, 148
Chaudhary, P., 171
Chaudry, A., 219–20
Chavis, D. M., 218–19
Chen, S. H., 31
child-centered play therapy (CCPT), 34
childhood abuse, 196–203
   case study, 196–97
   death from, 196
   defined, 197
   emotional, 198
   estimated number of victims, 196
   incidence of, 197
   physical, 198
   reporting, 201–2
   sexual, 198
   signs and symptoms of, 199–201
   societal impact of, 202–3
   types of, 198–99
   vulnerability to sex trafficking and, 131
childhood neglect, 131, 198, 199
child protective services (CPS), 201, 202
children and youth of color
   in juvenile justice system, 48–49
   LGBTQ+, 128, 224–25
Choi, S. K., 225
Christie-Mizell, C. A., 151
chronic stress, 103
cisgender, defined, 125*t*
Citizens Commission on Human Rights, 70–71
Clelland, T., 154
client failure, 3. *See also* systemic failure
cocaine, 173
Coercive Family Process Theory, 145
Cognitive Behavioral Intervention for Trauma in Schools, 243–44
cognitive behavioral therapy (CBT), 47, 48, 207
   conditions commonly used for, 48
   described, 48
   for internet gaming disorder, 168
   problematic sexual behavior-, 122–24
   in schools, 65–66
   for substance abuse, 48, 173
   trauma-focused (*see* trauma-focused cognitive behavioral therapy)
cognitive development theory, 27
cognitive processing therapy (CPT), 207
Cohen, J. A., 207
collaboration
   in school services, 71
   systemic, 16–18
collective efficacy, 216–19
Columbine High School shooting, 5, 148
coming out, 124
   average age of, 224–25
   defined, 125*t*
communities, 215–32
   antisocial behavior and, 176–77
   case studies, 215–16, 230–32
   challenges and oppression in, 222–27
   collective efficacy in, 216–19
   protective and moderating factors in, 227–29

communities (*cont.*)
　relationships in, 216–18
　rural (*see* rural communities)
　suicide prevention and, 114
　underserved, 219–22
　urban, 221–22
community-based interventions
　for antisocial behavior and
　　addictions, 183–84
　recommended programs for, 227–28
community-based participatory research
　(CBPR), 228
community-based services, 61
community engagement, 90
community mental health and youth
　services
　case study of systemic failure, 9–10
　systemic approach in, 8–10
Community Mental Health Centers Act of
　1963, 8, 67
community resources, 216–17, 219
Comprehensive Human Trafficking
　Assessment Tool, 132–33
concrete operational developmental
　stage, 27
conduct disorder (CD), 144–45, 165–
　66, 177–78
confidentiality, 70–71, 135
conformity. *See* pressure to conform
Conner, B. T., 149–50
consent, 70–71
consultation, 71
continuity of care, 42
conventional stage of moral
　development, 28
conversion therapy, 129
coping skills, 152–53
cost
　of depression, 104
　of mental health disorders, 59
　of suicide, 101
covert antisocial behavior, 174
covert bullying, 144
COVID-19 pandemic, 40, 58, 226–27, 229
　impact on childhood abuse, 197
　impact on LGBTQ+ youth, 128
　impact on substance use
　　disorders, 172–73

Coyne, Sarah M., 167–68
"coyotes" (immigrant foot guides), 82
CPS. *See* child protective services
CPT (cognitive processing therapy), 207
Crenshaw, K., 222
crime rates, 183–84, 217, 219, 224
criminal behavior, 149–50, 226
crisis residence, 43–44
Critical Race Theory (CRT), 223–24
cultural comfort, 91–92
cultural humility, 91–92
culturally responsive approach, 48–49
culture (refugee), 81–84
culture shock, 83–84
Cushman, P., 154
cyberbullying, 102–3, 122, 144, 174–75
　defined, 123*t*, 143
　increase in, 142–43
　prevalence of, 143
　sexting behaviors and, 170–71

DACA (Deferred Action for Childhood
　Arrivals), 85–86
Dale, J., 146
Damon, W., 228–29
danger to self or others criteria, 43–44
DARE. *See* Drug Abuse Resistance
　Education
DBT (dialectical behavior therapy), 168
DeBaryshe, B., 145
Deblinger, E., 207
Deferred Action for Childhood Arrivals
　(DACA), 85–86
de Moivre, Abraham, 22
Department of Defense, US, 204
Department of Health and Human
　Services, US, 17, 204–5, 219–20
Department of Justice, US, 46
Department of Justice Office for Victims of
　Crime, US, 131
Department of State, US, 12–13
deportation, parental, 84
depression, 40, 58–59, 101, 102
　bullying and, 144–45, 147
　case study, 110–11
　childhood abuse and, 198
　in children of color, 48–49
　cognitive behavioral therapy for, 48

homelessness and, 225–26
in LGBTQ+ youth, 129
major depressive disorder, 129
percentage of children with, 40
percentage of students with, 60
sexting behaviors and, 171
societal impact of, 104–5
stress and, 103–4
suicidal ideation and, 104
suicide and, 106–7
developmental task theory, 28–29, 30*b*, 33
developmental theories, 21
adolescent identity development theory, 26
cognitive development theory, 27
developmental task theory, 28–29, 30*b*, 33
intersection of, 29, 32*f*
moral development theory, 27–28
overview, 24–25
psychosocial identity development theory, 25–26
systemic perspective on, 29–35
DHS. *See* Division of Human Services
Diagnostic and Statistical Manual of Mental Disorders (DSM-5-TR), 23, 124–28, 167–68, 169–71, 203–4
dialectical behavior therapy (DBT), 168
diffusion, identity, 26
diversion programs, 46
Division of Human Services (DHS), 6–8
drug abuse. *See* substance use and abuse
Drug Abuse Resistance Education (DARE), 244–46
DSM. See *Diagnostic and Statistical Manual of Mental Disorders*
Duncan, B. L., 15

early adulthood developmental tasks, 29, 30*b*
early interventions
for antisocial behavior, 182
for immigrants and refugees, 90
eating disorders, 44
EBTs. *See* evidence-based treatments
economic downturn of 2007-2008, 60
ecstasy (Molly), 173
education
mental health, 113–14
in suicide aftermath, 117

Egan, V., 178–79
Eivers, A. R., 177–78
elderly population, 219–20
Elementary and Secondary Education Act, 67–68
EMDR. *See* eye-movement desensitization and reprocessing
emergency services, 201, 202
emotional childhood abuse, 198
emotional connection, 218
emotion-focused coping strategies, 152
empowerment, youth, 228–29
Erikson, Erik, 21, 25–26, 27, 33
ethics, 201, 202, 248
Evans, S. W., 70–71
Every Student Succeeds Act of 2015, 62, 67–68, 149
evidence-based treatments (EBTs), 46–48, 49
for antisocial behavior, 178–79, 180–81
for bullying, 149
in communities, 227–28
defined, 46–47
platforms for, 46–47
in schools, 61–62, 149
executive functioning (EF), 31
Expert Working Group Report (DOJ), 46
exploitation, 122, 123*t*
eye-movement desensitization and reprocessing (EMDR), 207–8

Facebook, 122
face-to-face relational bullying, 143
families. *See also* parents
antisocial behavior and, 175–76
psychiatric hospitalization and, 10
school performance and, 6–7
Family Acceptance Project (FAP) model, 129, 130*t*
Family Educational Rights and Privacy Act (FERPA), 17, 71
family-level functioning, 175–76
family therapy, 47–48
for antisocial behavior, 181–82
for gender dysphoria, 124–28
for substance abuse, 173
in suicide aftermath, 117
for trauma, 207

FAP. *See* Family Acceptance Project
Farrington, D. P., 151
Fedewa, A. L., 4–5
feedback effects, 15
Felitti, V. J., 62–63
females. *See* gender
Fergusson, A., 63
FERPA. *See* Family Educational Rights and Privacy Act
FFT (functional family therapy), 47
Finkelhor, D., 142
Fitzpatrick, K. M., 147
Florida, 69–70
Folkman, S., 152
foreclosure, identity, 26
formal operational developmental stage, 27
Forness, S. R., 58–59
foster care, 6–8, 12–13
Fowler, P. J., 177
Fox, C., 150
Fraser, S. L., 107–8
Freud, Sigmund, 21, 24, 25–26, 27
Frydenberg, E., 152
functional family therapy (FFT), 47
funding, for mental health services, 60, 67, 69–70, 105

gaming disorder, 167–68
gang violence, 81–82, 84–85, 200–1
gay, defined, 125*t*
gender
    alcohol abuse and, 171–72
    antisocial behavior and, 166, 174–75
    coping skills and, 152
    school climate and, 148
    school mental health services and, 68–69
    shopping addiction and, 170
gender and sexual identity classifications, 124–28
gender binary, defined, 125*t*
gender dysphoria, 124–28, 125*t*
gender-expansive, defined, 125*t*
gender expression, defined, 125*t*
gender-fluid, defined, 125*t*
gender identity, 128
    defined, 125*t*
    discrimination based on, 128

gender-nonconforming youth, 107, 125*t*
genderqueer, defined, 125*t*
generalized anxiety disorder, 129
generativity *vs.* stagnation (psychosocial identity development theory), 25
genetics, 173–74
Geoffroy, D., 107–8
Georgia, 148
Ghandour, R. M., 48–49
Gilligan, C., 28
Gilliland, B. E., 117
GLSEN, 148
Golden Gate Bridge jump survivors, 112
Goodram, B., 177–78
graduation rates, high school, 224
Grant, J. E., 169–70
Green, A. E., 131
Greene, M. B., 144
grooming, 122, 123*t*
Guatemalan immigrants, 81–82, 83, 86

Hagan, M. P., 180
Hall, G. Stanley, 21
hallucinations, 43–45
Hamilton, S. F., 228–29
Harding, D. J., 150
Havighurst, Robert J., 21, 28–29, 30*b*, 33
Health Insurance Portability and Accountability Act (HIPAA), 10, 17–18
    conditions for information disclosure, 17
    school mental health services and, 71
Health Resources and Services Administration, 69–70
Healthy Schools, Healthy Communities program, 69–70
Henggeler, S. W., 178
Herschel, A. D., 71
Hess, R. S., 177–78
HIPAA. *See* Health Insurance Portability and Accountability Act
Hispanic youth, 137, 224
HIV, 129
homelessness, 131, 225–26
homicidal ideation, 44–45
homicide, 60, 81–82, 217–18
homophobia, 125*t*, 224–25

INDEX 257

Honduran refugees, 81–82, 85
Hughes, T., 48–49
Human Rights Campaign, 124
human trafficking, 83, 198. *See also* sex trafficking

Ialongo, N. S., 107–8
ICD-11 *(International Classification of Diseases)*, 167–68
ICE (Immigration and Custom Enforcement), 85–86
ICYSHs (integrated community-based youth service hubs), 228
IDEA (Individuals with Disabilities Education Act), 178–79
identity achievement, 26
identity crisis, 122, 123*t*
identity diffusion, 26
identity foreclosure, 26
identity moratorium, 26
identity *vs.* role confusion (psychosocial identity development theory), 25, 26
immigrants, 80–95. *See also* refugees; unaccompanied immigrant minors
　barriers to engagement in mental health practice, 85–86
　case studies, 82, 83, 85
　cultural humility when engaging with, 91–92
　legal statuses and clinical implications, 93*t*
　number of US foreign-born population, 80
　postmigration experience of, 84–85
　socioecological model on, 86–87, 87*f*, 89–90
　trafficking and exploitation of, 83
　trauma during journey to US, 82–83
　trauma in country of origin, 81–82
　trauma-informed care for, 87–91
　undocumented, 80, 86, 93*t*, 132
Immigration and Custom Enforcement (ICE), 85–86
impairment, 23–24
incarceration, 41, 45, 46, 48–49, 202–3, 225–26. *See also* juvenile justice system
indicated interventions. *See* Tier 3 interventions

indirect effects, 243
Individuals with Disabilities Education Act (IDEA), 178–79
industry *vs.* inferiority (psychosocial identity development theory), 25
infancy and early childhood developmental stage, 239*t*
infancy and early childhood developmental tasks, 29, 30*b*
infant mortality rates, 219–20
influence, 218
initiative *vs.* guilt (psychosocial identity development theory), 25
inpatient counseling, 43–44
inpatient hospitalization, 115–16
in-school suspension, 177–78
Instagram, 122
Institutional Review Board (IRB), 241–42, 248
integrated community-based youth service hubs (ICYSHs), 228
integrated treatment, 38–39
integrative approach, 110–13
integrity *vs.* despair (psychosocial identity development theory), 25
Interagency Working Group on Youth Programs (IWGYP), 241
International Classification of Diseases (ICD-11), 167–68
internet addiction, 168–69
internet gaming disorder, 167–68
Interpersonal Theory of Suicide (ITS), 109
intersectionality, 222–23
intersex, defined, 125*t*
interventions
　for antisocial behavior, 180–85
　community-based (*see* community-based interventions)
　early (*see* early interventions)
　for immigrants and refugees, 90–91
　programs for, 237–38, 241
　for sexual issues, 122–24
　suicide, 114–16, 131
　tiered, 61–62, 64–65, 70–71
intimacy *vs.* isolation (psychosocial identity development theory), 25
IRB. *See* Institutional Review Board
"It's OK, to Not Be OK" (song), 68–69

IWGYP (Interagency Working Group on Youth Programs), 241

James, R. K., 117
Joiner, T. E., Jr., 109
Jones, J., 223
Justice Strategic Initiative, 204–5
juvenile justice system, 45–46, 48–49. *See also* incarceration
    defined, 45
    mental health services in, 49
    prevalence of mental health disorders in, 59
    problems with, 45–46
    vulnerability to sex trafficking, 131

Kim, K. H., 63
King, S. L., 180
Kirmayer, L. J., 107–8
Kline, D. M. S., 178
Kohlberg, Lawrence, 27–28, 33
Kutcher Adolescent Depression Scale, 110

Lacey, P., 63
lack of boundaries, 123*t*
Lambert, S. F., 107–8
Lanigan, J. D., 62–63
later maturity developmental tasks, 29, 30*b*
Lazarus, R. S., 152
Lee, V., 71–72
legislation and public policies, 67–68
lesbian, defined, 125*t*
Leuschner, V., 150–51
LGBTQ+ youth, 107, 121, 124–31
    barriers to, 224–25
    bullying of, 144
    of color, 128, 224–25
    defined, 125*t*
    depression in, 101
    terminology related to, 125*t*
    vulnerability to sex trafficking and, 131
Livingston, M. D., 5
LivingWorks, 115
loneliness, 147
Los Angeles Police Department, 244
Los Angeles School District, 244
Louisiana, 69–70

Luritsen, J. L., 176–77

major depressive disorder, 129
males. *See* gender
mandated reporting, 201
Mandelli, P., 103–4
Mannarino, A. P., 207
Marcia, James, 26
marijuana, 172–73
Marshmello, 68–69
Massachusetts, 69–70
Mazzone, A., 151
McMillan, D. W., 218–19
Medicaid, 67
medication. *See* psychiatric medication
meditation, 207
membership, 218
mental health
    bullying and, 146–47
    in childhood, 40
    common disorders in youth, 40, 58–59
    cost of disorders, 59
    in juvenile justice system, 59
    prevalence of disorders, 38, 40, 104
    response to the multifaceted nature of, 237–42
    in rural communities, 220–22
    stigma of disorders, 68–69
    stress and, 103–4
    trauma impact on, 103–4
    in urban communities, 221–22
    in youth, 58–59
mental health education, 113–14
Mental Health Planning Act of 1986, 8
mental health screening, 66–67
methamphetamines, 173
Meyer-Adams, N., 149–50
middle adulthood developmental tasks, 29
middle age developmental tasks, 30*b*
middle childhood developmental tasks, 29, 30*b*
middle school developmental stage, 239*t*
mindfulness strategies, 65–66
Mississippi, 220–21
Mississippi Delta, 247
Models for Change, 45
Moffit, T. E., 179
Molly (ecstasy), 173

Monitoring the Future, 172–73
mood disorders, 48–49
moral development theory, 27–28
moratorium, identity, 26
Morton, M. H., 225–26
motivational interviewing, 133
MST. *See* multisystemic therapy
multisystemic therapy (MST), 47, 243
    for antisocial behavior, 184–85, 187
    case study example, 50–52
    described, 47
    for substance abuse, 173

National Center for Mental Health Promotion and Youth Violence Prevention, 146
National Child Traumatic Stress Network (NCTSN), 87–88, 198
National Institute on Drug Abuse (NIDA), 242
National Mental Health Act of 1946, 8
National Survey on LGBTQ Mental Health, 128–29
National Survey Results on Drug Abuse, 172–73
National Youth Risk Behavior Survey (YRBS), 121, 149–50
NCLB (No Child Left Behind) Act of 2001, 149
NCTSN. *See* National Child Traumatic Stress Network
needs fulfillment, 218
neglect. *See* childhood neglect
Neighborhood Disorganization Theory, 226
neighborhood partnerships, 227
neighborhoods and antisocial behavior, 176–77
neighborhood sense of community (SOC), 218–19
neurofeedback, 207
New York, 113–14
NIDA (National Institute on Drug Abuse), 242
No Child Left Behind (NCLB) Act of 2001, 149
nonbinary youth
    defined, 125*t*

    generalized anxiety disorder in, 129
    suicidal attempts in, 128, 129
nonproductive coping strategies, 152
normal curve, 22
normality, defining, 21–29
Northern Triangle of Central America, 81–82

O'Connell, M. E., 237–38
ODD. *See* oppositional-defiant disorder
Ohio Scales, 15
Olafsen, R. N., 152–53
Olweus, D., 142–43, 145
oniomania. *See* shopping addiction
opioids, 173
oppositional-defiant disorder (ODD), 165–66, 177–78
outing, defined, 125*t*
out-of-school suspension, 177–78
outpatient counseling, 43
overt antisocial behavior, 174
overt bullying, 144, 153

Pabian, S., 147
pansexual, defined, 125*t*
parent-child relationship, 175–76
parenting abilities, 175–76
parent knowledge, 175–76
parents. *See also* families
    antisocial behavior in, 173–74
    bullying and, 145, 151
    consent for children's treatment, 70–71
    deportation of, 84
partial hospitalization, 10
passive consent, 70–71
passive suicidal ideation, 109
PATH WARM, 115
Patterson, G. R., 145
PBIS (Positive Behavioral Interventions and Supports), 178–79
Peckham, S., 149–50
peer groups, 179–80
peer mediation, 182–83
peer similarity, 179
people of color. *See* children and youth of color
perceived burdensomeness, 109
Perfect, M., 61

Peterson, C., 202–3
Phelps, C., 58
physical bullying, 143
physical childhood abuse, 198
Piaget, Jean Claude, 24, 27–28, 33
play therapy, 206, 207
police, 244–45
pornograpy, 124
Positive Behavioral Interventions and Supports (PBIS), 178–79
positive youth development, 228–29
postconventional stage of moral development, 28
posttraumatic stress disorder (PTSD), 103–4, 133, 209, 243–44
  correlation between trauma and, 203–4
  from sexual childhood abuse, 198
postvention services, 116–17
poverty, 41–42, 200, 219, 224, 225–26
  antisocial behavior and, 176–77, 181
  children in, 219–20
  in LGBTQ+ community, 225
  in rural communities, 221
preconventional stage of moral development, 28
pregnancy. See teen pregnancy and parenthood
preoperational developmental stage, 27
pressure to conform, 122, 123t
prevention
  of antisocial behavior, 182–83
  for immigrants and refugees, 90
  programs for, 237–38, 241
  school services for, 64–66
  of school violence, 150–51
  suicide (see suicide prevention)
Preventive Health and Health Services block grant, 69–70
privacy, 70–71
problematic sexual behavior-cognitive behavioral therapy (PSB-CBT), 122–24
problem-focused coping strategies, 152
process addictions, 163, 167–71
  defined, 167
  types of, 167–71
productive coping strategies, 152
pronouns, preferred, 129

protective factors
  against bullying, 151–53
  in communities, 227–29
  by developmental stage, 237–38, 239t
  program effectiveness in strengthening, 243
  against suicide, 107–8
PSB-CBT (problematic sexual behavior-cognitive behavioral therapy), 122–24
psychiatric hospitalization
  case study of systemic failure, 10–12
  systemic approach in, 10–12
psychiatric medication, 39, 40
psychoeducation, 207
psychological childhood abuse. See emotional childhood abuse
psychosexual development theory, 24, 25–26
psychosocial identity development theory, 25–26
PTSD. See posttramatic stress disorder
Pub. L. 114-95. See Every Student Succeeds Act of 2015
public health
  bullying and, 146
  childhood abuse and, 196, 198
  schools and, 57–58
  trauma and, 196
public policies and legislation, 67–68

queer, defined, 125t
questioning, defined, 125t
Quinn, K. P., 71–72

racism, 222, 223–25
Ramsey, E., 145
randomized controlled trials (RCTs), 241–42
Ray, D. C., 34
Rayner, C., 152–53
reading skills, 33–34
recidivism, 45, 46, 49
refugees, 80
  case study in systemic failure, 13–14
  cultural humility when engaging with, 91–92
  culture impact on experience of, 81–84

defined, 93t
  postmigration experience of, 84–85
  systemic approach to, 12–14
  trauma-informed care for, 87–91
relational approach, 243
relationships (community), 216–18
research ethics, 248
residential segregation, 224
residential treatment, 43–44, 115–16
  defined, 10
  indications and goals for, 44–45
resources
  community, 216–17, 219
  efficacy of, 14, 15
  sufficiency of, 14, 16
Response to Intervention model, 64–65
risk factors
  by developmental stage, 237–38, 239t
  program effectiveness in reducing, 243
  for suicide, 106–7
risky or unsafe behaviors, 122, 123t
Roehrig, C., 59
role models, 182–83
rural communities, 200–1, 215–16, 221–22
  issues in, 220–21
  number of people residing in, 41
  system of care in, 41, 50
Russell, R., 146
Ryan, T. G., 177–78

SADPERSONAS, 115
SADPERSONS, 115
Safe Schools/Healthy Students initiative, 69–70
Saluja, G., 147
Salvadoran immigrants, 81–82, 84–85
Samara, M., 146
same-gender loving, defined, 125t
SAMHSA. See Substance Abuse and Mental Health Services Administration
Sampson, R. J., 176–77
SBMH. See school-based mental health services
schemas, 27
SCHIP (State Children's Health Insurance Program), 67
Schoenwald, S. K., 178
school-based mental health (SBMH) services
  efficacy of, 64

  overview, 60–71
  school-based programming, 182–83
school climate, 148
schools, 56–74
  adverse childhood experiences and services, 62–63
  antisocial behavior in, 177–79
  bullying in, 156–57
  case studies of interventions, 56–57, 73–74
  case study of systemic failure, 7–8
  funding for mental health services, 60, 67, 69–70
  immigrant and refugee services in, 90
  limitations of services in, 68–71
  mental health promotion for staff, 65–66
  mental health screening in, 66–67
  number of students attending, 60
  partserships for serving youth in, 71–72
  prevalence of mental health disorders in, 60
  program effectiveness in, 243–44
  promoting mental health and prevention in, 64–66
  public health and, 57–58
  public policies and legislation on, 67–68
  special education in, 63–64
  suicide prevention strategies in, 113–14
  systemic approach in, 6–8
  time spent in, 6
  trauma-informed, 61–62, 67–68
  violence in, 150–51
school shootings, 5, 41, 61–62, 67–68, 69–70, 148
school-to-prison pipeline, 48–49, 178
SCI (Sense of Community Index), 218–19
segregation, residential, 224
self-harm/self-injury, 105
Sense of Community Index (SCI), 218–19
sensorimotor developmental stage, 27
Session Rating Scale, 15
sex and sexuality, 121–38. See also LGBTQ+ youth; sex trafficking; sexual activity; teen pregnancy and parenthood
  issues pertaining to, 121–22
  potential interventions, 122–24

sex assigned at birth, defined, 124–28, 125t
sexting, 122, 170–71
sex trafficking, 121, 131–34. *See also* human trafficking
  defined, 131
  signs of, 132f
  vulnerable groups, 131–32
sexual activity, 121, 122
sexual and gender minority (SGM) youth, 129
sexual assault, 124
  antisocial behavior and, 163, 165–66
  of immigrants and refugees, 13, 83, 85
sexual childhood abuse, 198
sexually transmitted diseases, 60
sexual orientation, 129
  defined, 125t
  discrimination based on, 128
Shapiro, F., 207
Shin, R. Q., 222–23
shopping addiction, 169–70
SIMPLESTEPS, 115
single parents, 175, 181, 224
smartphone addiction, 168–69
Smith, P. K., 146
Snapchat, 122
social anxiety, 147
social development and bullying, 145
social-emotional learning, 61–62
social loneliness, 147
social media
  addiction to, 168–69
  antisocial behavior on, 174–75
  LGBTQ+ youth and, 129
  sexual activity and, 122
  stress and, 102–3
  terms related to adolescent use of, 123t
societal impact
  of childhood abuse, 202–3
  of stress, depression, and suicide, 104–5
  of trauma, 204
Society for Adolescent Medicine, 146
socioecological model, 86–87, 87f, 89–90
special education, 63–64
Sperry, L. L., 58
Stacciarini, J. R., 228
State Children's Health Insurance Program (SCHIP), 67

Stewart, Potter, 22
stigma
  of mental health disorders, 68–69
  of suicide, 111–12, 117
  of teen pregnancy and parenthood, 135–36
strengths-based approach, 64–65, 129, 238
stress, 101, 102–4
  bullying and, 144–45, 147
  chronic, 103
  common stressors in youth, 102–3
  defined, 102
  mental health and, 103–4
  societal impact of, 104–5
stress hormones, 103
Substance Abuse and Mental Health Services Administration (SAMHSA), 47, 203, 204–6
substance dependence, defined, 171–72
substance use and abuse, 40, 163, 171–73
  case study of psychiatric hospitalization for, 10–12
  childhood abuse and, 198
  cognitive behavioral therapy for, 48, 173
  community influences and, 226–27
  decrease in, 172–73
  defined (substance abuse), 171–72
  as leading cause of death in youth, 226
  in LGBTQ+ youth, 129
  residential treatment for, 44
  in rural communities, 220–21
  in schools, 60
  sexting behaviors and, 171
  shopping addiction and, 169–70
  suicide and, 106–7
  vulnerability to sex trafficking and, 131
suicidal attempts, 41, 101, 104, 105, 106–7
  annual number of, 101
  in Black youth, 5
  in children, 106
  defined, 105–6
  in LGBTQ+ youth, 128, 129, 131
suicidal behaviors (suicidality), 40, 101, 105, 107, 112
  in children, 106
  defined, 105
  inpatient counseling for, 43–44
  inpatient hospitalization for, 115–16

protective factors against, 107–8
residential treatment for, 44–45
suicidal ideation, 101, 105, 112
   active, 109
   bullying and, 147
   in children, 106
   defined, 105–6
   depression and, 104
   homelessness and, 225–26
   inpatient hospitalization for, 115–16
   in LGBTQ+ youth, 101, 128, 129
   passive, 109
   residential treatment for, 44
suicidality. *See* suicidal behaviors
suicidal thoughts, 105–7, 108, 171
suicide, 60, 101–2
   aftermath and postvention services, 116–17
   annual number of deaths from, 101
   biases on, 111–12
   bullying and, 148
   in children, 106–8
   defined, 105
   discomfort discussing, 102
   increase in, 5, 101, 102
   Interpersonal Theory of, 109
   in LGBTQ+ youth, 107, 129, 224–25
   myths on, 111, 112
   precipitating factors *vs.* warning signs, 108
   protective factors, 107–8
   rank of as cause of death, 5, 101, 102
   rate of in children, 102
   risk factors for, 106–7
   in rural communities, 220–21
   screening for, 66–67
   sexting behaviors and, 171
   stigma of, 111–12, 117
   terminology for, 112
   in youth, 105–8
Suicide and Life-Threatening Behavior (journal), 109
suicide assessment, 114–15
suicide intervention, 114–16, 131
suicide prevention, 110–13
   community approach to, 114
   in schools, 113–14
   training needed in, 49

Suicide Prevention Resource Center, 117
suicidology, 106
supportive discipline, 175–76
suspension, school, 177–78
syphilis study, 248
systemic approach, 3–18
   to bullying, 154–56
   collaboration in, 16–18
   in community mental health and youth services, 8–10
   defined, 6
   efficacy of resources in, 14, 15
   failure in (*see* systemic failure)
   issues in, 3
   perspective on development, 29–35
   in psychiatric hospitalization, 10–12
   in refugee services, 12–14
   in schools and connected systems, 6–8
   sufficiency of resources in, 14, 16
   types of systems in, 14
systemic change, 237–49
   advocacy in, 247–49
   multifaceted nature of youth mental health and, 237–42
   principles of effective programs, 242–47
systemic collaboration, 16–18
systemic failure
   case studies, 7–8, 9–12, 13–14
   overview, 4–14
system of care, 38–52
   case study, 50–52
   continuity of care in, 42
   defining care for youth, 38–39
   effective services in, 46–48
   failure of, 41–42
   juvenile justice (*see* juvenile justice system)
   lack of integration in, 41
   suggested improvements for, 49–52
   treatment settings, 43–45
   withdrawal from services, 41–42

targeted interventions. *See* Tier 2 interventions
Teaching Tolerance (website), 111–12
team-based care, 71–72
teen pregnancy and parenthood, 121, 134–37
   antisocial behavior and, 175
   birth rate decrease, 134–35

teen pregnancy and parenthood (*cont.*)
  challenges and adversities, 134, 137
  confidentiality and, 135
  number of babies born, 134
  school services and, 60
Texas, 45, 201
Texas Department of Family Protective Services, 201
TF-CBT. *See* trauma-focused-cognitive behavioral therapy
therapeutic alliance, 116, 206
Thompson, R. E., 124
thwarted belongingness, 109
Tier 1 interventions (universal interventions), 61–62, 64–65, 70–71
Tier 2 interventions (targeted interventions), 61–62, 64–65
Tier 3 interventions (indicated interventions), 61–62, 64–65
TikTok, 122
TIME magazine, 224–25
Title V Maternal and Child Health Block grant, 69–70
Title XI funds for disadvantaged youth, 69–70
Title XX Social Services block grant, 69–70
tobacco taxes, 69–70
trafficking. *See* human trafficking; sex trafficking
Trafficking Victim Identification Tool (TVIT), 132–34
transgender youth, 224–25
  defined, 125*t*
  generalized anxiety disorder in, 129
  suicidal attempts in, 128, 129
  suicidal behaviors in, 107
transitioning, defined, 125*t*
transphobia, 224–25
trauma, 122–24, 196, 203–8, 243–44
  antisocial behavior and, 173–74
  case study, 208–9
  childhood abuse and, 196, 199
  defined, 203, 204–5
  executive functioning and, 31
  immigrants affected by (*see under* immigrants)
  lasting impact on mental health, 103–4
  societal impact of, 204
  subjective experience and, 203
  three E's in, 205
trauma-focused cognitive behavioral therapy (TF-CBT), 122–23, 133, 134, 207–8
trauma-informed care, 204–8
  for childhood abuse victims, 199
  four assumptions of, 205–6
  for immigrants and refugees, 87–91
  six principles of, 206
trauma-informed schools, 61–62, 67–68
trauma systems therapy (TST), 88, 89–90
trauma systems therapy for refugees (TST-R), 89–91
treatment settings, 43–45
Trevor Project, 129
Trevor Project Survey, 128
trust (community), 217–18
trust *vs.* mistrust (psychosocial identity development theory), 25
TST. *See* trauma systems therapy
Turnbull, A. P., 63
TVIT. *See* Trafficking Victim Identification Tool

UIMs. *See* unaccompanied immigrant minors
unaccompanied children (UAC), 80, 93*t*
unaccompanied immigrant minors (UIMs), 80–86, 237
  defined, 80–81
  postmigration experience of, 84–85
  trafficking and exploitation of, 83
  trauma during journey to US, 82–83
  trauma in country of origin, 81–82
unaccompanied refugee minors (URMs), 80, 93*t*
Unaccompanied Refugee Minors (URM) program, 12–13
underserved communities, 219–22
undocumented immigrants, 80, 86, 93*t*, 132
universal interventions. *See* Tier 1 interventions
universities (advocacy in), 247–49
urban communities, 221–22
US Naval Postgraduate School study, 5

Vandebosch, H., 147

Van der Kolk, Bessel, 203
Van Orden, K. A., 109
vaped nicotine, 172–73
Vera Institute of Justice, 133–34
verbal bullying, 143
Villages Children and Youth Program, 231–32
violence
   bullying and, 149–51
   gang, 81–82, 84–85, 200–1
   school, 150–51
   in urban communities, 222
Virginia, 113–14
Vygotsky, L. S., 27

Wainberg, M. L., 41
Ward, T., 166
weapons, carrying and using, 149–50, 163, 165–66, 169–70
weight-based bullying, 141–42, 174–75
wilderness challenge programs, 180–81
Williams, S., 66
Wolke, D., 146
working alliance. *See* therapeutic alliance
Working Alliance Inventory, 15
World Health Organization (WHO), 104, 106
World Report on Violence and Health, 150–51
wraparound services, 71–72

Ybarra, M. L., 124
yoga, 207
YOQ-TA, 15
young adulthood developmental stage, 239*t*
youth empowerment, 228–29
Youth Risk Behavior Surveillance System, 163
YRBS. *See* National Youth Risk Behavior Survey

zero tolerance school codes, 177–78